FAVORITE BRAND NAME™

Easy Asian

R E C I P E S

D1470594

Publications International, Ltd.

Favorite Brand Name Recipes at www.fbnr.com

Pictured on the front cover: Indonesian Chicken & Rice *(page 70)*.
Pictured on the back cover *(left to right):* Teriyaki Steak with Onions and Mushrooms *(page 88),* Hot & Sour Chicken *(page 56)* and Moo Shu Beef *(page 92)*.
Pictured on page 3 *(left to right):* Easy Make-at-Home Chinese Chicken *(page 64),* Asian Rice & Squash Noodles with Peanut Sauce *(page 52)* and Seafood & Vegetable Stir-Fry *(page 146)*.

ISBN: 0-7583-9683-7

Library of Congress Control Number: 2003109988

Manufactured in China.

8 7 6 5 4 3 2 1

Microwave Cooking: Microwave ovens vary in wattage. Use the cooking times as guidelines and check for doneness before adding more time.

Preparation/Cooking Times: Preparation times are based on the approximate amount of time required to assemble the recipe before cooking, baking, chilling or serving. These times include preparation steps such as measuring, chopping and mixing. The fact that some preparations and cooking can be done simultaneously is taken into account. Preparation of optional ingredients and serving suggestions is not included.

Contents

Pleasing Appetizers

Hong Kong Fried Rice Cakes

1 box (about 6 ounces) chicken-flavored rice mix
$\frac{1}{2}$ cup sliced green onions
2 eggs, beaten
2 tablespoons chopped fresh parsley
1 tablespoon hoisin sauce
1 tablespoons soy sauce
1 teaspoon minced fresh ginger
1 clove garlic, minced
2 to 3 tablespoons vegetable oil, divided

1. Prepare rice according to package directions, omitting butter. Cover and refrigerate one hour or until completely chilled. Add remaining ingredients, except oil, to rice; mix well. Form rice mixture into cakes, 3 inches in diameter.

2. Heat 1 tablespoon oil in large skillet over medium heat until hot. Cook 4 cakes at a time 3 to 4 minutes on each side or until golden brown. Add additional oil to skillet as needed.

Makes 4 to 6 servings

Hong Kong Fried Rice Cakes

Chicken Satay

1 pound boneless skinless chicken breast halves
1 recipe Peanut Dip (recipe follows), divided
    Cucumber slices
    Chopped fresh cilantro

1. Soak 8 (6-inch) bamboo skewers in hot water 20 minutes. Cut chicken lengthwise into 1-inch-wide strips; thread onto skewers.

2. Place skewers in large shallow glass dish. Pour ½ cup Peanut Dip over chicken, turning to coat evenly. Cover and marinate in refrigerator 30 minutes.

3. Place skewers on oiled grid and discard any remaining marinade. Grill over high heat 5 to 8 minutes or until chicken is no longer pink, turning once. Place on serving platter. Serve with cucumber, cilantro and remaining Peanut Dip.   *Makes 8 appetizer or 4 main-dish servings*

Prep Time: 15 minutes   **Marinate Time:** 30 minutes   **Cook Time:** 5 minutes

Peanut Dip

    ⅓ cup peanut butter
    ⅓ cup *French's*® Napa Valley Style Dijon Mustard
    ⅓ cup orange juice
    1 tablespoon chopped peeled fresh ginger
    1 tablespoon honey
    1 tablespoon *Frank's*® *RedHot*® Cayenne Pepper Sauce
    1 tablespoon teriyaki baste and glaze sauce
    2 cloves garlic, minced

Combine peanut butter, mustard, juice, ginger, honey, ***Frank's RedHot*** Sauce, teriyaki sauce and garlic in large bowl. Refrigerate until ready to serve.   *Makes 1 cup dip*

Prep Time: 10 minutes

Chicken Satay and Peanut Dip

Thai Lamb & Couscous Rolls

16 large napa or Chinese cabbage leaves, stems trimmed
2 tablespoons minced fresh ginger
1 teaspoon red pepper flakes
⅔ cup uncooked quick-cooking couscous
½ pound ground lean lamb
½ cup chopped green onions
3 cloves garlic, minced
¼ cup plus 2 tablespoons minced fresh cilantro or mint, divided
2 tablespoons reduced-sodium soy sauce
1 tablespoon lime juice
1 teaspoon dark sesame oil
1 cup plain nonfat yogurt

1. Place 4 cups water in medium saucepan; bring to a boil over high heat. Drop cabbage leaves into water; cook 30 seconds. Drain. Rinse under cold water until cool; pat dry with paper towels.

2. Place 1 cup water, ginger and red pepper in medium saucepan; bring to a boil over high heat. Stir in couscous; cover. Remove saucepan from heat; let stand 5 minutes.

3. Spray large saucepan with nonstick cooking spray; add lamb, onions and garlic. Cook and stir over medium-high heat 5 minutes or until lamb is no longer pink. Remove lamb from skillet; drain in colander.

4. Combine couscous, lamb, ¼ cup cilantro, soy sauce, lime juice and oil in medium bowl. Spoon evenly down centers of cabbage leaves. Fold ends of cabbage leaves over filling; roll up. Combine yogurt and remaining 2 tablespoons cilantro in small bowl; spoon evenly over rolls. Serve warm. Garnish as desired.

Makes 16 appetizers

Thai Lamb & Couscous Rolls

Chinatown Stuffed Mushrooms

24 large fresh mushrooms (about 1 pound), cleaned
and stems trimmed
½ pound ground turkey
1 clove garlic, minced
¼ cup fine dry bread crumbs
¼ cup thinly sliced green onions
3 tablespoons reduced-sodium soy sauce, divided
1 teaspoon minced fresh ginger
1 egg white, lightly beaten
⅛ teaspoon red pepper flakes (optional)

Remove stems from mushrooms; finely chop enough stems to equal 1 cup. Cook turkey with chopped stems and garlic in medium skillet over medium-high heat until turkey is no longer pink, stirring to separate turkey. Spoon off any fat. Stir in bread crumbs, green onions, 2 tablespoons soy sauce, ginger, egg white and pepper flakes, if desired; mix well.

Brush mushroom caps lightly on all sides with remaining 1 tablespoon soy sauce; spoon about 2 teaspoons stuffing into each mushroom cap.* Place stuffed mushrooms on rack of foil-lined broiler pan. Broil 4 to 5 inches from heat 5 to 6 minutes or until hot.   *Makes 24 appetizers*

*Mushrooms may be made ahead to this point; cover and refrigerate up to 24 hours. Add 1 to 2 minutes to broiling time for chilled mushrooms.

Pork and Crab Dumplings

1 cup finely chopped cooked pork tenderloin
1 (6-ounce) can flaked crab meat, drained
¼ cup finely chopped onion
2 tablespoons finely chopped water chestnuts
2 teaspoons soy sauce
¼ teaspoon salt
⅛ teaspoon black pepper
1 (3-ounce) package cream cheese, softened
About 20 wonton wrappers
6 tablespoons cooking oil
1 cup water
Chinese mustard
Soy sauce

In a medium bowl stir together well pork, crab, onion, water chestnuts, soy sauce, salt and pepper. Stir in cream cheese to blend thoroughly.

Spoon about 1 tablespoon filling in center of each wonton wrapper. Fold wrapper in half diagonally across filling to form triangle; moisten and pinch edges to seal. Place triangle with pinched edge upright and press gently to flatten bottom. Transfer to a baking sheet and cover with a dry cloth. Repeat with remaining wrappers and filling.

In a large skillet heat 2 tablespoons of the oil. Carefully place half the dumplings in skillet, not allowing sides to touch. Cook over medium heat 1 minute or until bottoms are browned. Carefully add ½ cup water to skillet. Reduce heat; cover and simmer 10 minutes. Uncover and cook 3 to 5 minutes or until water evaporates. Cook, uncovered, 1 minutes. Transfer dumplings to a baking sheet. Place in a preheated 250°F oven to keep warm. Repeat with remaining dumplings, oil and water. Serve with Chinese mustard and soy sauce for dipping. *Makes 20 dumplings*

Favorite recipe from **National Pork Board**

Apricot-Chicken Pot Stickers

2 cups plus 1 tablespoon water, divided
2 small boneless skinless chicken breasts (about 8 ounces)
2 cups chopped finely shredded cabbage
½ cup all-fruit apricot preserves
2 green onions with tops, finely chopped
2 teaspoons soy sauce
½ teaspoon grated fresh ginger
⅛ teaspoon black pepper
30 (3-inch) wonton wrappers
    Prepared sweet & sour sauce (optional)

1. Bring 2 cups water to boil in medium saucepan. Add chicken. Reduce heat to low; simmer, covered, 10 minutes or until chicken is no longer pink in center. Remove from saucepan; drain.

2. Add cabbage and remaining 1 tablespoon water to saucepan. Cook over high heat 1 to 2 minutes or until water evaporates, stirring occasionally. Remove from heat; cool slightly.

3. Finely chop chicken. Add to saucepan along with preserves, green onions, soy sauce, ginger and pepper; mix well.

4. To assemble pot stickers, remove 3 wonton wrappers at a time from package. Spoon slightly rounded tablespoonful of chicken mixture onto center of each wrapper; brush edges with water. Bring 4 corners together; press to seal. Repeat with remaining wrappers and filling.

5. Spray steamer with nonstick cooking spray. Assemble steamer so that water is ½ inch below steamer basket. Fill steamer basket with pot stickers, leaving enough space between them to prevent sticking. Cover; steam 5 minutes. Transfer pot stickers to serving plate. Serve with prepared sweet & sour sauce, if desired.   *Makes 10 servings (3 pot stickers each)*

Apricot-Chicken Pot Stickers

Crab Cakes Canton

7 ounces thawed frozen cooked crabmeat or imitation crabmeat, drained and flaked
1½ cups fresh whole wheat bread crumbs (about 3 slices bread)
¼ cup thinly sliced green onions
1 clove garlic, minced
1 teaspoon minced fresh ginger
2 egg whites, lightly beaten
1 tablespoon teriyaki sauce
2 teaspoons vegetable oil, divided
Prepared sweet and sour sauce (optional)

Combine crabmeat, bread crumbs, onions, garlic and ginger in medium bowl; mix well. Add egg whites and teriyaki sauce; mix well. Shape into patties about ½ inch thick and 2 inches in diameter.*

Heat 1 teaspoon oil in large nonstick skillet over medium heat until hot. Add about half of crab cakes to skillet. Cook 2 minutes per side or until golden brown. Remove to warm serving plate; keep warm. Repeat with remaining 1 teaspoon oil and crab cakes. Serve with sweet and sour sauce, if desired.

Makes 6 servings (12 cakes)

Crab cakes may be made ahead to this point; cover and refrigerate up to 24 hours before cooking.

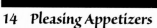

Crab Cakes Canton

Szechuan Cold Noodles

8 ounces vermicelli, broken in half or Chinese egg noodles
3 tablespoons soy sauce
3 tablespoons rice vinegar
2 tablespoons peanut or vegetable oil
1 large clove garlic, minced
1 teaspoon minced fresh ginger
1 teaspoon dark sesame oil (optional)
½ teaspoon crushed Szechuan peppercorns or red pepper flakes
½ cup coarsely chopped fresh cilantro (optional)
¼ cup chopped peanuts

1. Cook vermicelli according to package directions. Drain; keep warm.

2. Combine soy sauce, vinegar, peanut oil, garlic, ginger, sesame oil and peppercorns in large bowl. Add hot vermicelli; toss to coat. Sprinkle with cilantro and peanuts. Serve at room temperature or chilled.

Makes 4 servings

Chilled Shrimp in Chinese Mustard Sauce

1 cup water
½ cup dry white wine
2 tablespoons reduced-sodium soy sauce
½ teaspoon Szechuan or black peppercorns
1 pound raw large shrimp, peeled and deveined
¼ cup prepared sweet and sour sauce
2 teaspoons hot Chinese mustard

1. Combine water, wine, soy sauce and peppercorns in medium saucepan. Bring to a boil over high heat. Add shrimp; reduce heat to medium. Cover and simmer 2 to 3 minutes or until shrimp are opaque. Drain well. Cover and refrigerate until chilled.

2. Combine sweet and sour sauce and mustard in small bowl; mix well. Serve as a dipping sauce for shrimp.

Makes 6 servings

Beef and Lettuce Bundles

1 pound ground beef
½ cup sliced green onions
1 medium clove garlic, minced
⅔ cup chopped water chestnuts
½ cup chopped red bell pepper
1 tablespoon soy sauce
1 tablespoon seasoned rice vinegar
2 tablespoons chopped fresh cilantro
1 or 2 heads leaf lettuce, separated into leaves (discard outer leaves)
Hoisin sauce (optional)

Brown ground beef in medium skillet. Drain. Add onions and garlic. Cook until tender. Stir in water chestnuts, red pepper, soy sauce and vinegar. Cook, stirring occasionally, until red pepper is crisp-tender and most of liquid evaporates.

Stir in cilantro. Spoon ground beef mixture onto lettuce leaves; sprinkle with hoisin sauce, if desired. Wrap lettuce leaf around ground beef mixture to make appetizer bundle.

Makes 8 appetizer servings

Spicy Apricot Sesame Wings

⅓ cup *Frank's® RedHot®* Cayenne Pepper Sauce
½ cup *French's®* Napa Valley Style Dijon Mustard
2 tablespoons Oriental sesame oil
1 tablespoon red wine vinegar
½ cup apricot jam
2 pounds chicken wings, split and tips discarded
2 tablespoons toasted sesame seeds

1. Stir *Frank's RedHot* Sauce, mustard, sesame oil and vinegar in small measuring cup. Spoon ¼ cup *Frank's RedHot* Sauce mixture and apricot jam into blender or food processor. Cover; process until smooth. Reserve for basting and dipping sauce.

2. Place wings in large bowl. Pour remaining *Frank's RedHot* Sauce mixture over wings; toss to coat. Cover; marinate in refrigerator 20 minutes.

3. Place wings on oiled grid and discard any remaining marinade. Grill over medium heat 25 to 30 minutes or until crispy and no longer pink, turning often. Brush with ¼ cup of the reserved sauce during last 10 minutes of cooking. Place wings on serving platter; sprinkle with sesame seeds. Serve with remaining sauce.   *Makes 8 servings*

Prep Time: 15 minutes   **Marinate Time:** 20 minutes   **Cook Time:** 25 minutes

WOK'S COOKING?

To toast sesame seeds, place on baking sheet and bake at 375°F 8 to 10 minutes or until golden.

Spicy Apricot Sesame Wings

Chinese Vegetable Rolls

¼ **cup red wine**
2 **tablespoons teriyaki sauce**
2 **tablespoons Worcestershire sauce**
1 **cup diced zucchini**
1 **cup diced yellow squash**
1 **cup broccoli florets**
1 **cup cauliflower florets**
½ **cup diced carrots**
¼ **cup chopped red onion**
¼ **cup chopped fresh parsley**
¼ **teaspoon white pepper**
¼ **teaspoon garlic salt**
⅛ **teaspoon ground red pepper**
⅛ **teaspoon black pepper**
1 **package (16 ounces) egg roll wrappers**
1 **egg, beaten**
Peanut or corn oil for frying
Sweet and sour sauce, hot mustard sauce or soy sauce for
dipping

1. Combine wine, teriyaki sauce and Worcestershire sauce in large saucepan over medium heat. Stir in vegetables and seasonings. Cook and stir 5 to 6 minutes until flavors blend and vegetables are crisp-tender. Do not overcook.

2. Remove from heat. Immediately transfer vegetable mixture to bowl to prevent further cooking. Let stand at room temperature until cool.

3. Place about 2 tablespoons vegetable mixture on bottom half of 1 egg roll wrapper.

4. Moisten left and right edges of wrapper with egg. Fold bottom edge up to just cover filling.

5. Fold left and right edges over ½ inch; roll up jelly-roll fashion.

6. Moisten top edge with egg to seal. Repeat with remaining egg roll wrappers and vegetables.

7. Heat ½ inch oil in large, heavy saucepan over medium-high heat until oil reaches 365°F; adjust heat to maintain temperature. Fry egg rolls, a few at a time, in hot oil 2 minutes or until golden brown, turning once. Remove with slotted spoon; drain on paper towels.

8. Serve warm with sauces for dipping.   *Makes about 15 appetizers*

Mini-Marinated Beef Skewers

1 boneless beef top sirloin steak, cut 1 inch thick (about 1 pound)
2 tablespoons soy sauce
2 tablespoons dry sherry
1 tablespoon dark sesame oil
2 cloves garlic, minced
18 cherry tomatoes
   Lettuce leaves (optional)

1. Cut beef across the grain into ⅛-inch slices. Place in large plastic bag. Combine soy sauce, sherry, sesame oil and garlic in cup; pour over steak. Close bag securely; turn to coat. Marinate in refrigerator at least 30 minutes or up to 2 hours.

2. Soak 18 (6-inch) wooden skewers in water to cover 20 minutes.

3. Drain steak; discard marinade. Weave beef accordion-fashion onto skewers. Place on rack of broiler pan.

4. Broil 4 to 5 inches from heat 2 minutes. Turn skewers over; broil 2 minutes or until beef is barely pink in center.

5. Garnish each skewer with one cherry tomato; place on lettuce-lined platter. Serve warm or at room temperature.   *Makes 18 appetizers*

Gingered Chicken Pot Stickers

3 cups finely shredded cabbage

4 green onions with tops, finely chopped

1 egg white, lightly beaten

1 tablespoon light soy sauce

1 tablespoon minced fresh ginger

$1/4$ teaspoon red pepper flakes

$1/4$ pound ground chicken breast, cooked and drained

24 wonton wrappers, at room temperature

Cornstarch

$1/2$ cup water

1 tablespoon oyster sauce

2 teaspoons grated lemon peel

$1/2$ teaspoon honey

$1/8$ teaspoon red pepper flakes

1 tablespoon peanut oil

Steam cabbage 5 minutes, then cool to room temperature. Squeeze out any excess moisture; set aside. To prepare filling, combine green onions, egg white, soy sauce, ginger and $1/4$ teaspoon red pepper in large bowl; blend well. Stir in cabbage and chicken.

To prepare pot stickers, place 1 tablespoon filling in center of 1 wonton wrapper. Gather edges around filling, pressing firmly at top to seal. Repeat with remaining wrappers and filling. Place pot stickers on large baking sheet dusted with cornstarch. Refrigerate 1 hour or until cold. Meanwhile, to prepare sauce, combine remaining ingredients except oil in small bowl; mix well. Set aside.

Heat oil in large nonstick skillet over high heat. Add pot stickers and cook until bottoms are golden brown. Pour sauce over top. Cover and cook 3 minutes. Uncover and cook until all liquid is absorbed. Serve warm on tray as finger food or on small plates with chopsticks as first course.

Makes 8 appetizer servings

Gingered Chicken Pot Stickers

Szechuan Chicken Tenders

  2 tablespoons soy sauce
  1 tablespoon chili sauce
  1 tablespoon dry sherry
  2 cloves garlic, minced
  ¼ teaspoon red pepper flakes
 16 chicken tenders (about 1 pound)
  1 tablespoon peanut oil
    Hot cooked rice

Combine soy sauce, chili sauce, sherry, garlic and red pepper in shallow dish. Add chicken; coat well.

Heat oil in large nonstick skillet over medium heat until hot. Add chicken with marinade; cook 6 minutes, turning once, until chicken is browned and no longer pink in center.

Serve chicken with rice.   *Makes 4 servings*

Spring Rolls

  1 cup pre-shredded cabbage or coleslaw mix
  ½ cup finely chopped cooked ham
  ¼ cup finely chopped water chestnuts
  ¼ cup thinly sliced green onions
  3 tablespoons plum sauce, divided
  1 teaspoon dark sesame oil
  3 (6-inch) flour tortillas

continued on page 26

Szechuan Chicken Tenders

Spring Rolls, continued

Combine cabbage, ham, water chestnuts, onions, 2 tablespoons plum sauce and sesame oil in medium bowl. Mix well. Spread remaining 1 tablespoon plum sauce evenly over tortillas. Spread about ½ cup cabbage mixture on each tortilla to within ¼ inch of edge; roll up. Wrap each tortilla tightly in plastic wrap. Refrigerate at least 1 hour or up to 24 hours before serving. Cut each tortilla diagonally into 4 pieces.   *Makes 12 appetizers*

Lettuce Wrap

1½ **tablespoons LEE KUM KEE® Hoisin Sauce**
1 **tablespoon LEE KUM KEE® Panda Brand Oyster Flavored Sauce**
1 **tablespoon vegetable oil**
3 **ounces diced onion**
½ **pound ground chicken or turkey**
⅔ **cup diced cucumbers**
Large lettuce leaves
Additional LEE KUM KEE® Hoisin Sauce

Combine 1½ tablespoons Hoisin Sauce and Oyster Sauce in small bowl; set aside. Heat skillet over medium heat. Add oil. Sauté onion. Add chicken, cucumber and sauce mixture. Heat through. To serve, wrap chicken mixture in lettuce leaves. Serve with additional Hoisin Sauce for dipping.   *Makes 4 servings*

Asian Kabobs

1 pound ground pork
1⅓ cups *French's®* French Fried Onions, slightly crushed
2 egg whites
2 tablespoons reduced-sodium soy sauce
1 tablespoon *Frank's® RedHot®* Cayenne Pepper Sauce
1 tablespoon grated fresh ginger *or* 1 teaspoon ground ginger
1 can (20 ounces) pineapple chunks, drained
2 medium green or red bell peppers, cut into 1-inch pieces
Peach or apricot dipping sauce, heated

Preheat oven to 400°F. Combine pork, French Fried Onions, egg whites, soy sauce, **Frank's RedHot** Sauce and ginger in large bowl; mix well. Shape into 1-inch balls, using 1 level tablespoon for each. Place on greased rack in foil-lined baking pan. Bake 15 minutes or until browned and no longer pink in center.

Thread meatballs, pineapple and bell peppers alternately onto 6-inch wooden skewers. Arrange kabobs on serving platter. Serve with dipping sauce.

Makes 10 appetizer servings (about 2½ dozen meatballs)

Prep Time: 35 minutes   **Cook Time:** 15 minutes

Chicken Kabobs with Thai Dipping Sauce

1 pound boneless skinless chicken breasts, cut into 1-inch cubes
1 small cucumber, seeded and cut into small chunks
1 cup cherry tomatoes
2 green onions, cut into 1-inch pieces
$^2/_3$ cup teriyaki baste & glaze sauce
$^1/_3$ cup _Frank's_® _RedHot_® Cayenne Pepper Sauce
$^1/_3$ cup peanut butter
3 tablespoons frozen orange juice concentrate, undiluted
2 cloves garlic, minced

Thread chicken, cucumber, tomatoes and onions alternately onto metal skewers; set aside.

To prepare Thai Dipping Sauce, combine teriyaki baste & glaze sauce, **_Frank's RedHot_** Sauce, peanut butter, orange juice concentrate and garlic; mix well. Reserve $^2/_3$ cup sauce for dipping.

Brush skewers with some of remaining sauce. Place skewers on oiled grid. Grill over hot coals 10 minutes or until chicken is no longer pink in center, turning and basting often with remaining sauce. Serve skewers with reserved Thai Dipping Sauce. Garnish as desired.

Makes 6 appetizer servings

Prep Time: 15 minutes   **Cook Time:** 10 minutes

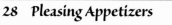

Chicken Kabobs with Thai Dipping Sauce

Sizzling Sides

Carrots Chinoise

8 ounces medium carrots, peeled
2 teaspoons vegetable oil
$\frac{1}{4}$ cup water
1 package (6 ounces) frozen Chinese pea pods, partially thawed
1 can (8 ounces) sliced water chestnuts, drained
1 teaspoon sesame oil
$\frac{1}{2}$ teaspoon salt
$\frac{1}{8}$ teaspoon black pepper

Cut carrots diagonally into thin slices.

Heat wok over medium-high heat 1 minute or until hot. Drizzle vegetable oil into wok and heat 30 seconds. Add carrots; stir-fry until lightly browned. Reduce heat to medium.

Add water; cover and cook about 4 minutes or until carrots are crisp-tender.

Add pea pods, water chestnuts, sesame oil, salt and black pepper; stir-fry until heated through. Transfer to serving dish.

Makes 4 servings

Carrots Chinoise

Thai Fried Rice

2½ cups water

1⅓ cups long-grain white rice

8 ounces ground pork or pork sausage

1 tablespoon vegetable oil

1 medium onion, thinly sliced

1 tablespoon finely chopped fresh ginger

1 jalapeño pepper,* seeded and finely chopped

3 cloves garlic, minced

½ teaspoon ground turmeric or paprika

2 tablespoons fish sauce

2 cups chopped cooked vegetables such as broccoli, zucchini, red
    bell peppers, carrots, bok choy or spinach

3 eggs, lightly beaten

3 green onions, thinly sliced

½ cup cilantro leaves

*Jalapeños can sting and irritate the skin; wear rubber gloves when handling peppers and do not touch eyes. Wash hands after handling.

1. Bring water and rice to a boil in medium saucepan over high heat. Reduce heat to medium-low; cover and simmer 20 minutes or until water is absorbed.

2. Transfer rice to large bowl and fluff with fork. Let cool to room temperature, 30 to 40 minutes, stirring occasionally. Cover and refrigerate until cold, at least 1 hour or up to 24 hours.

3. When rice is cold, cook pork in wok or medium skillet over medium-high heat until no longer pink. Drain off excess fat; transfer pork to bowl and set aside.

4. Heat wok or large skillet over medium-high heat. Add oil and swirl to coat surface. Add onion, ginger, jalapeño, garlic and turmeric; stir-fry 4 to 6 minutes or until onion is very tender.

5. Stir in fish sauce; mix well. Stir in cold rice, vegetables and pork; cook and stir 3 to 4 minutes or until heated through.

continued on page 34

Thai Fried Rice

Thai Fried Rice, continued

6. Push rice to side of wok and pour eggs into center. Cook eggs 2 to 3 minutes or just until set, lifting and stirring to scramble. Stir rice into eggs.

7. Stir in green onions. Transfer to serving bowl; sprinkle with cilantro. Garnish as desired.

Makes 4 servings

Chinese Spinach Toss

    3 to 4 cups fresh bean sprouts *or* 2 cans (16 ounces each) bean
       sprouts, well drained
⅓ cup honey
⅓ cup white wine or rice vinegar
2 tablespoons vegetable oil
2 teaspoons soy sauce
1 to 2 teaspoons grated fresh gingerroot
6 cups washed and torn fresh spinach
1 cup diced peeled jicama
1 cup crisp Chinese noodles

Place bean sprouts in large glass or ceramic bowl. Combine honey, vinegar, oil, soy sauce and gingerroot in small bowl; pour over bean sprouts. Cover and refrigerate at least 1 hour, tossing occasionally. Just before serving, add spinach and jicama; toss gently to coat. Top each serving with noodles.

Makes 6 servings

Favorite recipe from ***National Honey Board***

Zucchini Shanghai Style

4 dried Chinese black mushrooms
½ cup fat-free reduced-sodium chicken broth
2 tablespoons ketchup
2 teaspoons dry sherry
1 teaspoon reduced-sodium soy sauce
1 teaspoon red wine vinegar
¼ teaspoon sugar
1½ teaspoons vegetable oil, divided
1 teaspoon minced fresh ginger
1 clove garlic, minced
1 large tomato, peeled, seeded and chopped
1 green onion, finely chopped
4 tablespoons water, divided
1 teaspoon cornstarch
1 pound zucchini (about 3 medium), diagonally cut into
    1-inch pieces
½ small yellow onion, cut into wedges and separated

1. Soak mushrooms in warm water 20 minutes. Drain, reserving ¼ cup liquid. Squeeze out excess water. Discard stems; slice caps. Combine reserved ¼ cup mushroom liquid, chicken broth, ketchup, sherry, soy sauce, vinegar and sugar in small bowl. Set aside.

2. Heat 1 teaspoon oil in large saucepan over medium heat. Add ginger and garlic; stir-fry 10 seconds. Add mushrooms, tomato and green onion; stir-fry 1 minute. Add chicken broth mixture; bring to a boil over high heat. Reduce heat to medium; simmer 10 minutes.

3. Combine 1 tablespoon water and cornstarch in small bowl; set aside. Heat remaining ½ teaspoon oil in large nonstick skillet over medium heat. Add zucchini and yellow onion; stir-fry 30 seconds. Add remaining 3 tablespoons water. Cover and cook 3 to 4 minutes or until vegetables are crisp-tender, stirring occasionally. Add tomato mixture to skillet. Stir cornstarch mixture and add to skillet. Cook until sauce boils and thickens. *Makes 4 servings*

Stir-Fried Broccoli

1 pound broccoli
1 medium onion
2 ribs celery
4 ounces fresh bean sprouts
1 tablespoon cornstarch
1 tablespoon cold water
1 tablespoon oyster sauce
¼ teaspoon salt
¼ teaspoon sugar
1 tablespoon vegetable oil
2 cloves garlic, minced
¾ cup vegetable or chicken broth
¼ cup pimiento strips, drained

Cut woody stems from broccoli; discard. Cut stems diagonally into slices. Cut tops into flowerets; rinse. Cut onion into wedges. Cut celery diagonally into ¼-inch-thick slices. Rinse bean sprouts and drain. Remove any green hulls. Set aside.

Combine cornstarch, water, oyster sauce, salt and sugar in small bowl; stir until smooth. Set aside.

Heat wok over high heat about 1 minute or until hot. Drizzle oil into wok and heat 30 seconds. Add broccoli stems, onion and celery; stir-fry 2 to 3 minutes or until vegetables are crisp-tender. Add broccoli flowerets and garlic; stir-fry 30 seconds. Add broth. Cover and cook about 3 minutes or until broccoli is crisp-tender.

Stir cornstarch mixture until smooth. Add to wok. Cook and stir until sauce boils and thickens.

Add sprouts and pimiento; stir-fry just until heated through. Transfer to serving dish.

Makes 6 servings

Stir-Fried Broccoli

Thai-Style Warm Noodle Salad

8 ounces uncooked angel hair pasta
½ cup chunky peanut butter
¼ cup soy sauce
¼ to ½ teaspoon red pepper flakes
2 green onions, thinly sliced
1 carrot, shredded

1. Cook pasta according to package directions.

2. While pasta is cooking, blend peanut butter, soy sauce and red pepper flakes in serving bowl until smooth.

3. Drain pasta, reserving 5 tablespoons water. Mix hot pasta water with peanut butter mixture until smooth; toss pasta with sauce. Stir in green onions and carrot. Serve warm or at room temperature.

Makes 4 servings

Prep and Cook Time: 12 minutes

WOK'S COOKING?

This salad is as versatile as it is easy to make. It can be prepared a day ahead and served warm or cold—perfect for potlucks, picnics and even lunch boxes. You can also make it into a heartier meal by mixing in any leftover cooked chicken or beef.

Thai-Style Warm Noodle Salad

Sesame Snow Peas

½ **pound snow peas (Chinese pea pods)**
2 **teaspoons sesame oil**
2 **teaspoons vegetable oil**
2 **green onions, cut into ¼-inch slices**
1 **medium carrot, julienned**
½ **teaspoon grated fresh gingerroot** *or* ¼ **teaspoon ground ginger**
1 **teaspoon soy sauce**
1 **tablespoon sesame seeds, toasted***

*To toast sesame seeds, heat small skillet over medium heat. Add sesame seeds; cook and stir about 5 minutes or until golden. Set aside.

1. To de-stem peas decoratively, pinch off stem end from each pod, pulling strings down the pod to remove if present. (Young tender pods may have no strings.)

2. Make a "V-shaped" cut at opposite end of pod with utility knife.

3. To stir-fry, place wok or large skillet over high heat. (Test hot pan by adding drop of water to pan; if water sizzles, pan is sufficiently hot.) Add sesame and vegetable oils, swirling to coat sides. Heat oils until hot, about 30 seconds. Add onions, peas, carrot and gingerroot; briskly toss and stir with wok utensil or spoon, keeping vegetables in constant motion about 4 minutes or until peas are bright green and crisp-tender.

4. Stir in soy sauce. Transfer to warm serving dish; sprinkle with reserved sesame seeds. Serve immediately.

Makes 4 side-dish servings

Sesame Snow Peas

Rice Noodles with Peppers

3½ ounces dried Chinese rice noodles or rice sticks
⅓ cup chicken broth
3 tablespoons soy sauce
2 tablespoons tomato paste
1 tablespoon peanut or vegetable oil
1 medium green bell pepper, cut into thin strips
1 medium red bell pepper, cut into thin strips
1 medium onion, cut into thin wedges
2 cloves garlic, minced

1. Place rice noodles in bowl; cover with warm water. Soak 15 minutes to soften. Drain; cut into 3-inch pieces.

2. Combine broth, soy sauce and tomato paste in small bowl.

3. Heat wok or large skillet over medium-high heat. Add oil; heat until hot. Add bell peppers, onion and garlic; stir-fry 4 to 5 minutes until vegetables are crisp-tender.

4. Stir in broth mixture; heat through. Add noodles; stir-fry 3 minutes or until heated through.

Makes 6 servings

Sesame Broccoli

1 bag (16 ounces) BIRDS EYE® frozen Broccoli Cuts
1 tablespoon sesame seeds
1 tablespoon oil
Dash soy sauce (optional)

- Cook broccoli according to package directions.

- Cook sesame seeds in oil 1 to 2 minutes or until golden brown, stirring frequently.

- Toss broccoli with sesame seed mixture. Add soy sauce, salt and pepper to taste.

Makes 4 to 6 servings

Prep Time: 1 minute   **Cook Time:** 8 to 9 minutes

Japanese Pear Salad

2 tablespoons packed brown sugar
2 tablespoons rice vinegar, red wine vinegar or balsamic vinegar
2 fresh Northwest Anjou or Bosc pears, cored and sliced
⅓ cup thinly sliced mushrooms
¼ cup each thinly sliced green pepper and radishes
4 Green Onion Brushes (recipe follows)

Combine sugar and vinegar; gently toss pears in mixture. Allow to stand 30 minutes to 1 hour to blend flavors; stir occasionally. Drain pears and arrange with vegetables on individual trays or plates.   *Makes 4 servings*

Green Onion Brushes: Cut 3-inch piece off root ends of 4 green onions. Cut three 1-inch lengthwise slashes through root end; rotate onion half-turn and make three more 1-inch lengthwise slashes. Place in iced water. Drain before using.

Favorite recipe from ***Pear Bureau Northwest***

Curried Rice & Green Beans

2 teaspoons vegetable oil
2 cups sliced mushrooms
1 clove garlic, minced
½ teaspoon curry powder
¼ teaspoon cumin seed (optional)
1 cup fat-free reduced-sodium chicken broth
1 cup frozen cut green beans or fresh sliced green beans
½ cup uncooked long-grain white rice
4 slices Canadian bacon, cut into short thin strips
¼ teaspoon black pepper

1. Heat oil in small saucepan. Add mushrooms and garlic. Cook and stir over medium-low heat about 5 minutes. Stir in curry powder and cumin seed, if desired. Cook and stir 30 seconds.

2. Add chicken broth; bring to a boil. Stir in green beans and rice. Reduce heat to low; cover and simmer about 18 minutes or until rice is tender and liquid is absorbed.

3. Stir in Canadian bacon and pepper. Heat just until bacon is hot.   *Makes 6 servings*

Curried Rice & Green Beans

Stewed Mushrooms on Asparagus with Vegetarian Oyster Sauce

7 ounces asparagus, trimmed
Salt
Vegetable oil
2 slices ginger
4 ounces fresh black mushrooms
4 ounces baby corn
3 tablespoons LEE KUM KEE® Vegetarian Oyster Flavored Sauce
¼ teaspoon sugar
1 teaspoon cornstarch mixed with 1 tablespoon water
¼ teaspoon LEE KUM KEE® Sesame Oil

1. Cook asparagus in boiling water with salt and vegetable oil 3 minutes. Remove and arrange on plate.

2. Heat 2 tablespoons vegetable oil in wok. Sauté ginger until fragrant. Add mushrooms and baby corn. Stir-fry 1 minute.

3. Combine Vegetarian Oyster Flavored Sauce, ⅔ cup water and sugar in small bowl; add to wok. Simmer 5 minutes. Add cornstarch mixture; simmer until thickened. Place mixture over asparagus and sprinkle with Sesame Oil.   *Makes 4 to 6 servings*

Spicy Sesame Noodles

6 ounces uncooked dry soba (buckwheat) noodles
2 teaspoons dark sesame oil
1 tablespoon sesame seeds
¹/₂ cup fat-free reduced-sodium chicken broth
1 tablespoon creamy peanut butter
4 teaspoons reduced-sodium soy sauce
¹/₂ cup thinly sliced green onions
¹/₂ cup minced red bell pepper
1¹/₂ teaspoons finely chopped, seeded jalapeño pepper*
1 clove garlic, minced
¹/₄ teaspoon red pepper flakes

*Jalapeño peppers can sting and irritate the skin; wear rubber gloves when handling peppers and do not touch eyes. Wash hands after handling.

1. Cook noodles according to package directions. (Do not overcook.) Rinse noodles thoroughly with cold water to stop cooking and remove salty residue; drain. Place noodles in large bowl; toss with oil.

2. Place sesame seeds in small skillet. Cook over medium heat about 3 minutes or until seeds begin to pop and turn golden brown, stirring frequently. Remove from heat; set aside.

3. Combine chicken broth and peanut butter in small bowl with wire whisk until blended. (Mixture may look curdled.) Stir in soy sauce, green onions, bell pepper, jalapeño pepper, garlic and red pepper flakes.

4. Pour mixture over noodles; toss to coat. Cover and let stand 30 minutes at room temperature or refrigerate up to 24 hours. Sprinkle with toasted sesame seeds before serving.

Makes 6 servings

Indian-Style Vegetable Stir-Fry

1 teaspoon canola oil
1 teaspoon curry powder
1 teaspoon ground cumin
⅛ teaspoon red pepper flakes
1½ teaspoons minced seeded jalapeño pepper*
2 cloves garlic, minced
¾ cup chopped red bell pepper
¾ cup thinly sliced carrots
3 cups cauliflower florets
½ cup water, divided
½ teaspoon salt
2 teaspoons finely chopped fresh cilantro (optional)

*Jalapeño peppers can sting and irritate the skin; wear rubber gloves when handling peppers and do not touch eyes. Wash hands after handling.

1. Heat oil in large nonstick skillet over medium-high heat. Add curry powder, cumin and red pepper flakes; cook and stir about 30 seconds.

2. Stir in jalapeño pepper and garlic. Add bell pepper and carrots; mix well. Add cauliflower; reduce heat to medium.

3. Stir in ¼ cup water; cook and stir until water evaporates. Add remaining ¼ cup water; cover and cook about 8 to 10 minutes or until vegetables are crisp-tender, stirring occasionally.

4. Add salt; mix well. Sprinkle with cilantro and garnish with mizuna* and additional red bell pepper, if desired.   *Makes 6 servings*

Mizuna is a Japanese salad green that can be found from spring through summer at specialty produce markets.

Indian-Style Vegetable Stir-Fry

Sweet and Sour Vegetables

3 cups broccoli florets
2 medium carrots, diagonally sliced
1 large red bell pepper, cut into short, thin strips
¼ cup water
2 teaspoons cornstarch
1 teaspoon sugar
⅓ cup unsweetened pineapple juice
1 tablespoon reduced-sodium soy sauce
1 tablespoon rice vinegar
½ teaspoon dark sesame oil

1. Combine broccoli, carrots and bell pepper in large nonstick skillet with tight fitting lid. Add water; bring to a boil over high heat. Reduce heat to medium. Cover and steam 4 minutes or until vegetables are crisp-tender.

2. Meanwhile, combine cornstarch and sugar in small bowl. Blend in pineapple juice, soy sauce and vinegar until smooth.

3. Transfer vegetables to colander; drain. Stir pineapple mixture and add to skillet. Cook and stir 2 minutes or until sauce boils and thickens.

4. Return vegetables to skillet; toss with sauce. Stir in oil. Garnish with green onions and fresh cilantro, if desired.   *Makes 4 side-dish servings*

Sweet and Sour Vegetables

Asian Rice & Squash Noodles with Peanut Sauce

2 boxes UNCLE BEN'S® COUNTRY INN® Oriental Fried Rice
1 medium spaghetti squash
4 tablespoons peanut butter
2 tablespoons soy sauce
1 tablespoon grated gingerroot
6 green onions, sliced

PREP: CLEAN: Wash hands. Carefully cut squash in half lengthwise. Remove seeds and place flesh-side down in microwavable baking dish. Add ½ cup water; cover with plastic wrap.

COOK: Microwave squash at HIGH 9 to 10 minutes or until skin is firm but soft. Remove from dish and allow to cool until safe to handle. Spoon out flesh into bowl (it will come out in strands like spaghetti). Meanwhile, prepare rice according to package directions. In large nonstick skillet, combine peanut butter, soy sauce and gingerroot. Heat slightly; add squash and rice. Mix thoroughly.

SERVE: Garnish rice and squash mixture with green onions.

CHILL: Refrigerate leftovers immediately.

Makes 6 servings

Prep Time: 5 minutes   **Cook Time:** 25 minutes

WOK'S COOKING?

Squash can also be baked in 350°F oven 45 to 50 minutes (omit plastic wrap).

Asian Rice & Squash Noodles
with Peanut Sauce

Cauliflower and Potato Masala

    2 tablespoons vegetable oil
    1 teaspoon minced garlic
    1 teaspoon finely chopped fresh ginger
    1 teaspoon salt
    1 teaspoon cumin seeds
    1 teaspoon ground coriander
1½ cups chopped tomatoes, fresh or canned
    1 head cauliflower (about 1¼ pounds), broken into florets
    8 ounces medium red potatoes, peeled and cut into wedges
    ½ teaspoon Garam Masala (recipe follows)
    2 tablespoons chopped fresh cilantro

1. Heat oil in large saucepan over medium-high heat. Add seasonings; cook and stir until fragrant.

2. Add tomatoes; cook and stir 1 minute. Add cauliflower and potatoes; mix well. Reduce heat to low; cover and cook about 30 minutes or until vegetables are tender. Stir in Garam Masala; mix well. Pour into serving bowl; sprinkle with cilantro. Garnish as desired.   *Makes 6 servings*

Garam Masala

    2 teaspoons cumin seeds
    2 teaspoons whole black peppercorns
1½ teaspoons coriander seeds
    1 teaspoon fennel seeds
    ¾ teaspoon whole cloves
    ½ teaspoon whole cardamom seeds, pods removed
    1 cinnamon stick, broken

Preheat oven to 250°F. Combine all ingredients and spread on baking sheet; bake 30 minutes, stirring occasionally. Grind warm spices in spice mill or clean coffee grinder. Store in refrigerator.

Makes about 3 tablespoons

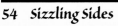

Cauliflower and Potato Masala

Happy Chicken

Hot & Sour Chicken

4 to 6 boneless skinless chicken breasts (about 1 to 1½ pounds)
1 package (1 ounce) dry hot-and-sour soup mix
1 cup chicken or vegetable broth

Slow Cooker Directions
Place chicken in slow cooker. Add soup mix and broth. Cover and cook on LOW 5 to 6 hours. Serve and garnish as desired.   *Makes 4 to 6 servings*

WOK'S COOKING?

This dish can be served over steamed white rice and topped with crispy Chinese noodles. Or, for a colorful variation, serve it over a bed of snow peas and sugar snap peas tossed with diced red bell pepper.

Hot & Sour Chicken

Crispy Mandarin Chicken

1 pound boneless, skinless chicken breast halves
½ cup soy sauce
¼ cup hoisin sauce
¼ cup honey
2 cloves garlic, minced
¾ cup CRISCO® Oil*
1 cup plus 1 tablespoon cornstarch, divided
1 can (11 ounces) mandarin oranges in light syrup, undrained
2 tablespoons balsamic vinegar
1 teaspoon minced fresh ginger
2 tablespoons water

Use your favorite Crisco Oil product.

Rinse chicken; pat dry. Cut into ¾-inch-wide strips.

Combine soy sauce, hoisin sauce, honey and garlic in 9-inch square glass dish. Add chicken, turning to coat. Refrigerate 45 minutes, turning once.

Heat oil in medium skillet on medium heat.

Remove chicken from marinade. Reserve marinade. Coat chicken with 1 cup cornstarch. Fry in hot oil about 3 minutes per side or until golden brown and no longer pink in center, reducing heat if necessary. Drain on paper towels.

Drain syrup from oranges into medium saucepan. Add reserved marinade, vinegar and ginger. Simmer 10 minutes or until slightly thickened. Combine water and remaining 1 tablespoon cornstarch. Stir into saucepan. Cook and stir until mixture comes to a boil. Remove from heat. Stir in oranges. Spoon over chicken. *Makes 4 servings*

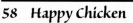

Orange Chicken Oriental

3 **whole boneless skinless chicken breasts, cut into 2-inch strips**
½ **teaspoon salt**
¼ **teaspoon ground ginger**
2 **tablespoons vegetable oil**
1 **small garlic clove, minced**
1 **can (8¼ ounces) pineapple chunks, undrained**
1 **cup Florida orange juice, divided**
1 **teaspoon instant chicken bouillon granules**
2 **tablespoons wine vinegar**
⅓ **cup sliced celery**
1 **small green bell pepper, cut into ¼-inch strips**
1 **small onion, sliced**
1 **small tomato, cut in wedges**
3 **tablespoons flour**
2 **tablespoons soy sauce**
1 **tablespoon sugar**
 Hot cooked rice

Sprinkle chicken with salt and ginger. Heat oil in large skillet over medium heat; add chicken and garlic and cook 5 minutes. Add liquid from pineapple, ¾ cup of the orange juice, the bouillon and vinegar. Cover; simmer 10 minutes or until chicken is tender.

Add celery, green pepper and onion. Cover; cook 5 minutes longer. Add tomato wedges and pineapple chunks. In small bowl, blend together flour, soy sauce, sugar and remaining ¼ cup orange juice. Add to skillet and cook, stirring constantly, until mixture thickens and comes to a boil; cook 1 minute longer. Serve over rice, if desired. *Makes 4 servings*

Favorite recipe from ***Florida Department of Citrus***

Indian Chicken with Couscous

1 pound boneless skinless chicken breasts
2 teaspoons olive oil
1 cup chopped onion
1 cup chopped green bell pepper
1 teaspoon chili powder
1 teaspoon curry powder
$\frac{1}{2}$ teaspoon ground red pepper
1 can (14$\frac{1}{2}$ ounces) Mexican-style stewed tomatoes, undrained
$\frac{1}{3}$ cup golden raisins
1$\frac{1}{3}$ cups reduced-sodium chicken broth
1$\frac{1}{3}$ cups uncooked quick-cooking couscous
$\frac{1}{2}$ cup plain nonfat yogurt
$\frac{1}{4}$ cup sliced green onions

1. Cut chicken into $\frac{1}{4}$-inch slices; cut each slice into 1-inch strips.

2. Heat oil in large nonstick skillet over medium-high heat until hot. Add chicken; cook and stir 5 minutes or until chicken is no longer pink. Remove chicken from skillet; set aside.

3. Add onion, bell pepper, chili powder, curry powder and red pepper to same skillet; cook and stir 5 minutes or until vegetables are tender.

4. Stir chicken, tomatoes with juice and raisins into skillet; bring to a boil over high heat. Cover; reduce heat to medium-low. Simmer 15 minutes. Uncover; simmer 5 minutes, stirring occasionally.

5. Meanwhile, place chicken broth in small saucepan; bring to a boil over high heat. Stir in couscous; cover. Remove saucepan from heat; let stand 5 minutes.

6. Spoon $\frac{1}{2}$ cup couscous onto each serving plate; top with $\frac{3}{4}$ cup chicken mixture, 2 tablespoons yogurt and 1 tablespoon green onions. *Makes 4 servings*

Indian Chicken with Couscous

Chicken Ribbons Satay

½ cup creamy peanut butter
½ cup water
¼ cup soy sauce
4 cloves garlic, sliced
3 tablespoons lemon juice
2 tablespoons firmly packed brown sugar
¾ teaspoon ground ginger
½ teaspoon crushed red pepper flakes
4 boneless skinless chicken breast halves
Sliced green onion tops for garnish

Combine peanut butter, water, soy sauce, garlic, lemon juice, brown sugar, ginger and red pepper flakes in a small saucepan. Cook over medium heat 1 minute or until smooth; cool. Remove garlic from sauce; discard. Reserve half of sauce for dipping. Cut chicken lengthwise into 1-inch-wide strips. Thread onto 8 metal or bamboo skewers. (Soak bamboo skewers in water at least 20 minutes to keep them from burning.)

Oil hot grid to help prevent sticking. Grill chicken, on a covered grill, over medium-hot KINGSFORD® Briquets, 6 to 8 minutes until chicken is no longer pink in center, turning once. Baste with sauce once or twice during cooking. Serve with reserved sauce garnished with sliced green onion.   *Makes 4 servings*

Chicken Ribbons Satay

Easy Make-at-Home Chinese Chicken

3 tablespoons frozen orange juice concentrate, thawed
2 tablespoons reduced-sodium soy sauce
2 tablespoons water
¾ teaspoon cornstarch
¼ teaspoon garlic powder
2 carrots, peeled
1 (12-ounce) package cut-up broccoli and cauliflower florets
Nonstick cooking spray
2 teaspoons canola oil
¾ pound boneless skinless chicken breasts, cut into bite-size pieces
1⅓ cups hot cooked rice

1. For sauce, stir together orange juice concentrate, soy sauce, water, cornstarch and garlic powder; set aside.

2. Use bottle opener or ice pick to make 4 to 5 lengthwise cuts down each carrot, not cutting completely through carrot. Cut crosswise into ¼-inch-thick slices, forming flowers.

3. Spray nonstick wok or large skillet with cooking spray. Add carrots to wok. Stir-fry over high heat 1 minute. Add broccoli and cauliflower to wok. Stir-fry 2 to 3 minutes or until vegetables are crisp-tender. Remove vegetables from wok or skillet; set aside.

4. Add oil to wok. Stir-fry chicken in hot oil 2 to 3 minutes or until no longer pink. Push chicken to sides of wok. Add sauce mixture; cook and stir until boiling. Return all vegetables to wok; cook and stir until mixture is heated through. Serve with hot cooked rice. *Makes 4 servings*

Easy Make-at-Home Chinese Chicken

Bangkok Chicken

- **1 pound boneless skinless chicken breasts**
- **2 tablespoons chopped green onion**
- **3 cloves garlic, halved**
- **1 teaspoon anchovy paste *or* 1 canned anchovy fillet**
- **¼ teaspoon red pepper flakes**
- **3 tablespoons vegetable oil**
- **1 cup drained canned button mushrooms or straw mushrooms**
- **1 cup drained canned baby corn**
- **3 tablespoons reduced-sodium soy sauce**
- **2 teaspoons sugar**
- **¾ cup fresh basil leaves**
- **Boston or romaine lettuce leaves**
- **Red jalapeño or red Thai chili pepper* flowers for garnish**

*Jalapeño peppers and Thai chilies can sting and irritate the skin; wear rubber gloves when handling peppers and do not touch eyes. Wash hands after handling.

Rinse chicken and pat dry with paper towels. Cut chicken crosswise into ¼-inch-thick slices; set aside.

Place onion, garlic, anchovy paste and red pepper flakes in food processor or blender; process until smooth. Set aside.

Heat wok over high heat about 1 minute or until hot. Drizzle oil into wok and heat 30 seconds. Add chicken; stir-fry until chicken is no longer pink in center. Remove chicken to large bowl. Reduce heat to medium.

Add onion mixture to wok; stir-fry 1 minute. Add mushrooms and corn; mix well. Add soy sauce and sugar; stir until sugar dissolves. Return chicken to wok; stir-fry until heated through. Add basil; toss gently to combine.

Line serving platter with lettuce leaves. Spoon chicken onto lettuce. Garnish, if desired.

Makes 4 servings

Indian Curry Stir-Fry

Cucumber-Mint Raita (recipe follows)
2 small (about 4-inch diameter) acorn squash
Nonstick cooking spray
1 medium onion, thinly sliced
1 tablespoon minced fresh ginger
1 medium red bell pepper, diced
1½ teaspoons curry powder
4 cloves garlic, minced
12 ounces ground chicken
2 tablespoons chopped fresh cilantro

1. Prepare Cucumber-Mint Raita. Cut squash in half through stem ends; discard seeds. Place squash halves cut sides down on plate; microwave at HIGH 10 to 12 minutes, or until tender when pierced. Cover; let stand 3 minutes or until ready to fill.

2. Spray large nonstick skillet with cooking spray; heat over high heat. Add onion and ginger; stir-fry 4 minutes or until onion is golden. Add bell pepper, curry powder and garlic; stir-fry 30 seconds or until fragrant. Add chicken; stir-fry 4 minutes or until chicken is browned and no longer pink in center. Remove from heat. Stir in cilantro. Spoon into squash halves. Serve with raita on side.

Makes 4 servings

Cucumber-Mint Raita

1 cup (8 ounces) plain nonfat yogurt
½ cup diced cucumber
2 tablespoons minced fresh mint leaves
1 to 2 tablespoons lemon juice
1 to 3 teaspoons honey (optional)

Combine yogurt, cucumber and mint in small bowl. Stir in lemon juice and honey to taste, if desired.

Makes 1¼ cups

Plum Chicken

6 ounces fresh uncooked Chinese egg noodles
¼ cup plum preserves or jam
3 tablespoons rice wine vinegar
3 tablespoons reduced-sodium soy sauce
1 tablespoon cornstarch
3 teaspoons oil, divided
1 small red onion, thinly sliced
2 cups fresh pea pods, diagonally sliced
12 ounces boneless skinless chicken breasts, cut into thin strips
4 medium plums or apricots, pitted and sliced

1. Cook noodles according to package directions, omitting salt. Drain and keep warm.

2. Stir together plum preserves, rice wine vinegar, soy sauce and cornstarch; set aside.

3. Heat 2 teaspoons oil in large nonstick skillet or wok. Add onion and cook 2 minutes or until slightly softened. Add pea pods and cook 3 minutes. Remove vegetables to medium bowl.

4. Heat remaining 1 teaspoon oil in skillet. Add chicken and cook over medium-high heat 2 to 3 minutes or until no longer pink. Push chicken to one side of skillet.

5. Stir sauce; add to skillet. Cook and stir until thick and bubbly. Stir in vegetables and plums; coat evenly. Cook 3 minutes or until heated through. Toss with noodles and serve immediately.

Makes 4 servings

Plum Chicken

Indonesian Chicken & Rice

12 TYSON® Fresh Chicken Breast Tenders, cut into halves
1 cup UNCLE BEN'S® ORIGINAL CONVERTED® Brand Rice
1 green onion, chopped
2 tablespoons peanut oil, divided
1 tablespoon soy sauce
¼ teaspoon garlic powder
1 can (14½ ounces) low-sodium chicken broth
¼ cup cashews, chopped

PREP: Mix green onion, 1 tablespoon oil, soy sauce and garlic powder in reclosable plastic bag. CLEAN: Wash hands. Add chicken to bag; close bag and toss to coat well. Refrigerate 10 to 15 minutes.

COOK: Meanwhile, prepare rice according to package directions, substituting chicken broth for water. In large skillet, heat remaining 1 tablespoon oil over medium-high heat. Add chicken and marinade. Sauté 10 to 15 minutes or until internal juices of chicken run clear. (Or insert instant-read meat thermometer in thickest part of chicken. Temperature should read 170°F.)

SERVE: Serve chicken over cooked rice and garnish with cashews and additional green onions, if desired.

CHILL: Refrigerate leftovers immediately.

Makes 4 servings

Prep Time: 10 minutes   **Cook Time:** 25 minutes

Indonesian Chicken & Rice

Fried Noodles with Chicken Marinade

4 tablespoons vegetable oil, divided
2 ounces shredded chicken fillet
5 ounces bean sprouts
4 ounces shredded carrot
12 ounces cooked noodles
6 tablespoons LEE KUM KEE® Chicken Marinade
2 ounces shredded ham
½ teaspoon salt
1 green onion, shredded

1. Heat 2 tablespoons oil in wok; stir-fry chicken until half done. Add bean sprouts and carrot; cook until tender. Remove to serving dish.

2. Heat remaining 2 tablespoons oil in wok. Stir-fry noodles, Chicken Marinade, ham and salt. Mix well; add to chicken mixture. Garnish with onion.   *Makes 4 servings*

Chicken Tandoori with Jarlsberg Lite™

8 ounces (1 cup) plain yogurt
1 tablespoon minced garlic (3 to 4 cloves)
2 teaspoons fresh thyme *or* 1 teaspoon dried thyme leaves
2 teaspoons paprika
2 teaspoons ground cumin
    Pinch ground cloves (optional)
4 boneless skinless chicken breast halves, flattened to ¼ inch
    (about 1½ pounds)
¼ cup seasoned dry bread crumbs
1 cup (4 ounces) shredded JARLSBERG LITE™ Cheese

Mix first six ingredients in large glass bowl; reserve ¼ cup. Add chicken to bowl, turning to coat evenly. Marinate in refrigerator 2 hours.

Remove chicken from yogurt mixture; discard yogurt mixture. Mix reserved ¼ cup yogurt mixture, bread crumbs and cheese. Spread one quarter of the cheese mixture on each chicken breast. Roll up from pointed end and secure with toothpicks.

Broil on rack of broiler pan, 10 to 12 inches from heat source, 12 to 15 minutes or until done, turning after 5 minutes.

Remove toothpicks. Serve with brown rice and vinegared cucumbers. Garnish with lemon slices and cilantro, if desired.

Makes 4 servings

Chicken Teriyaki

  1 pound boneless skinless chicken tenders
  1 can (6 ounces) pineapple juice
¼ cup soy sauce
  1 tablespoon sugar
  1 tablespoon minced fresh ginger
  1 tablespoon minced garlic
  1 tablespoon vegetable oil
  1 tablespoon molasses
24 cherry tomatoes (optional)
  2 cups hot cooked rice

Slow Cooker Directions
Combine all ingredients except rice in slow cooker. Cover; cook on LOW 2 hours or until chicken is tender. Serve chicken and sauce over rice.

Makes 4 servings

Combination Chop Suey

2 whole chicken breasts
4 cups chicken broth
1 cup water
4 teaspoons soy sauce
2 teaspoons cornstarch
1 teaspoon instant chicken bouillon granules
3 tablespoons vegetable oil
8 ounces boneless lean pork, finely chopped
½ head bok choy or napa cabbage (about 8 ounces), finely
 chopped
4 ounces fresh green beans, trimmed and cut into 1-inch pieces
3 ribs celery, diagonally cut into ½-inch pieces
2 yellow onions, chopped
1 large carrot, chopped
8 ounces medium shrimp, peeled and deveined
1 can (8 ounces) sliced bamboo shoots, drained
Steamed Rice (recipe follows, optional)

1. Combine chicken and broth in large saucepan. Bring to a boil over medium-high heat. Reduce heat to low; cover. Simmer 20 to 30 minutes or until chicken is no longer pink in center. Remove from heat. Let stand until chicken is cool. Remove skin and bones from chicken. Coarsely chop chicken.

2. Combine water, soy sauce, cornstarch and bouillon granules; set aside.

3. Heat oil in wok or large skillet over high heat. Add pork; stir-fry until no longer pink in center, about 5 minutes. Remove from wok; set aside.

continued on page 76

Combination Chop Suey

Combination Chop Suey, continued

4. Add cabbage, beans, celery, onions and carrot to wok; stir-fry until crisp-tender, about 3 minutes. Stir soy sauce mixture; add to wok. Cook and stir until liquid boils and thickens, about 3 minutes. Add chicken, shrimp, pork and bamboo shoots. Cook and stir until shrimp turn pink and are cooked through, about 3 minutes. Serve over hot Steamed Rice and garnish, if desired.

Makes 4 to 6 servings

Steamed Rice

1 cup uncooked long-grain rice
2 cups water
1 teaspoon salt
1 tablespoon oil

1. Place rice in strainer; rinse under cold running water to remove excess starch. Combine rice, water, salt and oil in 3-quart saucepan.

2. Cook over medium-high heat until water comes to a boil. Reduce heat to low; cover. Simmer 15 to 20 minutes or until rice is tender.

3. Remove from heat; let stand 5 minutes. Uncover; fluff rice lightly with fork. *Makes 3 cups*

Teriyaki Plum Chicken

½ **cup LA CHOY® Teriyaki Sauce**
½ **cup plum jam**
2 **tablespoons WESSON® Vegetable Oil**
2 **plums, finely chopped**
1½ **to 2 pounds chicken pieces**
   Fresh plum slices (optional)

In a large bowl, combine *all* ingredients *except* chicken and plum slices; mix well. Add chicken, cover and marinate in refrigerator at least 2 hours. Place chicken on grill over medium-hot coals. Grill, basting occasionally with marinade and turning often, for 20 minutes or until meat is no longer pink. Garnish with fresh plum slices, if desired.   *Makes 4 servings*

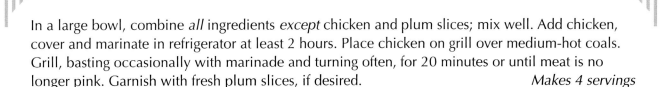

Curried Chicken & Rice

1 (5.9-ounce) package RICE-A-RONI® Chicken & Garlic Flavor
2 tablespoons margarine or butter
1 teaspoon curry powder
¼ teaspoon ground ginger
⅛ teaspoon cayenne pepper
1 pound boneless, skinless chicken thighs or breasts, cut into ¾-inch pieces
½ cup thinly sliced carrots
½ cup golden or dark raisins
1 cup broccoli flowerets
Optional condiments: mango chutney, toasted sliced almonds, chopped cilantro, plain yogurt

1. In large skillet over medium heat, sauté rice-vermicelli mix with margarine until vermicelli is golden brown. Add curry powder, ginger and cayenne pepper; sauté 15 seconds.

2. Slowly stir in 2 cups water, chicken, carrots, raisins and Special Seasonings; bring to a boil. Reduce heat to low. Cover; simmer 10 minutes.

3. Add broccoli; simmer 5 to 10 minutes or until rice is tender and chicken is no longer pink inside. Let stand 3 to 5 minutes before serving. Serve with desired condiments.

                                                                Makes 4 servings

Prep Time: 15 minutes   **Cook Time:** 30 minutes

Thai Stir Fry

1 package BUTTERBALL® Chicken Breast Tenders
1 tablespoon oil
½ cup red and yellow bell pepper strips
1 clove garlic, minced
1 tablespoon chopped fresh cilantro
1 teaspoon grated fresh ginger
2 tablespoons reduced sodium soy sauce
1 teaspoon brown sugar

Heat oil in large skillet over medium heat until hot. Cook and stir chicken about 6 minutes on each side or until golden brown. Add bell peppers, garlic, cilantro, ginger, soy sauce and brown sugar to skillet. Reduce heat to low; cover and simmer 4 minutes longer. Serve over rice or lo mein noodles, if desired.

Makes 4 servings

Tandoori Chicken Drumsticks

1½ pounds chicken drumsticks
½ cup plain yogurt
4 tablespoons PATAK'S® Tandoori Paste
4 tablespoons chunky-style peanut butter
2 teaspoons cider vinegar

Remove skin from drumsticks and gently score. In large bowl, combine yogurt, tandoori paste, peanut butter and vinegar. Place drumsticks in marinade. Cover and refrigerate at least 1 hour. Grill drumsticks over medium coals 20 to 25 minutes or until cooked through, turning occasionally and basting with remaining sauce.

Makes 4 servings

Thai Stir Fry

Coconut Chicken Curry

    1 tablespoon vegetable oil
    4 boneless skinless chicken breasts
    3 medium potatoes, peeled and chopped
    1 medium onion, sliced
    1 can (14 ounces) coconut milk
    1 cup chicken broth
 1½ teaspoons curry powder
    1 teaspoon hot pepper sauce (optional)
    ½ teaspoon salt
    ½ teaspoon black pepper
    1 package (10 ounces) frozen peas
      Hot cooked rice (optional)

Slow Cooker Directions

1. Heat oil in medium skillet over medium-high heat. Brown chicken breasts on both sides. Place potatoes and onion in slow cooker. Top with chicken breasts.

2. Combine coconut milk, broth, curry powder, pepper sauce, if desired, salt and pepper in medium bowl. Pour over chicken. Cover; cook on LOW 6 to 8 hours.

3. About 30 minutes before serving, add peas to slow cooker. Slice chicken and serve over hot cooked rice, if desired.

Makes 4 servings

WOK'S COOKING?

Curry powder is a blend of many different spices, herbs and seeds. Depending on what region of India the powder is made, the flavor can range from mild to pungent. Milder powders are used with fish and eggs, while stronger ones are used to season meats and fish.

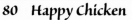

Coconut Chicken Curry

Orange Chicken Stir-Fry

½ cup orange juice
2 tablespoons sesame oil, divided
2 tablespoons soy sauce
1 tablespoon dry sherry
2 teaspoons grated fresh ginger
1 teaspoon grated orange peel
1 clove garlic, minced
1½ pounds boneless skinless chicken breasts, cut into strips
3 cups mixed fresh vegetables, such as green bell pepper, red bell pepper, snow peas, carrots, green onions, mushrooms and/or onions
1 tablespoon cornstarch
½ cup unsalted cashew bits or halves
3 cups hot cooked rice

Combine orange juice, 1 tablespoon oil, soy sauce, sherry, ginger, orange peel and garlic in large glass bowl. Add chicken; marinate in refrigerator 1 hour. Drain chicken, reserving marinade. Heat remaining 1 tablespoon oil in large skillet or wok over medium-high heat. Add chicken; stir-fry 3 minutes or until chicken is light brown. Add vegetables; stir-fry 3 to 5 minutes or until vegetables are crisp-tender. Combine cornstarch and marinade; add to skillet and stir until sauce boils and thickens. Stir in cashews; cook 1 minute more. Serve over hot rice.   *Makes 6 servings*

Favorite recipe from **USA Rice Federation**

Orange Chicken Stir-Fry

Ginger Chicken Stir-Fry

1 bag SUCCESS® Rice
¼ cup reduced-sodium soy sauce
¼ cup water
1 pound chicken breasts, skinned, boned and cut into 1½-inch
   pieces
2 tablespoons sesame oil
½ cup chopped onion
1 package (16 ounces) frozen broccoli, cauliflower and carrot
   mixture,* thawed and drained
⅓ cup dry white wine *or* chicken broth
1 teaspoon ground ginger
1 tablespoon cornstarch
1 tablespoon water

*Or, use 1 (16 ounce) package frozen vegetable mixture of your choice.

Prepare rice according to package directions.

Combine soy sauce and water in shallow baking dish. Add chicken; turn over to coat. Cover; marinate in refrigerator at least 2 hours. Drain marinade. Heat sesame oil in large skillet or wok over medium-high heat. Add chicken and onion; stir-fry until chicken is no longer pink in center. Stir in vegetables, wine and ginger. Reduce heat to low; cover. Simmer until vegetables are crisp-tender, 4 to 5 minutes. Combine cornstarch and water in small bowl; mix well. Gradually add to chicken mixture, stirring constantly; cook until sauce is thickened. Serve over hot rice.

Makes 6 servings

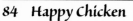

Chicken Tikka (Tandoori-Style Grilled Chicken)

2 chickens (3 pounds each), cut up
1 pint nonfat yogurt
½ cup *Frank's® RedHot®* Cayenne Pepper Sauce
1 tablespoon grated peeled fresh ginger
3 cloves garlic, minced
1 tablespoon paprika
1 tablespoon cumin seeds, crushed *or* 1½ teaspoons ground cumin
2 teaspoons salt
1 teaspoon ground coriander

Remove skin and visible fat from chicken pieces. Rinse with cold water and pat dry. Randomly poke chicken all over with tip of sharp knife. Place chicken in resealable plastic food storage bags or large glass bowl. Combine yogurt, **Frank's RedHot** Sauce, ginger, garlic, paprika, cumin, salt and coriander in small bowl; mix well. Pour over chicken pieces, turning pieces to coat evenly. Seal bags or cover bowl and marinate in refrigerator 1 hour or overnight.

Place chicken on oiled grid, reserving marinade. Grill over medium coals 45 minutes or until chicken is no longer pink near bone and juices run clear, turning and basting often with marinade. (Do not baste during last 10 minutes of cooking.) Discard any remaining marinade. Serve warm.

Makes 6 to 8 servings

Prep Time: 15 minutes   **Marinate Time:** 1 hour   **Cook Time:** 45 minutes

Slow-Simmered Curried Chicken

1½ cups chopped onions
1 medium green bell pepper, chopped
1 pound boneless skinless chicken breast or thighs, cut into
　　bite-size pieces
1 cup medium salsa
2 teaspoons grated fresh ginger
½ teaspoon garlic powder
½ teaspoon red pepper flakes
¼ cup chopped fresh cilantro
1 teaspoon sugar
1 teaspoon curry powder
¾ teaspoon salt
　Hot cooked rice

Slow Cooker Directions

1. Place onions and bell pepper in bottom of slow cooker. Top with chicken. Combine salsa, ginger, garlic powder and pepper flakes in small bowl; spoon over chicken. Cover; cook on LOW 5 to 6 hours or until chicken is tender.

2. Combine cilantro, sugar, curry powder and salt in small bowl. Stir mixture into slow cooker. Cover; cook on HIGH 15 minutes or until hot. Serve with rice.　　　　　*Makes 4 servings*

Slow-Simmered Curried Chicken

Beef Delights

Teriyaki Steak with Onions and Mushrooms

    1 boneless sirloin steak, about 1 inch thick (1½ pounds)
    ¾ cup light teriyaki sauce, divided
    1 tablespoon vegetable oil
    1 can (8 ounces) sliced mushrooms, drained
    1 small red or green bell pepper, cut into strips
  1⅓ cups *French's*® French Fried Onions, divided

1. Brush each side of steak with 1 tablespoon teriyaki sauce. Heat oil in grill pan or heavy skillet over medium-high heat. Cook steak for 3 to 4 minutes per side or until desired doneness. Remove steak; keep warm.

2. Add mushrooms and bell pepper to pan; cook until pepper is crisp-tender. Stir in remaining teriyaki sauce and ⅔ *cup* French Fried Onions; heat through.

3. Serve mushroom mixture over steak. Sprinkle with remaining onions.   *Makes 6 servings*

Prep Time: 5 minutes   **Cook Time:** 15 minutes

Teriyaki Steak with Onions and Mushrooms

Apricot Beef with Sesame Noodles

1 pound beef, cut for stroganoff or stir-fry
3 tablespoons Dijon-style mustard
3 tablespoons soy sauce
2 packages (3 ounces each) uncooked ramen noodles
2 tablespoons vegetable oil
2 cups (6 ounces) snow peas
1 medium red bell pepper, cut into cubes
¾ cup apricot preserves
½ cup beef broth
3 tablespoons chopped green onions
2 tablespoons toasted sesame seeds, divided

1. Combine beef, mustard and soy sauce in medium resealable plastic food storage bag. Shake to evenly distribute marinade; refrigerate 4 hours or overnight.

2. Cook noodles according to package directions, omitting seasoning packets.

3. Heat oil in large skillet over medium-high heat until hot. Add beef with marinade; stir-fry 2 minutes. Add snow peas and bell pepper; stir-fry 2 minutes. Add noodles, preserves, broth, onions and 1 tablespoon sesame seeds. Cook 1 minute or until heated through. Top with remaining sesame seeds before serving. *Makes 4 to 6 servings*

Tip: Toast sesame seeds in a dry, heavy skillet over medium heat 2 minutes or until golden, stirring frequently.

Apricot Beef with Sesame Noodles

Moo Shu Beef

½ pound deli roast beef, cut ⅛ inch thick
1 tablespoon dry sherry
3 teaspoons reduced-sodium soy sauce, divided
2 teaspoons cornstarch, divided
1 teaspoon minced fresh ginger
1 clove garlic, minced
½ teaspoon sugar
¼ cup cold water
¼ cup beef broth
3 tablespoons peanut or vegetable oil, divided
1 egg, lightly beaten
1 cup shredded carrots
1 can (8 ounces) sliced bamboo shoots, drained and cut into
    thin strips
3 green onions with tops, cut into ½-inch pieces
    Hoisin or plum sauce
8 flour tortillas (7 to 8 inches), warmed

1. Cut beef into thin strips. Combine sherry, 1 teaspoon soy sauce, 1 teaspoon cornstarch, ginger, garlic and sugar in large bowl; stir until smooth. Add beef and toss to coat. Marinate 10 minutes.

2. Stir water, broth and remaining 2 teaspoons soy sauce into remaining 1 teaspoon cornstarch in small bowl until smooth; set aside.

3. Heat wok over high heat about 1 minute or until hot. Drizzle 1 tablespoon oil into wok and heat 30 seconds. Pour egg into wok; tilt to coat bottom. Scramble egg, breaking into small pieces as it cooks. Remove from wok.

continued on page 94

Moo Shu Beef

Moo Shu Beef, continued

4. Add remaining 2 tablespoons oil to wok and heat 30 seconds. Add carrots; stir-fry 1 minute. Add beef mixture, bamboo shoots and green onions; stir-fry 1 minute. Stir broth mixture until smooth; add to wok. Cook and stir 1 minute or until sauce boils and thickens. Cook 1 minute more. Stir in egg.

5. Spread equal amount of hoisin sauce on each tortilla. Spoon beef mixture over sauce. Fold bottom of tortilla up over filling, then fold sides over filling. Transfer to serving plate.

Makes 4 servings

Note: Hoisin sauce is a thick, dark brown sauce made from soybeans, flour, sugar, spices, garlic, chili and salt. It has a sweet, spicy flavor.

Broccoli Beef

2 tablespoons vegetable oil
1 teaspoon chopped shallots
10 ounces sliced beef
**6 tablespoons LEE KUM KEE® Stir-Fry Sauce, LEE KUM KEE® Spicy
   Stir-Fry Sauce or LEE KUM KEE® Stir-Fry Sauce Kung Pao,
   divided**
1 cup cooked broccoli florets

Heat skillet over medium heat. Add oil. Sauté shallots. Add beef and 2 tablespoons Stir-Fry Sauce; stir-fry. When beef is half done, add broccoli and remaining 4 tablespoons Stir-Fry Sauce. Cook and stir until beef is done and broccoli is tender and heated through.

Makes 4 servings

Sesame Steak

Sauce

¼ cup LA CHOY® Soy Sauce

¼ cup BUTTERBALL® Chicken Broth

1½ tablespoons cornstarch

1 tablespoon dry sherry

¼ teaspoon Oriental sesame oil

Steak and Vegetables

2 tablespoons dry sherry

1 tablespoon LA CHOY® Soy Sauce

1 tablespoon cornstarch

1 pound round steak, sliced into thin 2-inch strips

4 tablespoons WESSON® Oil, divided

1 teaspoon *each:* minced fresh garlic and gingerroot

1 cup chopped red bell pepper

1 cup sliced fresh mushrooms

1 package (10 ounces) frozen French-cut green beans,
thawed and drained

1 can (14 ounces) LA CHOY® Bean Sprouts, drained

1 can (8 ounces) LA CHOY® Sliced Water Chestnuts, drained

½ cup sliced green onions

2 tablespoons toasted sesame seeds

In small bowl, combine sauce ingredients; set aside. In medium bowl, combine sherry, soy sauce and cornstarch; mix well. Add steak; toss gently to coat. In large nonstick skillet or wok, heat 3 tablespoons oil. Add half of steak mixture; stir-fry until lightly browned. Remove steak from skillet; set aside. Repeat with remaining steak mixture. Heat remaining 1 tablespoon oil in same skillet. Add garlic and ginger; cook and stir 10 seconds. Add bell pepper; stir-fry 1 minute. Add mushrooms and green beans; stir-fry 1 minute. Stir sauce; add to skillet with bean sprouts and water chestnuts. Cook, stirring constantly, until sauce is thick and bubbly. Return steak to skillet; heat thoroughly, stirring occasionally. Sprinkle with green onions and sesame seeds. Garnish, if desired.

Makes 4 to 6 servings

Thai-Style Beef & Rice

1 (6.2-ounce) package RICE-A-RONI® Fried Rice
2 tablespoons margarine or butter
1 pound boneless sirloin or top round steak, cut into thin strips
2 cloves garlic, minced
¼ teaspoon crushed red pepper flakes
1 tablespoon sesame oil or vegetable oil
2 cups fresh or frozen snow peas, halved if large
½ cup red and/or yellow bell pepper strips
3 tablespoons soy sauce
1 tablespoon peanut butter
¼ cup chopped cilantro (optional)

1. In large skillet over medium heat, sauté rice-vermicelli mix with margarine until vermicelli is golden brown.

2. Slowly stir in 2 cups water and Special Seasonings; bring to a boil. Reduce heat to low. Cover; simmer 15 to 20 minutes or until rice is tender. Let stand 3 minutes.

3. Meanwhile, toss steak with garlic and red pepper flakes; set aside. In another large skillet or wok over medium-high heat, heat oil until hot. Add snow peas and bell pepper; stir-fry 2 minutes. Add meat mixture; stir-fry 2 minutes. Add soy sauce and peanut butter; stir-fry 1 minute or until meat is barely pink inside and vegetables are crisp-tender. Serve meat mixture over rice; sprinkle with cilantro, if desired.

Makes 4 servings

Prep Time: 15 minutes   **Cook Time:** 30 minutes

Thai-Style Beef & Rice

Malaysian Curried Beef

2 tablespoons vegetable oil
2 large yellow onions, chopped
1 piece fresh ginger (about 1-inch square), minced
2 tablespoons curry powder
2 cloves garlic, minced
1 teaspoon salt
2 large baking potatoes (1 pound), peeled and cut into chunks
1 cup beef broth
1 pound ground beef chuck
2 ripe tomatoes (12 ounces), peeled and cut into chunks
   Hot cooked rice
   Purple kale and watercress sprigs for garnish

1. Heat wok over medium-high heat 1 minute or until hot. Drizzle oil into wok and heat 30 seconds. Add onions and stir-fry 2 minutes. Add ginger, curry, garlic and salt to wok. Cook and stir about 1 minute or until fragrant. Add potatoes; cook and stir 2 to 3 minutes.

2. Add beef broth to potato mixture. Cover and bring to a boil. Reduce heat to low; simmer about 20 minutes or until potatoes are fork-tender.

3. Stir ground beef into potato mixture. Cook and stir about 5 minutes or until beef is browned and no pink remains; spoon off fat, if necessary.

4. Add tomato chunks and stir gently until thoroughly heated. Spoon beef mixture into serving dish. Top center with rice. Garnish, if desired.

Makes 4 servings

Korean Beef Short Ribs

2½ pounds flanken-style beef short ribs, cut ⅜ to ½ inch thick*
¼ cup soy sauce
¼ cup water
¼ cup chopped green onions
1 tablespoon sugar
2 teaspoons dark sesame oil
2 teaspoons grated fresh ginger
2 cloves garlic, minced
½ teaspoon black pepper
1 tablespoon sesame seeds, toasted

*Flanken-style ribs can be ordered from your butcher. They are cross-cut short ribs sawed through the bones, ⅜ to ½ inch thick.

1. Place ribs in large resealable plastic food storage bag. Combine soy sauce, water, green onions, sugar, oil, ginger, garlic and pepper in small bowl; pour over ribs. Seal bag tightly, turning to coat. Marinate in refrigerator at least 4 hours or up to 24 hours, turning occasionally.

2. Prepare barbecue grill for direct cooking.

3. Drain ribs; reserve marinade. Place ribs on grid. Grill ribs, on covered grill, over medium-hot coals 5 minutes. Brush tops lightly with reserved marinade; turn and brush again. Discard remaining marinade. Continue to grill, covered, 5 to 6 minutes for medium or until desired doneness is reached. Sprinkle with sesame seeds.

Makes 4 to 6 servings

Szechwan Beef Lo Mein

1 pound well-trimmed boneless beef top sirloin steak, 1 inch thick
4 cloves garlic, minced
2 teaspoons minced fresh ginger
¾ teaspoon red pepper flakes, divided
1 tablespoon vegetable oil
1 can (about 14 ounces) vegetable broth
1 cup water
2 tablespoons reduced-sodium soy sauce
1 package (8 ounces) frozen mixed vegetables for stir-fry
1 package (9 ounces) refrigerated angel hair pasta
¼ cup chopped fresh cilantro (optional)

1. Cut steak crosswise into ⅛-inch strips; cut strips into 1½-inch pieces. Toss steak with garlic, ginger and ½ teaspoon red pepper flakes.

2. Heat oil in large nonstick skillet over medium-high heat. Add half of steak to skillet; cook and stir 3 minutes or until meat is barely pink in center. Remove from skillet; set aside. Repeat with remaining steak.

3. Add vegetable broth, water, soy sauce and remaining ¼ teaspoon red pepper flakes to skillet; bring to a boil over high heat. Add vegetables; return to a boil. Reduce heat to low; simmer, covered, 3 minutes or until vegetables are crisp-tender.

4. Uncover; stir in pasta. Return to a boil over high heat. Reduce heat to medium; simmer, uncovered, 2 minutes, separating pasta with two forks. Return steak and any accumulated juices to skillet; simmer 1 minute or until pasta is tender and steak is hot. Sprinkle with cilantro, if desired.

Makes 4 servings

Szechwan Beef Lo Mein

Korean Broiled Beef (Bulgogi)

1½ **pounds boneless beef top sirloin steak**
  2 **tablespoons Sesame Salt (recipe follows)**
  ¼ **cup soy sauce**
  2 **tablespoons rice wine, beef broth or water**
  1 **tablespoon sesame oil**
  1 **tablespoon sugar**
  ¼ **teaspoon black pepper**
  3 **green onions, green parts only, diagonally sliced**
  2 **cloves garlic, sliced**
    Leaf lettuce
    Cooked rice, roasted garlic, kimchee or Korean hot bean paste
      (optional)
    Carrot ribbon and additional green onion slices for garnish

1. Trim fat from beef; discard. Slice beef across grain into ⅛-inch-thick strips forming 3-inch-long strips.

2. Prepare Sesame Salt.

3. To prepare marinade, combine soy sauce, rice wine, Sesame Salt, sesame oil, sugar and pepper in large bowl. Add green onions, garlic and beef; toss to coat. Cover and refrigerate at least 30 minutes.

4. Preheat broiler. Spray broiler rack with nonstick cooking spray. Place strips of beef on broiler rack; set pan about 4 inches from heat source. Broil 2 minutes; turn beef and broil 1 minute for medium or until desired doneness.

5. Line platter with leaf lettuce; arrange beef on top. Serve as is or use lettuce leaves to wrap beef with choice of accompaniments and eat burrito-style. Garnish, if desired.   *Makes 4 servings*

Sesame Salt: Heat small skillet over medium heat. Add ¼ cup sesame seeds; cook and stir about 5 minutes or until seeds are golden. Cool. Process toasted sesame seeds and ¼ teaspoon salt in clean coffee or spice grinder. Refrigerate in covered glass jar.

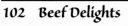

Korean Broiled Beef (Bulgogi)

Japanese-Style Steak with Garden Sunomono

Garden Sunomono

    1 medium cucumber, peeled and seeded, thinly sliced
    ½ teaspoon salt
    ¼ cup rice wine vinegar
    3 tablespoons sugar
    1 cup thinly sliced radishes
    ½ cup carrot cut into julienne strips

Japanese-Style Steak

    3 New York strip steaks, cut ¾-inch thick (8 ounces each)
    ¼ cup soy sauce
    3 tablespoons dry sherry
    1 teaspoon dark sesame oil
    ½ teaspoon ground ginger
    1 large clove garlic, minced

1. For sunomono, place cucumber in colander; sprinkle with salt. Let stand 20 minutes. Squeeze out liquid; rinse with water. Squeeze again.

2. Blend vinegar and sugar in medium bowl, stirring until sugar dissolves. Add cucumber, radishes and carrot. Cover; refrigerate 30 minutes to 2 hours, stirring occasionally.

3. Place steaks in shallow baking dish. Blend soy sauce, sherry, sesame oil, ginger and garlic in small bowl; pour over steaks. Cover; refrigerate 30 minutes to 2 hours, turning steaks occasionally.

4. To complete recipe, preheat broiler. Remove steaks from marinade; place on broiler pan rack. Discard marinade. Broil 2 to 3 inches from heat 5 to 6 minutes per side or until desired doneness.

5. Transfer steaks to cutting board; slice across the grain into ½-inch slices. Serve with sunomono.

Makes 4 servings

Serving Suggestion: Serve the steak with jasmine or white rice.

Beef with Leeks and Tofu

8 ounces boneless beef top sirloin, top loin or tenderloin steaks
2 cloves garlic, minced
8 ounces firm tofu, drained
¾ cup chicken broth
¼ cup soy sauce
1 tablespoon dry sherry
1 tablespoon cornstarch
4 teaspoons peanut or vegetable oil, divided
1 large or 2 medium leeks, sliced (white and light green portion)
1 large red bell pepper, cut into short, thin strips
1 tablespoon dark sesame oil (optional)
Hot cooked spaghetti (optional)

1. Cut beef lengthwise in half, then crosswise into ⅛-inch slices; cut each slice into 2-inch pieces. Toss beef with garlic in medium bowl. Press tofu lightly between paper towels; cut into ¾-inch triangles or squares.

2. Blend broth, soy sauce and sherry into cornstarch in small bowl until smooth.

3. Heat large, deep skillet over medium-high heat. Add 2 teaspoons peanut oil; heat until hot. Add half of beef mixture; stir-fry 2 minutes or until beef is barely pink in center. Remove to large bowl. Repeat with remaining beef. Remove and set aside.

4. Add remaining 2 teaspoons peanut oil to skillet. Add leek and red pepper; stir-fry 3 minutes or until red pepper is crisp-tender. Stir broth mixture and add to skillet along with tofu. Stir-fry 2 minutes or until sauce boils and thickens and tofu is hot, stirring frequently.

5. Return beef along with any accumulated juices to skillet; heat through. Stir in sesame oil, if desired. Serve over spaghetti, if desired. *Makes 4 servings*

Green Dragon Stir-Fry

2 tablespoons vegetable oil, divided
1 pound beef flank steak, very thinly sliced
1 bunch asparagus *or* 8 ounces green beans, cut into 2-inch pieces
1 green bell pepper, cut into strips
1 cup julienned carrots
3 large green onions, sliced
1 tablespoon minced fresh ginger
1 clove garlic, minced
¼ cup water
1 tablespoon soy sauce
1 tablespoon TABASCO® brand Green Pepper Sauce
½ teaspoon salt
2 cups hot cooked rice (optional)

Heat 1 tablespoon oil in 12-inch skillet over medium-high heat. Add flank steak; cook until well browned on all sides, stirring frequently. Remove steak to plate with slotted spoon.

Heat remaining 1 tablespoon oil in skillet over medium heat. Add asparagus, green bell pepper, carrots, green onions, ginger and garlic; cook about 3 minutes, stirring frequently. Add water, soy sauce, TABASCO® Green Pepper Sauce, salt and steak; heat to boiling over high heat.

Reduce heat to low; simmer, uncovered, 3 minutes, stirring occasionally. Serve with rice, if desired.

Makes 4 servings

WOK'S COOKING?

Stir-fry is also delicious served over ramen or soba noodles.

Green Dragon Stir-Fry

Vietnamese Loin Steaks with Black Bean Relish

1 stalk lemongrass, outer leaves removed and upper stalk trimmed
1 tablespoon sugar
1 tablespoon fish sauce
1 teaspoon minced garlic
½ to 1 teaspoon hot chili oil
2 boneless beef top loin steaks (8 ounces each), about 1 inch thick
1 can (about 8¾ ounces) whole baby corn (about 8 cobs), rinsed
    and drained
1 can (about 15 ounces) black beans, rinsed and drained
1 cup diced mango
½ green bell pepper, cut into strips
2 tablespoons chopped red onion
1 jalapeño pepper,* seeded and sliced (optional)
  Juice of ½ lemon
½ teaspoon vegetable oil
½ teaspoon honey
⅛ teaspoon salt

*Jalapeños can sting and irritate the skin; wear rubber gloves when peppers handling
and do not touch eyes. Wash hands after handling.

1. Flatten lemongrass with meat mallet and mince. Combine with sugar, fish sauce, garlic and chili oil in baking dish. Cut each steak lengthwise into 2 strips. Place in dish with marinade, coating both sides. Cover; refrigerate 1 hour, turning once.

2. Halve corn cobs diagonally; combine with beans, mango, bell pepper, onion and jalapeño, if desired, in large bowl. Combine lemon juice, oil, honey and salt in small bowl; stir into bean mixture.

3. Grill steaks on covered grill over medium-hot coals 10 minutes for medium-rare or until desired doneness is reached, turning once. Serve with relish. *Makes 4 servings*

Vietnamese Loin Steak with Black Bean Relish

Masaman Curry Beef

Masaman Curry Paste (page 112) *or* ½ cup canned Masaman
    curry paste
2 pounds boiling potatoes
4 tablespoons vegetable oil, divided
1 medium onion, cut into strips
1½ pounds boneless beef chuck or round, cubed
2 cans (about 14 ounces each) unsweetened coconut milk
3 tablespoons fish sauce
1 large red bell pepper, cut into strips
½ cup roasted peanuts, chopped
2 tablespoons lime juice
¼ cup slivered fresh basil leaves or chopped fresh cilantro
    Hot cooked rice or noodles (optional)
    Lime wedges for garnish

1. Prepare Masaman Curry Paste; set aside.

2. Peel potatoes and cut into 1½-inch pieces. Place in bowl with cold water to cover; set aside.

3. Heat 1 tablespoon oil in wok or large skillet over medium-high heat. Add onion; stir-fry 6 to 8 minutes or until golden. Transfer onion to bowl with slotted spoon.

4. Add 1 tablespoon oil to wok. Increase heat to high. Add half the beef; stir-fry 2 to 3 minutes until browned on all sides.

5. Transfer beef to another bowl; set aside. Repeat with remaining beef, adding 1 tablespoon oil to prevent sticking if necessary. Set aside.

6. Reduce heat to medium. Add remaining 1 tablespoon oil and curry paste to wok; cook and stir 1 to 2 minutes or until very fragrant. Add coconut milk and fish sauce; stir to scrape bits of cooked meat and spices from bottom of wok.

continued on page 112

Masaman Curry Beef

7. Return beef to wok. Increase heat to high and bring to a boil. Reduce heat to low; cover and simmer 45 minutes or until meat is fork-tender.

8. Drain potatoes; add to wok with onions. Cook 20 to 30 minutes more or until potatoes are fork-tender. Stir in bell pepper; cook 1 to 2 minutes more or until pepper is heated through.

9. Stir in peanuts and lime juice. Pour into serving bowl and sprinkle with basil. Serve with rice or noodles and garnish, if desired.

Makes 6 servings

Masaman Curry Paste

6 tablespoons coarsely chopped ginger
3 tablespoons coarsely chopped garlic (10 to 12 cloves)
2 tablespoons ground cumin
2 tablespoons ground mace or nutmeg
4 teaspoons packed brown sugar
2 teaspoons grated lemon peel
2 teaspoons ground cinnamon
2 to 4 teaspoons ground red pepper*
2 teaspoons paprika
2 teaspoons black pepper
2 teaspoons anchovy paste *or* 1 minced anchovy fillet
1 teaspoon turmeric
1 teaspoon ground cloves

*Use 2 teaspoons ground red pepper for mild paste and up to 4 teaspoons for very hot paste.

Place all ingredients in food processor or blender; process until mixture forms dry paste.

Makes about ½ cup

Asian Ramen Beef with Almonds

1 pound roast beef, sliced ⅛-inch thick
4 tablespoons teriyaki marinade
⅔ cup slivered almonds, toasted and divided
1 pound broccoli cole slaw
2 packages oriental flavor ramen noodles, broken into small pieces
  (reserve seasoning packets)
4 teaspoons butter or margarine

1. In large saucepan, bring 2 quarts of water to full boil.

2. Trim any visible fat from deli roast beef and cut into julienne strips. In microwave safe bowl, toss beef with teriyaki sauce and set aside.

3. Toast almonds on cookie sheet under broiler about 2 minutes or until lightly browned. Set aside 2 tablespoons to use for garnish.

4. Add broccoli slaw to boiling water and cook over high heat for 3 minutes. To broccoli, add ramen noodles and oriental seasoning packets, reserving ½ teaspoon of seasoning, and cook an additional 3 minutes. Drain in colander. Return to pan and toss with butter, reserved oriental seasoning and toasted almonds. Cover and keep warm.

5. Warm beef in microwave at 50 percent power for 3 minutes.

6. To serve, place noodle and broccoli mixture on platter leaving a well in the center of the platter for beef. Mound beef in center. Garnish with 2 tablespoons reserved almonds and optional garnish, if desired.

Makes 4 servings

Optional Garnish: Break ½ package of ramen noodles into small pieces. Mix with ½ tablespoon teriyaki marinade. Sprinkle around edge of platter.

Favorite recipe from **North Dakota Beef Commission**

Quick 'n' Tangy Beef Stir-Fry

Sauce

    ½ **cup** *French's*® **Worcestershire Sauce**
    ½ **cup water**
    2 **tablespoons sugar**
    2 **teaspoons cornstarch**
    ½ **teaspoon ground ginger**
    ½ **teaspoon garlic powder**

Stir-fry

    1 **pound thinly sliced beef steak**
    3 **cups sliced bell peppers**

1. Combine ingredients for sauce. Marinate beef in ¼ *cup* sauce 5 minutes. Heat *1 tablespoon oil* in large skillet or wok over high heat. Stir-fry beef in batches 5 minutes or until browned.

2. Add peppers; cook 2 minutes. Add remaining sauce; stir-fry until sauce thickens. Serve over hot cooked rice or ramen noodles, if desired. *Makes 4 servings*

Prep Time: 10 minutes   **Cook Time:** about 10 minutes

Quick 'n' Tangy Beef Stir-Fry

Szechuan Grilled Flank Steak

1 beef flank steak (1¼ to 1½ pounds)
¼ cup soy sauce
¼ cup seasoned rice vinegar
2 tablespoons dark sesame oil
4 cloves garlic, minced
2 teaspoons minced fresh ginger
½ teaspoon red pepper flakes
¼ cup water
½ cup thinly sliced green onions
2 to 3 teaspoons sesame seeds, toasted
Hot cooked rice (optional)

1. Place steak in large resealable plastic food storage bag. To prepare marinade, combine soy sauce, vinegar, oil, garlic, ginger and red pepper in small bowl; pour over steak. Press air from bag and seal; turn to coat. Marinate in refrigerator 3 hours, turning once.

2. To prevent sticking, spray grid with nonstick cooking spray. Prepare coals for grilling. Drain steak, reserving marinade in small saucepan. Place steak on grid over medium heat; grill, uncovered, 17 to 21 minutes for medium rare to medium or until desired doneness, turning once.

3. Add water to reserved marinade. Bring to a boil over high heat. Reduce heat to low; simmer 5 minutes. Transfer steak to carving board. Slice steak across grain into thin slices. Drizzle steak with boiled marinade. Sprinkle with green onions and sesame seeds. Serve with rice.

Makes 4 to 6 servings

Szechuan Grilled Flank Steak

Pork Specialties

Cantonese Pork

1 tablespoon vegetable oil
1 pork tenderloin (about 2 pounds), cut into strips
1 can (8 ounces) pineapple chunks in juice, undrained
1 can (8 ounces) tomato sauce
2 cans (4 ounces each) sliced mushrooms, drained
1 medium onion, thinly sliced
3 tablespoons brown sugar
2 tablespoons Worcestershire sauce
1½ teaspoons salt
1½ teaspoons white vinegar
    Hot cooked rice

Slow Cooker Directions

1. Heat oil in large nonstick skillet over medium-low heat. Brown pork on all sides. Drain excess fat; discard.

2. Place pork and remaining ingredients in slow cooker. Cover and cook on HIGH 4 hours or on LOW 6 to 8 hours. Serve over rice. *Makes 8 servings*

Cantonese Pork

Oriental-Style Ground Pork

1 package (8 ounces) shredded carrots
1 tablespoon sugar
1 teaspoon distilled white vinegar or rice vinegar
2 green onions with tops
1 teaspoon cornstarch
½ teaspoon chili powder
¼ cup chicken broth
1 tablespoon reduced-sodium soy sauce
1 tablespoon vegetable oil
1 pound ground pork
8 large mushrooms, sliced
   Boston lettuce leaves

1. Combine carrots, sugar and vinegar in medium bowl; set aside.

2. Slice green onions diagonally into 1-inch pieces.

3. Combine cornstarch and chili powder in small bowl. Stir broth and soy sauce into cornstarch mixture until smooth. Set aside.

4. Heat wok over medium-high heat 1 minute or until hot. Drizzle oil into wok and heat 30 seconds. Add pork; stir-fry until well browned. Add mushrooms; stir-fry until tender.

5. Stir broth mixture until smooth and add to wok. Cook until sauce boils and thickens. Add green onions; stir-fry 1 minute.

6. Line serving plate with lettuce leaves. Arrange carrot mixture in layer over leaves. Top with pork mixture. (Traditionally, the lettuce leaves are eaten as a wrapper to hold the ground meat mixture.)

Makes 4 servings

Oriental-Style Ground Pork

Peanut Pork Tenderloin

$\frac{1}{3}$ **cup chunky unsweetened peanut butter**
$\frac{1}{3}$ **cup regular or light canned coconut milk**
$\frac{1}{4}$ **cup lemon juice or dry white wine**
3 **tablespoons soy sauce**
3 **cloves garlic, minced**
2 **tablespoons sugar**
1 **piece (1-inch cube) fresh ginger, minced**
$\frac{1}{2}$ **teaspoon salt**
$\frac{1}{4}$ **to** $\frac{1}{2}$ **teaspoon cayenne pepper**
$\frac{1}{4}$ **teaspoon ground cinnamon**
$1\frac{1}{2}$ **pounds pork tenderloin**

Combine peanut butter, coconut milk, lemon juice, soy sauce, garlic, sugar, ginger, salt, cayenne pepper and cinnamon in 2-quart glass dish until blended. Add pork; turn to coat. Cover and refrigerate at least 30 minutes or overnight. Remove pork from marinade; discard marinade. Grill pork on covered grill over medium KINGSFORD® Briquets about 20 minutes until just barely pink in center, turning 4 times. Cut crosswise into $\frac{1}{2}$-inch slices. Serve immediately.

Makes 4 to 6 servings

Chinese Pork & Vegetable Stir-Fry

2 tablespoons BERTOLLI® Olive Oil, divided
1 pound pork tenderloin or boneless beef sirloin, cut into ¼-inch slices
6 cups assorted fresh vegetables*
1 can (8 ounces) sliced water chestnuts, drained
1 envelope LIPTON® Recipe Secrets® Onion Soup Mix
¾ cup water
½ cup orange juice
1 tablespoon soy sauce
¼ teaspoon garlic powder

*Use any of the following to equal 6 cups: broccoli florets, snow peas, thinly sliced red or green bell peppers or thinly sliced carrots.

In 12-inch skillet, heat 1 tablespoon oil over medium-high heat; brown pork. Remove and set aside.

In same skillet, heat remaining 1 tablespoon oil and cook assorted fresh vegetables, stirring occasionally, 5 minutes. Stir in water chestnuts and onion soup mix blended with water, orange juice, soy sauce and garlic powder. Bring to a boil over high heat. Reduce heat to low and simmer, uncovered, 3 minutes. Return pork to skillet and cook 1 minute or until heated through.

Makes about 4 servings

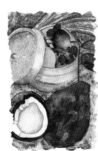

WOK'S COOKING?

Pick up pre-sliced vegetables from your local salad bar.

Stir-Fried Pork Lo Mein

Nonstick cooking spray
6 green onions, cut into 1-inch pieces
½ teaspoon garlic powder
½ teaspoon ground ginger
6 ounces pork loin roast, thinly sliced
3 cups shredded green cabbage
½ cup shredded carrots
½ cup trimmed snow peas
½ cup reduced-sodium chicken broth
2 tablespoons hoisin sauce (optional)
1 tablespoon reduced-sodium soy sauce
2 teaspoons cornstarch
8 ounces hot cooked linguine

1. Spray wok with cooking spray. Heat over medium heat until hot. Add onions, garlic powder and ginger; stir-fry 30 seconds. Add pork; stir-fry 2 minutes or until pork is no longer pink. Add vegetables; stir-fry 3 minutes or until vegetables are crisp-tender.

2. Blend chicken broth, hoisin sauce, soy sauce and cornstarch in small bowl. Add to wok. Cook and stir until mixture boils and thickens. Serve vegetables and sauce over pasta.

Makes 4 servings

Stir-Fried Pork Lo Mein

Tandoori Pork Sauté

Nutty Rice (recipe follows)
8 ounces lean pork, cut into 2×½-inch strips
½ cup sliced onion
1 clove garlic, minced
4 fresh California plums, halved, pitted and cut into thick wedges
1 cup plain low-fat yogurt
1 tablespoon all-purpose flour
1½ teaspoons grated fresh ginger
½ teaspoon ground turmeric
⅛ teaspoon ground black pepper
Additional plum wedges, orange sections and sliced green onions

Prepare Nutty Rice. Cook pork in nonstick skillet 2 minutes or until browned, turning occasionally. Transfer to platter. Add onion and garlic to skillet; cook 1 minute. Add plums; cook and stir 1 minute. Remove from heat and return pork to pan. Combine yogurt and flour; add to skillet. Stir in ginger, turmeric and pepper. Bring to a boil; reduce heat and simmer 10 minutes, stirring occasionally. Serve over Nutty Rice and surround with plum wedges, orange sections and green onions.

Makes 4 servings

Nutty Rice: Bring 2 cups water to a boil in medium saucepan. Add ¾ cup brown rice and ¼ cup wheat berries. (Or, omit wheat berries and use 1 cup brown rice.) Return to a boil. Reduce heat to low; cover and simmer 40 to 45 minutes or until rice is tender and liquid is absorbed.

Favorite recipe from **California Tree Fruit Agreement**

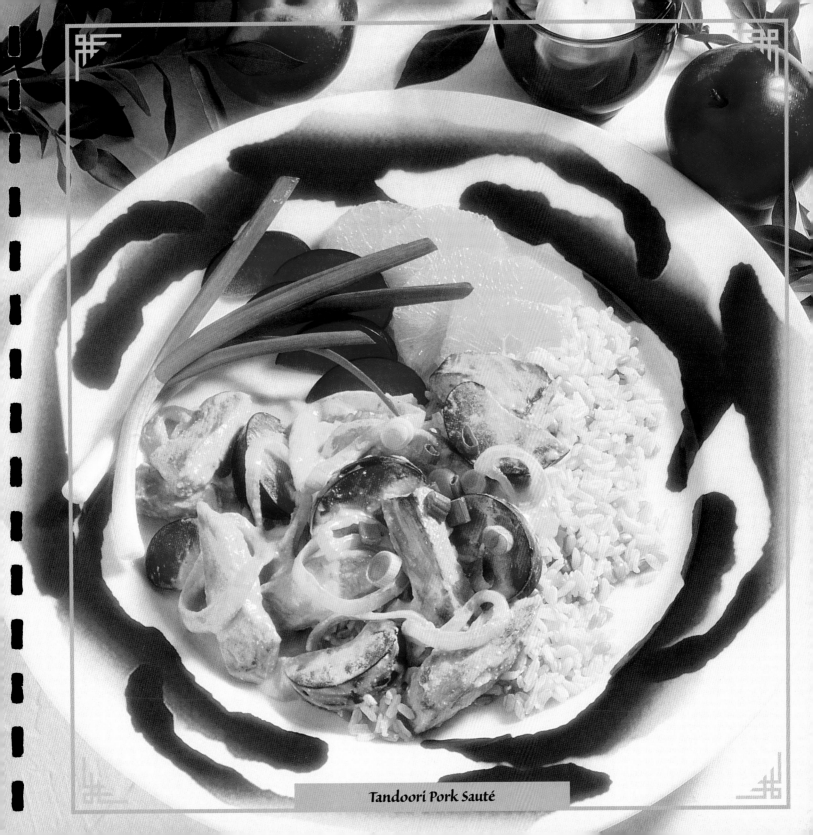

Tandoori Pork Sauté

Szechuan Pork & Vegetables

4 butterflied pork loin chops, ½ inch thick (1 to 1¼ pounds)
¼ cup plus 1 tablespoon stir-fry sauce, divided
¾ teaspoon bottled minced ginger *or* ½ teaspoon ground ginger
1 package (16 ounces) frozen Asian-style vegetables, thawed
1 can (5 ounces) crisp chow mein noodles
2 tablespoons chopped green onion

1. Heat large, deep nonstick skillet over medium heat until hot. Add pork. Spoon 1 tablespoon stir-fry sauce over pork; sprinkle with ginger. Cook 3 minutes. Turn pork; cook 3 minutes. Transfer chops to plate; set aside.

2. Add vegetables and remaining ¼ cup stir-fry sauce to skillet. Cook over medium-low heat 3 minutes; add pork. Cook 3 minutes or until pork is no longer pink in center, stirring vegetables and turning chops once.

3. While pork is cooking, arrange chow mein noodles around edges of 4 serving plates. Transfer chops to plates. Top noodles with vegetable mixture. Sprinkle with green onion.

Makes 4 servings

Prep and Cook Time: 12 minutes

Szechuan Pork & Vegetables

Stir-Fried Pork with Oranges and Snow Peas

1 cup uncooked rice
1 tablespoon vegetable oil
1 pound lean boneless pork, cut into ¼-inch-wide strips
½ pound snow peas, trimmed
½ cup bottled stir-fry sauce
2 tablespoons thawed frozen orange juice concentrate
1 can (11 ounces) mandarin orange sections, drained

1. Cook rice according to package directions.

2. Heat oil in wok or large skillet over high heat until hot. Stir-fry pork 3 minutes or until brown.

3. Add snow peas; stir-fry 2 to 3 minutes or until crisp-tender. Add stir-fry sauce and juice concentrate; stir until well blended. Gently stir in orange sections. Serve with rice.

Makes 4 servings

Prep and Cook Time: 20 minutes

Honey Sesame Tenderloin

1 pound whole pork tenderloin
½ cup soy sauce
2 cloves garlic, minced
1 tablespoon grated fresh ginger
1 tablespoon sesame oil
¼ cup honey
2 tablespoons packed brown sugar
4 tablespoons sesame seeds

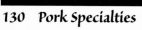

Combine soy sauce, garlic, ginger and sesame oil. Place tenderloin in resealable plastic food storage bag; pour in soy sauce mixture. Marinate 2 hours or overnight in refrigerator. Preheat oven to 375°F. Remove pork from marinade; pat dry with paper towel. Mix honey and brown sugar on plate. Place sesame seeds on another plate. Roll pork in honey mixture; roll in sesame seeds. Roast in shallow pan 20 to 30 minutes or until meat thermometer inserted in thickest part registers 160°F. Serve immediately.

Makes 4 servings

Favorite recipe from **National Pork Board**

Peking Pork Chops

6 pork chops, about 1 inch thick
¹⁄₂ cup soy or teriyaki sauce
¹⁄₄ cup brown sugar
¹⁄₄ cup Chinese ketchup or ketchup
1 teaspoon ground ginger
1 to 2 cloves garlic, crushed
Salt
Black pepper

Slow Cooker Directions

1. Trim excess fat from pork chops. Place in slow cooker.

2. Combine soy sauce, brown sugar, ketchup, ginger and garlic in small bowl; pour over meat. Cover; cook on LOW 4 to 6 hours or until pork is tender. Season with salt and pepper, if desired.

Makes 6 servings

Serving Suggestion: Serve with steamed white or jasmine rice and Chinese noodles.

Javanese Pork Saté

1 pound boneless pork loin
½ cup minced onion
2 tablespoons peanut butter
2 tablespoons lemon juice
2 tablespoons soy sauce
1 tablespoon brown sugar
1 tablespoon vegetable oil
1 clove garlic, minced
   Dash hot pepper sauce

Cut pork into ½-inch cubes; place in shallow dish. In blender or food processor combine remaining ingredients. Blend until smooth. Pour over pork. Cover and marinate in refrigerator 10 minutes. Thread pork onto skewers.

Grill or broil 10 to 12 minutes, turning occasionally, until done. Serve with hot cooked rice and vegetables, if desired.   *Makes 4 servings*

Favorite recipe from **National Pork Board**

WOK'S COOKING?

If using bamboo skewers, soak in water for about 30 minutes before using to make them more pliable and to prevent them from burning.

Javanese Pork Saté

Fried Noodle and Pork Stir-Fry

Noodle Bundles (recipe follows)
$\frac{1}{2}$ cup stir-fry sauce
$\frac{1}{4}$ cup red wine
1 teaspoon hot sauce
$\frac{1}{2}$ teaspoon cornstarch
$\frac{3}{4}$ pound boneless pork tenderloin, cut into thin pieces
2 tablespoons peanut oil, divided
1 carrot, thinly sliced
1 medium onion, chopped
2 ribs celery, thinly sliced
1 medium red bell pepper, cut into thin strips

Prepare Noodle Bundles; set aside and keep warm.

Stir together stir-fry sauce, red wine, hot sauce and cornstarch in small bowl; set aside.

Heat 1 teaspoon oil in wok or large skillet over high heat. Add pork. Stir-fry 3 minutes; remove. Add remaining teaspoon of oil to wok. Add carrot to wok; stir-fry 1 minute. Add remaining vegetables; stir-fry 3 minutes or until vegetables are tender. Return pork to wok; add sauce mixture. Cook and stir until mixture boils and sauce is slightly thickened. Serve over noodle bundles.

Makes 4 to 6 servings

Noodle Bundles: Cook 8 ounces pasta according to package directions; rinse and drain. Arrange pasta into 4 to 6 bundles. Heat 1 tablespoon peanut oil in large nonstick skillet over medium-high heat. Add 2 or 3 bundles to skillet; cook 5 minutes or until bottom of bundles are golden. Repeat with remaining bundles, adding more oil to pan as needed.

Fried Noodle and Pork Stir-Fry

Citrus Sweet & Sour Pork

1²⁄₃ cups orange-pineapple juice
2 pounds lean pork tenderloin, cut into ¹⁄₂-inch cubes
1 cup water
¹⁄₄ cup stir-fry sauce
2 cloves garlic, minced
¹⁄₃ cup sugar
¹⁄₄ cup cornstarch
¹⁄₄ cup rice vinegar
1 green pepper, cut into strips
1 red pepper, cut into strips
1 medium onion, sliced
2 seedless tangerines, peeled and sectioned
Hot cooked rice

Combine juice, pork, water, stir-fry sauce and garlic in large saucepan. Bring to a boil. Reduce heat; cover. Simmer 45 to 60 minutes or until meat is tender. Strain cooking liquid; reserve for sauce. Set meat aside.

Combine sugar and cornstarch in large saucepan. Add vinegar; stir until smooth. Gradually stir in reserved cooking liquid. Cook over medium heat, stirring constantly, until sauce thickens and comes to a boil. Add peppers and onion; simmer 5 minutes. Add meat and tangerine sections to sauce; heat thoroughly. Serve over hot cooked rice.

Makes 6 servings

Exotic Pork & Vegetables

¼ **cup water**
2 **teaspoons cornstarch**
4 **tablespoons peanut oil, divided**
6 **whole dried hot red chili peppers**
4 **cloves garlic, sliced**
1 **pork tenderloin (about ¾ pound), thinly sliced**
1 **large carrot, peeled**
2 **ounces fresh oyster, shiitake or button mushrooms,* cut into**
   halves
1 **baby eggplant, thinly sliced**
5 **ounces fresh snow peas, ends trimmed**
3 **tablespoons brown sugar**
2 **tablespoons fish sauce**
1 **tablespoon dark sesame oil**
   Hot cooked rice

Or, substitute ½ ounce dried Oriental mushrooms, soaked according to package directions.

1. Combine water and cornstarch in cup; set aside.

2. Heat wok or large skillet over high heat 1 minute or until hot. Drizzle 2 tablespoons peanut oil into wok and heat 30 seconds. Add peppers and garlic; stir-fry about 1 minute. Add pork; stir-fry 3 to 4 minutes or until no longer pink in center. Remove pork mixture to bowl and set aside.

3. Add remaining 2 tablespoons peanut oil to wok. Add carrot, mushrooms, and eggplant; stir-fry 2 minutes. Add snow peas and pork mixture; stir-fry 1 minute.

4. Stir cornstarch mixture; add to wok. Cook 1 minute or until thickened. Stir in brown sugar, fish sauce and sesame oil; cook until heated through. Serve over rice.   *Makes 4 servings*

Moo Shu Pork

1 cup DOLE® Pineapple Juice
1 tablespoon low-sodium soy sauce
2 teaspoons sesame seed oil
2 teaspoons cornstarch
8 ounces pork tenderloin, cut into thin strips
1½ cups Oriental-style mixed vegetables
¼ cup hoisin sauce (optional)
8 (8-inch) flour tortillas, warmed
2 green onions, cut into thin strips

• **Stir** juice, soy sauce, sesame seed oil and cornstarch in shallow, nonmetallic dish until blended; remove ½ cup mixture for sauce.

• **Add** pork to remaining juice mixture in shallow dish. Cover and marinate 15 minutes in refrigerator. Drain pork; discard marinade.

• **Cook** and stir pork in large, nonstick skillet over medium-high heat 2 minutes or until pork is lightly browned. Add vegetables; cook and stir 3 to 4 minutes or until vegetables are tender-crisp. Stir in reserved ½ cup juice mixture; cook 1 minute or until sauce thickens.

• **Spread** hoisin sauce onto center of each tortilla, if desired; top with moo shu pork. Sprinkle with green onions. Fold opposite sides of tortilla over filling; fold remaining sides of tortilla over filling. Garnish with slivered green onions, kumquats and fresh herbs, if desired.   *Makes 4 servings*

Prep Time: 10 minutes   **Marinate Time:** 15 minutes   **Cook Time:** 10 minutes

Moo Shu Pork

Honey Nut Stir-Fry

1 pound pork steak, pork loin or boneless chicken breast
¾ cup orange juice
⅓ cup honey
3 tablespoons soy sauce
1 tablespoon cornstarch
¼ teaspoon ground ginger
2 tablespoons vegetable oil, divided
2 large carrots, sliced diagonally
2 stalks celery, sliced diagonally
½ cup cashews or peanuts
Hot cooked rice

Cut pork into thin strips; set aside. Combine orange juice, honey, soy sauce, cornstarch and ginger in small bowl; mix well. Heat 1 tablespoon oil in large skillet over medium-high heat. Add carrots and celery; stir-fry about 3 minutes. Remove vegetables; set aside. Pour remaining 1 tablespoon oil into skillet. Add pork; stir-fry about 3 minutes. Return vegetables to skillet; add honey mixture and nuts. Cook and stir over medium-high heat until sauce comes to a boil and thickens. Serve over rice.
Makes 4 to 6 servings

Favorite recipe from **National Honey Board**

Honey Nut Stir-Fry

Stir-Fried Pork with Green Beans and Baby Corn

¾ **pound pork tenderloin**
4 **teaspoons cornstarch, divided**
2 **tablespoons soy sauce**
1 **tablespoon rice wine or dry sherry**
1 **teaspoon sugar**
½ **teaspoon dark sesame oil**
⅓ **cup plus 2 tablespoons water, divided**
2 **tablespoons peanut oil, divided**
1 **pound fresh green beans, trimmed and cut into 1½-inch pieces**
2 **cloves garlic, minced**
1 **teaspoon finely chopped ginger**
1 **tablespoon black bean sauce**
1 **can (15 ounces) whole baby corn, drained and rinsed**

1. Slice pork across grain into thin slices; cut slices into ¾-inch strips.

2. Combine 1 teaspoon cornstarch, soy sauce, rice wine, sugar and sesame oil in medium bowl; mix well. Add pork; toss to coat. Set aside to marinate 20 to 30 minutes. Combine remaining 3 teaspoons cornstarch and ⅓ cup water in small cup; set aside.

3. Heat 1 tablespoon peanut oil in wok or large skillet over high heat. Add beans; stir-fry about 4 minutes. Add remaining 2 tablespoons water; reduce heat to medium-low. Cover and simmer 10 to 12 minutes or until crisp-tender. Remove from wok; set aside.

4. Heat remaining 1 tablespoon peanut oil in wok over high heat. Add garlic, ginger and pork; stir-fry about 3 minutes or until meat is no longer pink in center. Add black bean sauce; stir-fry 1 minute.

5. Return beans to wok. Stir cornstarch mixture; add to wok. Bring to a boil; cook until sauce thickens. Stir in baby corn; heat through. *Makes 4 servings*

Stir-Fried Pork with Green Beans and Baby Corn

Pork Tenderloin with Mandarin Salsa

1½ pounds boneless pork loin chops, cut into ¼ inch strips
1 cup orange juice
1 medium green pepper, finely chopped
1 can (10½ ounces) mandarin orange segments, drained and chopped
1⅓ cup red onion, chopped, divided
½ cup frozen whole kernel corn, thawed
2 tablespoons olive oil, divided
4 teaspoons bottled minced garlic, divided
1½ teaspoons chili powder, divided
1¼ teaspoon salt, divided
1½ teaspoons cumin
¼ teaspoon black pepper

1. Combine pork and orange juice in medium bowl. Set aside.

2. In another medium bowl, combine bell pepper, orange segments, ⅓ cup onion, corn, 1 tablespoon oil, 1 teaspoon garlic, ¼ teaspoon chili powder and ¼ teaspoon salt. Set aside.

3. Heat remaining 1 tablespoon oil in large nonstick skillet over medium-high heat. Add remaining 1 cup onion and 3 teaspoons garlic. Cook and stir 5 minutes or until softened and starting to brown.

4. While onion and garlic are cooking, drain pork reserving orange juice. Toss pork remaining 1¼ teaspoons chili powder, cumin, remaining 1 teaspoon salt and ¼ teaspoon pepper. Add pork to skillet; cook and stir 5 minutes or until pork is cooked through and lightly browned. Add ⅓ cup reserved orange juice marinade to skillet. Bring mixture to a boil. Reduce heat to medium; simmer 1 to 2 minutes or until liquid thickens slightly. Serve immediately with mandarin salsa.

Makes 4 servings

Serving Suggestion: Serve with rice and a mix of steamed broccoli florets and baby carrots.

Prep and Cook Time: 21 minutes

Pork Tenderloin with Mandarin Salsa

Fish & Shellfish Dishes

Seafood & Vegetable Stir-Fry

2 teaspoons olive oil
$\frac{1}{2}$ medium red or yellow bell pepper, cut into strips
$\frac{1}{2}$ medium onion, cut into small wedges
10 snow peas, trimmed and cut diagonally into halves
1 clove garlic, minced
6 ounces frozen cooked medium shrimp, thawed
2 tablespoons stir-fry sauce
1 cup hot cooked rice

1. Heat oil in large nonstick skillet over medium-high heat. Add vegetables; stir-fry 4 minutes. Add garlic; stir fry 1 minute or until vegetables are crisp-tender.

2. Add shrimp and stir-fry sauce. Stir-fry 1 to 2 minutes or until hot. Serve over rice.

Makes 2 servings

Seafood & Vegetable Stir-Fry

Grilled Swordfish with Hot Red Sauce

2 to 3 green onions
4 swordfish or halibut steaks (about 1½ pounds total)
2 tablespoons hot bean paste*
2 tablespoons soy sauce
2 tablespoons Sesame Salt (recipe page 102)
1 tablespoon dark sesame oil
4 teaspoons sugar
4 cloves garlic, minced
⅛ teaspoon black pepper

*Available in specialty stores or Asian markets.

1. Spray grid of grill or broiler rack with nonstick cooking spray. Prepare coals for grilling or preheat broiler.

2. Cut off and discard root ends of green onions. Finely chop enough green onions to measure ¼ cup; set aside. Prepare Sesame Salt; set aside.

3. Rinse swordfish and pat dry with paper towels. Place in shallow glass dish.

4. Combine green onions, hot bean paste, soy sauce, Sesame Salt, sesame oil, sugar, garlic and pepper in small bowl; mix well.

5. Spread half of marinade over fish; turn fish over and spread with remaining marinade. Cover with plastic wrap and refrigerate 30 minutes.

6. Remove fish from marinade; discard remaining marinade. Place fish on prepared grid. Grill fish over medium-hot coals or broil 4 to 5 minutes per side or until fish is opaque and flakes easily with fork. Garnish as desired.

Makes 4 servings

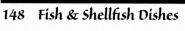

Grilled Swordfish With Hot Red Sauce

Lemon Sesame Scallops

1 tablespoon sesame seeds
8 ounces whole wheat spaghetti
3 tablespoons sesame oil, divided
1 pound sea scallops
¼ cup chicken broth or clam juice
3 tablespoons lemon juice
2 tablespoons oyster sauce
1 tablespoon soy sauce
1 tablespoon cornstarch
½ teaspoon grated lemon peel
1 tablespoon vegetable oil
2 carrots, cut into julienne strips
1 yellow bell pepper, cut into thin strips
4 slices peeled fresh ginger
1 clove garlic, minced
6 ounces fresh snow peas, trimmed or 1 (6-ounce) package frozen
    snow peas, thawed
2 green onions, thinly sliced

1. To toast sesame seeds, heat small skillet over medium heat. Add sesame seeds; cook and stir about 5 minutes or until golden. Set aside.

2. Cook spaghetti according to package directions; drain. Place spaghetti in large bowl; toss with 2 tablespoons sesame oil. Cover to keep warm.

3. Rinse scallops and pat dry with paper towels; set aside. Combine broth, lemon juice, oyster sauce, soy sauce, cornstarch and lemon peel in 1-cup glass measure; set aside. Heat remaining 1 tablespoon sesame oil and vegetable oil in large skillet or wok over medium heat. Add carrots and bell pepper; stir-fry 4 to 5 minutes or until crisp-tender. Transfer to large bowl; set aside.

continued on page 152

Lemon Sesame Scallops

Lemon Sesame Scallops, continued

4. Add ginger and garlic to skillet. Stir-fry 1 minute over medium high-heat. Add scallops; stir-fry 1 minute. Add snow peas and onions; stir-fry 2 to 3 minutes or until peas turn bright green and scallops turn opaque. Remove slices of ginger; discard. Transfer scallop mixture to bowl with vegetable mixture, leaving any liquid in skillet.

5. Stir broth mixture; add to liquid in skillet. Cook and stir 5 minutes or until thickened. Return scallop mixture to skillet; cook 1 minute. Serve immediately over warm spaghetti; sprinkle with sesame seeds.

Makes 4 servings

Asian Salmon Steaks

3 tablespoons reduced-sodium soy sauce
3 tablespoons lime juice
1 tablespoon honey
2 cloves garlic, pressed through garlic press
½ teaspoon ground ginger
4 salmon steaks
Minced fresh cilantro, for garnish

Combine soy sauce, lime juice, honey, garlic and ginger in jar with tight-fitting lid. Cover and shake well. Place salmon steaks in glass dish; spoon about 1 tablespoon marinade over each salmon steak. Refrigerate 10 to 30 minutes.

Remove salmon from marinade; discard marinade. Place salmon on lightly greased broiler pan. Brush fish with some marinade from jar. Broil 10 minutes for each of inch thickness of fish, turning and basting once. Serve garnished with minced cilantro.

Makes 4 servings

Favorite recipe from **National Fisheries Institute**

Fish Cakes with Thai Salsa

2 cans (14½ ounces each) DEL MONTE® Diced Tomatoes with
    Garlic & Onion, undrained
¾ cup sliced green onions
1 tablespoon minced gingerroot
¼ teaspoon crushed red pepper flakes
⅓ cup chopped cilantro
3½ cups cooked, flaked fish (1¾ to 2 pounds uncooked halibut,
    salmon or snapper)
2 eggs, beaten
½ cup Italian-seasoned dry bread crumbs
¼ cup mayonnaise
1 to 2 tablespoons butter

1. Combine tomatoes with ½ cup green onions, ginger and red pepper flakes in medium saucepan. Cook, uncovered, over high heat until thickened, stirring occasionally. Stir in cilantro. Cool.

2. Combine fish, eggs, crumbs, mayonnaise, remaining ¼ cup green onions and ⅓ cup tomato salsa mixture in medium bowl. Season with black pepper, if desired. Form into 16 patties.

3. Melt butter in large skillet over high heat. Reduce heat to medium-low; cook patties about 3 minutes on each side or until golden brown on both sides. Serve over salad greens, if desired. Top with salsa. Drizzle with Oriental sesame oil and garnish, if desired.

Makes 16 (2½-inch) cakes

Note: To cook fish, place in microwavable dish; cover. Microwave at HIGH 7 to 9 minutes or until fish flakes easily when tested with a fork, rotating twice; drain.

Prep and Cook Time: 35 minutes

Asian Honey-Tea Grilled Prawns

Marinade
  1 cup brewed double-strength orange-spice tea, cooled
  ¼ cup honey
  ¼ cup rice vinegar
  ¼ cup soy sauce
  1 tablespoon fresh ginger, peeled and finely chopped
  ½ teaspoon ground black pepper

Prawns
  1½ pounds medium shrimp, peeled and deveined
     Salt
  2 green onions, thinly sliced

In plastic bag, combine marinade ingredients. Remove ½ cup marinade; set aside for dipping sauce. Add shrimp to marinade in bag, turning to coat. Close bag securely and marinate in refrigerator 30 minutes or up to 12 hours.

Remove shrimp from marinade; discard marinade. Thread shrimp onto 8 skewers, dividing evenly. Grill over medium coals 4 to 6 minutes or until shrimp turn pink and are just firm to the touch, turning once. Season with salt, as desired.

Meanwhile prepare dipping sauce by placing reserved ½ cup marinade in small saucepan. Bring to a boil over medium-high heat. Boil 3 to 5 minutes or until slightly reduced. Stir in green onions.

Makes 4 servings

Favorite recipe from **National Honey Board**

Asian Honey-Tea Grilled Prawns

Albacore Stir-Fry

3 tablespoons vegetable oil
½ cup sliced onion
1 clove garlic, minced or pressed
1 bag (16 ounces) frozen Oriental vegetables, thawed and drained*
1 (7-ounce) pouch of STARKIST® Premium Albacore Tuna
3 tablespoons soy sauce
1 tablespoon lemon juice
1 tablespoon water
1 teaspoon sugar
2 cups hot cooked rice

*You can use 4 cups fresh vegetables, such as carrots, pea pods, broccoli, bell peppers, mushrooms, celery and bean sprouts instead of the frozen vegetables.

In wok or large skillet, heat oil over medium-high heat; sauté onion and garlic until onion is soft. Add vegetables; cook about 3 to 4 minutes or until vegetables are crisp-tender. Add tuna, soy sauce, lemon juice, water and sugar. Cook 1 more minute; serve over rice.   *Makes 4 servings*

WOK'S COOKING?

To make rice, bring 4 cups of water with 2 teaspoon of salt to a boil in a medium saucepan over medium-high heat. Slowly add 2 cups of rice so that the water continues to boil. Stir briefly. Reduce heat to low. Cook, covered, for 14 minutes or until the rice is tender.

Albacore Stir-Fry

Teriyaki Scallops

2 tablespoons soy sauce
1 tablespoon mirin or sweet cooking rice wine
2 teaspoons sake or dry sherry
1 teaspoon sugar
1 pound large scallops
8 ounces asparagus, diagonally sliced into 2-inch lengths
¼ teaspoon salt
1 tablespoon vegetable oil

1. Combine soy sauce, mirin, sake and sugar in medium bowl; stir until sugar is dissolved. Add scallops; let stand 10 minutes, turning occasionally.

2. Meanwhile, bring 2½ cups water and salt to a boil in medium saucepan over high heat. Add asparagus; reduce heat to medium-high. Cook 3 to 5 minutes or until crisp-tender. Drain asparagus; keep warm.

3. Drain scallops, reserving marinade.

4. Preheat broiler. Line broiler pan with foil; brush broiler rack with vegetable oil. Place scallops on rack; brush lightly with marinade. Broil about 4 inches from heat source 4 to 5 minutes or until brown. Turn scallops with tongs; brush lightly with marinade. Broil 4 to 5 minutes or just until scallops are opaque in center. Serve immediately with asparagus. Garnish as desired.

Makes 4 servings

WOK'S COOKING?

Mirin is a sweet wine made from rice. It can be found at Japanese markets and in the gourmet section of many supermarkets. Mirin is also referred to as rice wine.

Teriyaki Scallops

Steamed Fish over Fragrant Thai Noodles

1 pound thin rice noodles or angel hair pasta
4 cups broccoli, chopped
2 cups assorted sliced mushrooms
2 cups carrots, julienned
1½ cups bean sprouts
1 pound sole fillets
¾ cup unseasoned rice vinegar
½ cup reduced-sodium soy sauce
2 tablespoons minced fresh ginger
1 clove garlic, minced
¼ cup peanut butter
¾ cup thinly sliced green onions
½ cup finely chopped dry-roasted peanuts
¾ cup minced cilantro (optional)

Bring 3 quarts water to a boil over high heat. Add the noodles and cook until al dente, about 3 minutes. Drain the noodles and set aside. In a wok or skillet coated with cooking spray, stir-fry the broccoli, mushrooms, carrots, and bean sprouts until softened. Toss the noodles and vegetables and set aside. Steam the sole fillets by placing the fillets on a glass plate and cover with plastic wrap or a glass lid. Microwave on high for 3 to 4 minutes. (Or bake the fillets wrapped in foil in a 450°F oven for 4 to 6 minutes.)

To make the dressing, combine the rice vinegar, soy sauce, ginger and garlic in a small bowl. Microwave the peanut butter on high until a liquid-like consistency. Whisk the peanut butter into the dressing. Pour the dressing over the noodles and vegetables and toss well. Arrange the steamed fish fillets on top. Garnish with green onions, peanuts and cilantro.   *Makes 6 servings*

Favorite recipe from **Peanut Advisory Board**

Oriental Baked Seafood

¼ **cup chopped California Almonds**
2 **cups water**
½ **teaspoon salt**
1 **cup long-grain white rice**
1 **tablespoon grated fresh ginger**
1 **tablespoon sesame oil**
1 **teaspoon grated lemon peel**
1 **pound halibut**
½ **pound large scallops**
¼ **pound medium shrimp, shelled and deveined**
1 **clove garlic, minced**
1 **tablespoon light soy sauce**
½ **cup slivered green onions**

Preheat oven to 350°F. Spread almonds in shallow baking pan. Toast in oven 5 to 8 minutes until lightly browned, stirring occasionally; cool. Bring water and salt to a boil in medium saucepan. Stir in rice, ginger, sesame oil and lemon peel. Bring to a boil; cover and reduce heat to low. Simmer 20 to 25 minutes or until water is absorbed. Meanwhile, preheat oven to 400°F or preheat broiler or grill. Remove skin and bones from halibut; cut into large pieces. Cut 4 (12-inch) squares of foil. Divide halibut, scallops and shrimp among foil. Sprinkle seafood with garlic and soy sauce; seal squares tightly. Bake 12 minutes or broil or grill 4 inches from heat 15 minutes, turning once. Stir almonds into rice. Pour seafood mixture and juices over rice. Sprinkle with green onions.

Makes 4 servings

Microwave Directions: Spread almonds in shallow pan. Cook at HIGH (100% power) 2 minutes, stirring often; cool. Combine water, salt, rice, sesame oil, ginger and lemon peel in 3-quart microwave-safe dish. Cover with plastic wrap. Cook at HIGH (100% power) 12 minutes, stirring halfway through. Let stand 10 minutes. Prepare fish packets as above using parchment paper instead of foil. Bring edges up and seal with rubber band. Place packets in microwave-safe baking dish. Cook at HIGH (100% power) 5 minutes, rotating dish. Serve as directed.

Favorite recipe from **Almond Board of California**

Pad Thai (Thai Fried Noodles)

7¼ cups water, divided
12 ounces dried thin rice stick noodles
4 tablespoons vegetable oil, divided
3 tablespoons light brown sugar
3 tablespoons soy sauce
2 tablespoons lime juice
1 tablespoon anchovy paste
2 eggs, lightly beaten
12 ounces medium shrimp, peeled and deveined
2 cloves garlic, minced
1 tablespoon paprika
¼ to ½ teaspoon ground red pepper
8 ounces fresh bean sprouts, divided
½ cup coarsely chopped unsalted dry-roasted peanuts
4 green onions with tops, cut into 1-inch lengths
½ lime, cut lengthwise into 4 wedges, for garnish

1. Place 6 cups water in wok; bring to a boil over high heat. Add noodles; cook 2 minutes or until tender but still firm, stirring frequently. Drain and rinse under cold running water to stop cooking. Drain again and place noodles in large bowl. Add 1 tablespoon oil; toss lightly to coat. Set aside.

2. Combine remaining 1¼ cups water, brown sugar, soy sauce, lime juice and anchovy paste in small bowl; set aside.

3. Heat wok over medium heat about 30 seconds or until hot. Drizzle 1 tablespoon oil into wok and heat 15 seconds. Add eggs and cook 1 minute or just until set on bottom. Turn eggs over and stir to scramble until cooked but not dry. Transfer to medium bowl; set aside.

4. Heat wok over high heat until hot. Drizzle 1 tablespoon oil into wok and heat 15 seconds. Add shrimp and garlic; stir-fry 2 minutes or until shrimp begin to turn pink and opaque. Add shrimp to eggs.

continued on page 164

Pad Thai (Thai Fried Noodles)

Pad Thai, continued

5. Heat wok over medium heat until hot. Drizzle remaining 1 tablespoon oil into wok and heat 15 seconds. Stir in paprika and red pepper. Add noodles and anchovy mixture; cook and stir about 5 minutes or until noodles are softened. Stir in ¾ of bean sprouts. Add peanuts and green onions; toss and cook about 1 minute or until onions begin to wilt.

6. Add eggs and shrimp; stir-fry until heated through. Transfer to serving plate and garnish with remaining bean sprouts and lime wedges.   *Makes 4 servings*

Hoisin-Flavored Mushrooms and Shrimp

  2 tablespoons vegetable oil
  1 pound fresh white mushrooms, sliced (about 5 cups)
  1 tablespoon minced fresh ginger
  1 teaspoon minced garlic
1⅓ cups uncooked orzo pasta
  2 cans (about 14 ounces each) chicken broth
  ¼ cup hoisin sauce
    Pinch ground red pepper
 12 ounces cooked cleaned deveined shrimp
  ½ cup green onions, cut into 1-inch pieces

In large saucepan, heat oil until hot; add mushrooms, ginger and garlic. Cook until mushrooms release their liquid, about 5 minutes. Stir in pasta, chicken broth, hoisin sauce and pepper; bring to a boil. Simmer, covered, stirring occasionally until pasta is firm-tender and some liquid remains, about 10 minutes. Stir in shrimp and onions; cook until shrimp are heated through, 1 to 2 minutes.

Makes 4 servings

Favorite recipe from **Mushroom Council**

Oriental Baked Cod

2 tablespoons reduced-sodium soy sauce
2 tablespoons apple juice
1 tablespoon finely chopped fresh ginger
2 cloves garlic, minced
1 teaspoon crushed Szechuan peppercorns
4 cod fillets (about 1 pound)
4 green onions, thinly sliced

1. Preheat oven to 375°F. Spray roasting pan with nonstick cooking spray.

2. Combine soy sauce, apple juice, ginger, garlic and Szechuan peppercorns in small bowl; mix well.

3. Place cod fillets in prepared pan; pour soy sauce mixture over fish. Bake about 10 minutes or until fish is opaque and flakes easily when tested with fork.

4. Transfer fish to serving dish; pour pan juices over fish and sprinkle with green onions. Garnish, if desired.

Makes 4 servings

Smucker's® Mandarin Shrimp and Vegetable Stir-Fry

1 cup SMUCKER'S® Orange Marmalade
3 tablespoons soy sauce
2 tablespoons white vinegar
2 teaspoons hot pepper sauce
1 tablespoon plus 1½ teaspoons cornstarch
2 tablespoons vegetable oil
1 tablespoon fresh ginger, chopped
1 tablespoon chopped fresh garlic
24 fresh jumbo shrimp, peeled and deveined
1 red bell pepper, chopped
1 yellow or green bell pepper, chopped
3 cups broccoli florets (about 1 bunch)
½ cup water
1 cup chopped green onions
Salt and pepper, to taste

Combine SMUCKER'S® Orange Marmalade, soy sauce, vinegar, hot pepper sauce and cornstarch in small bowl. Stir to dissolve cornstarch and set aside.

Place large skillet or wok over high heat. Heat for 1 minute, then add oil. Heat oil for 30 seconds, then add ginger, garlic and shrimp. Stir-fry for 2 to 3 minutes until shrimp begin to turn pink. Remove shrimp; set aside.

Add bell peppers and broccoli to skillet and cook over high heat for 1 minute. Add water; cover and reduce heat to medium. Cook vegetables 4 to 5 minutes or until tender.

Uncover skillet and increase heat to high. Add shrimp and SMUCKER'S® Orange Marmalade mixture. Cook for 2 minutes until sauce is thickened and shrimp are completely cooked. Season with salt and freshly ground black pepper.

Stir in green onions and serve with boiled rice.   *Makes 4 to 6 servings*

Smucker's® Mandarin Shrimp and Vegetable Stir Fry

Vegetarian Options

Orange Ginger Tofu & Noodles

⅔ cup orange juice

3 tablespoons reduced-sodium soy sauce

½ to 1 teaspoon minced ginger

1 clove garlic, minced

¼ teaspoon red pepper flakes

5 ounces extra-firm tofu, well drained and cut into ½-inch cubes

1½ teaspoons cornstarch

1 teaspoon canola or peanut oil

2 cups fresh cut-up vegetables, such as broccoli, carrots, onion and snow peas

1½ cups hot cooked vermicelli

1. Combine orange juice, soy sauce, ginger, garlic and red pepper in resealable plastic food storage bag; add tofu. Marinate 20 to 30 minutes; drain. Reserve marinade and stir into cornstarch.

2. Heat oil in large nonstick skillet or wok over medium-high heat. Add vegetables; stir-fry 2 to 3 minutes or until vegetables are crisp-tender. Add tofu; stir-fry 1 minute. Stir reserved marinade mixture; add to skillet. Bring to a boil; boil 1 minute. Serve over vermicelli.   *Makes 2 servings*

Orange Ginger Tofu & Noodles

Whole Wheat Pasta with Cucumber and Spicy Peanut Sauce

1 cup hot water
¾ cup creamy peanut butter
3 tablespoons soy sauce
3 tablespoons lemon juice
2 garlic cloves, minced
1 teaspoon dried hot red pepper flakes
1 teaspoon sugar
20 ounces whole wheat pasta
2 cucumbers, peeled, seeded and cut diagonally into ⅛-inch slices
1 cup thinly sliced scallions
1 cup red peppers, thinly sliced and 1 inch in length
Salt and pepper to taste

In blender, combine hot water, peanut butter, soy sauce, lemon juice, garlic, red pepper flakes and sugar until smooth. In pot of boiling salted water, boil pasta until just tender; transfer to colander and rinse briefly under cold water. Drain pasta well. In large bowl, toss noodles with peanut sauce, cucumbers, scallions and red peppers. Add salt and pepper to taste. Serve immediately at room temperature. *Makes 8 servings*

Favorite recipe from **Peanut Advisory Board**

Szechuan Vegetable Stir-Fry

8 ounces firm tofu, drained and cut into cubes
1 cup canned vegetable broth, divided
½ cup orange juice
⅓ cup soy sauce
1 to 2 teaspoons hot chili oil
½ teaspoon fennel seeds
½ teaspoon black pepper
2 tablespoons cornstarch
3 tablespoons vegetable oil
1 cup sliced green onions and tops
3 medium carrots, peeled and diagonally sliced
3 cloves garlic, minced
2 teaspoons minced fresh ginger
¼ pound button mushrooms, sliced
1 medium red bell pepper, seeded and cut into 1-inch squares
¼ pound fresh snow peas, cut diagonally in half
8 ounces broccoli florets, steamed
½ cup peanuts
4 to 6 cups hot cooked rice

1. Place tofu in 8-inch round or square glass baking dish. Combine ½ cup broth, orange juice, soy sauce, chili oil, fennel seeds and black pepper in 2-cup measure; pour over tofu. Let stand 15 to 60 minutes. Drain, reserving marinade.

2. Combine cornstarch and remaining ½ cup broth in medium bowl. Add reserved marinade; set aside.

3. Heat vegetable oil in wok or large skillet over high heat until hot. Add onions, carrots, garlic and ginger; stir-fry 3 minutes. Add tofu, mushrooms, bell pepper and snow peas; stir-fry 2 to 3 minutes or until vegetables are crisp-tender. Add broccoli; stir-fry 1 minute or until heated through. Stir cornstarch mixture. Add to wok; cook 1 to 2 minutes or until bubbly. Stir in peanuts. Serve over rice.   *Makes 4 to 6 servings*

Mu Shu Vegetables

Peanut Sauce (recipe page 174)
3 tablespoons reduced-sodium soy sauce
2 tablespoons dry sherry
1½ tablespoons minced fresh ginger
2 teaspoons cornstarch
1½ teaspoons sesame oil
3 cloves garlic, minced
1 tablespoon peanut oil
3 leeks, washed and cut into 2-inch slivers
3 carrots, peeled and julienned
1 cup thinly sliced fresh shiitake mushrooms
1 small head Napa or Savoy cabbage, shredded (about 4 cups)
2 cups mung bean sprouts, rinsed and drained
8 ounces firm tofu, drained and cut into 2½×¼-inch strips
12 (8-inch) fat-free flour tortillas, warmed
¾ cup finely chopped honey roasted peanuts

Prepare Peanut Sauce; set aside. Combine soy sauce, sherry, ginger, cornstarch, sesame oil and garlic in small bowl until smooth; set aside.

Heat wok over medium-high heat 1 minute or until hot. Drizzle peanut oil into wok and heat 30 seconds. Add leeks, carrots and mushrooms; stir-fry 2 minutes. Add cabbage; stir-fry 3 minutes or until just tender. Add bean sprouts and tofu; stir-fry 1 minute or until hot. Stir soy sauce mixture and add to wok. Cook and stir 1 minute or until thickened.

Spread each tortilla with about 1 teaspoon Peanut Sauce. Spoon ½ cup vegetable mixture on bottom half of tortilla; sprinkle with 1 tablespoon peanuts.

Fold bottom edge of tortilla over filling; fold in side edges. Roll up to completely enclose filling. Or, spoon ½ cup vegetable mixture on one half of tortilla. Fold bottom edge over filling. Fold in one side edge. Serve with Peanut Sauce. *Makes 6 servings*

continued on page 174

Mu Shu Vegetables

Mu Shu Vegtables, continued

Peanut Sauce: Combine 3 tablespoons sugar, 3 tablespoons dry sherry, 3 tablespoons reduced-sodium soy sauce, 3 tablespoons water and 2 teaspoons white wine vinegar in small saucepan. Bring to a boil over medium-high heat, stirring constantly. Boil 1 minute or until sugar melts. Stir in ⅓ cup peanut butter until smooth; cool to room temperature.

Makes ⅔ cup

Bean Threads with Tofu and Vegetables

8 ounces firm tofu, drained and cubed
1 tablespoon dark sesame oil
3 teaspoons reduced-sodium soy sauce, divided
1 can (about 14 ounces) fat-free reduced-sodium chicken broth
1 package (3¾ ounces) bean threads
1 package (16 ounces) frozen mixed vegetable medley such as broccoli, carrots and red pepper, thawed
¼ cup rice wine vinegar
½ teaspoon red pepper flakes

1. Place tofu on shallow plate; drizzle with oil and 1½ teaspoons soy sauce.

2. Combine broth and remaining 1½ teaspoons soy sauce in deep skillet or large saucepan. Bring to a boil over high heat; reduce heat. Add bean threads; simmer, uncovered, 7 minutes or until noodles absorb liquid, stirring occasionally to separate noodles.

3. Stir in vegetables and vinegar; heat through. Stir in tofu mixture and red pepper flakes; heat through about 1 minute.

Makes 6 servings

Bean Threads with Tofu and Vegetables

Indian Vegetable Curry

2 to 3 teaspoons curry powder
1 can (16 ounces) sliced potatoes, drained
1 bag (16 ounces) BIRDS EYE® frozen Farm Fresh Mixtures
   Broccoli, Cauliflower and Carrots
1 can (15 ounces) chick-peas, drained
1 can (14½ ounces) stewed tomatoes
1 can (13¾ ounces) vegetable or chicken broth
2 tablespoons cornstarch

- Stir curry powder in large skillet over high heat until fragrant, about 30 seconds.

- Stir in potatoes, vegetables, chick-peas and tomatoes; bring to a boil. Reduce heat to medium-high; cover and cook 8 minutes.

- Blend broth with cornstarch; stir into vegetables. Cook until thickened.

Makes about 6 servings

Prep Time: 5 minutes   **Cook Time:** 15 minutes

WOK'S COOKING?

Serve Indian Vegetable Curry with white or brown rice for a heartier main dish.

Indian Vegetable Curry

Hot Sesame Noodles

1 package (16 ounces) uncooked linguini
1 teaspoon Oriental sesame oil
3 tablespoons olive oil
3 tablespoons sesame seeds
2 cloves garlic, minced
⅔ cup chunky peanut butter
1 cup chicken broth
⅓ cup reduced-sodium soy sauce
3 to 4 tablespoons *Frank's® RedHot®* Cayenne Pepper Sauce
1½ teaspoons sugar
1 large green onion, sliced

1. Cook linguini according to package directions. Rinse under cold water; drain well. Toss linguini with sesame oil in large bowl.

2. Heat olive oil in large nonstick skillet over medium heat. Add sesame seeds and garlic; cook and stir constantly 1 minute or until seeds are golden. Add peanut butter; stir until well blended. Stir in broth, soy sauce, **Frank's RedHot** Sauce and sugar. Bring just to a boil.

3. Pour sauce over linguini; toss to coat evenly. Sprinkle with green onions. Serve immediately.

Makes 4 servings (2 cups sauce)

Note: Sesame noodles may be served cold, if desired. Chill linguini and sauce separately. Toss just before serving.

Prep Time: 20 minutes   **Cook Time:** 15 minutes

Lentil Rice Curry

2 tablespoons olive oil
1 cup sliced green onions
2 tablespoons minced fresh ginger
2 teaspoons curry powder
3 cloves garlic, minced
½ teaspoon ground cumin
½ teaspoon ground turmeric
3 cups water
1 can (about 14 ounces) stewed tomatoes, undrained
½ teaspoon salt
1 cup red lentils
1 large head cauliflower (about 1¼ pounds), cut into florets
1 tablespoon lemon juice
  Hot cooked rice

1. Heat oil in large saucepan over medium heat until hot. Add onions, ginger, curry, garlic, cumin and turmeric; cook and stir 5 minutes. Add water, tomatoes and salt; bring to a boil over high heat.

2. Meanwhile, rinse lentils under cold running water, picking out any debris or blemished lentils. Add lentils to saucepan. Reduce heat to low. Cover and simmer 35 to 40 minutes or until lentils are tender. Add cauliflower and lemon juice. Cover and simmer 8 to 10 minutes more or until cauliflower is tender.

3. Spoon lentil mixture over. Garnish, if desired.   *Makes 6 servings*

Tofu Stir-Fry

2 cups uncooked instant rice
2 teaspoons vegetable oil
2 cups broccoli florets
1 large carrot, sliced
½ green bell pepper, sliced
¼ cup frozen chopped onion
½ cup teriyaki sauce
½ cup orange juice
1 tablespoon cornstarch
1 teaspoon bottled minced garlic
½ teaspoon ground ginger
¼ to ½ teaspoon hot pepper sauce
1 package (10½ ounces) reduced-fat firm tofu, drained and cubed

1. Cook rice according to package directions.

2. While rice is cooking, heat oil in large skillet. Add broccoli, carrot, bell pepper and onion; cook and stir 3 minutes.

3. Combine teriyaki sauce, orange juice, cornstarch, garlic, ginger and pepper sauce in small bowl; mix well. Pour sauce over vegetables in skillet. Bring to a boil; cook and stir 1 minute.

4. Add tofu to skillet; stir gently to coat with sauce. Serve over rice.   *Makes 4 servings*

Prep and Cook Time: 18 minutes

Tofu Stir-Fry

Cavatelli and Vegetable Stir-Fry

¾ cup cavatelli or elbow macaroni

6 ounces fresh snow peas, cut lengthwise into halves

½ cup thinly sliced carrot

1 teaspoon minced fresh ginger

½ cup chopped yellow or green bell pepper

½ cup chopped onion

¼ cup chopped fresh parsley

1 tablespoon chopped fresh oregano *or* 1 teaspoon dried oregano
   leaves, crushed

1 tablespoon reduced-fat margarine

2 tablespoons water

1 tablespoon reduced-sodium soy sauce

Prepare cavatelli according to package directions, omitting salt; drain.

Coat wok or large skillet with nonstick cooking spray. Add snow peas, carrot and ginger; stir-fry 2 minutes over medium-high heat. Add bell pepper, onion, parsley, oregano and margarine. Stir-fry 2 to 3 minutes or until vegetables are crisp-tender. Stir in water and soy sauce. Stir in pasta; heat through.

Makes 4 servings

Cavatelli and Vegetable Stir-Fry

Buddha's Delightful Vegetables

1½ cups chicken broth
3 tablespoons low-sodium soy sauce
2 tablespoons plus 1 teaspoon sesame oil, divided
1½ tablespoons rice wine or sake
1 tablespoon sugar
1 tablespoon cornstarch
3 dried red chili peppers
½ cup sliced green onions
1 tablespoon minced garlic
2 carrots, thinly sliced into coins
2 cups small broccoli florets
1 red bell pepper, cut into thin strips
2 cups shredded napa cabbage
1 cup baby corn
1 (8-ounce) can sliced water chestnuts
Hot cooked rice

Combine chicken broth, soy sauce, 1 teaspoon oil, rice wine, sugar and cornstarch in small bowl; blend well and set aside.

Heat wok. Add remaining 2 tablespoons oil; heat until very hot. Add chilies; stir-fry until darkened. Add onions and garlic; stir-fry 1 minute. Add carrots; stir-fry 4 minutes. Add broccoli and bell pepper; stir-fry 1 minute. Add cabbage; stir-fry 1 minute. Add baby corn and water chestnuts; stir-fry 30 seconds. Add reserved chicken broth mixture to wok and mix well. Cover wok; cook until vegetables are crisp-tender. Serve over rice. *Makes 8 servings*

Favorite recipe from **The Sugar Association, Inc.**

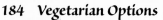

Stuffed Hairy Gourd Vegetarian Style

15 ounces hairy gourd
2 tablespoons vegetable oil
2 ounces diced carrot
5 Chinese dry mushrooms, rehydrated and diced
2 ounces diced baby corn
2 ounces diced celery
2 ounces diced dried bean curd
1 ounce dried black fungus, soaked
4 tablespoons LEE KUM KEE® Vegetarian Oyster Flavored Sauce
½ teaspoon sugar
1 teaspoon cornstarch mixed with 1 tablespoon water

1. Peel hairy gourd and cut into halves; scrape away pith. Cook in boiling water 3 minutes. Rinse and drain.

2. Heat oil in wok. Add carrot, mushrooms, baby corn, celery, bean curd and black fungus; stir-fry until fragrant. Combine 1 cup water, Vegetarian Stir Fry Sauce and sugar in small bowl; add to wok with hairy gourd. Stir until mixture comes to a boil. Lower heat and simmer 5 minutes or until hairy gourd softens.

3. Remove hairy gourd and arrange on plate. Add cornstarch mixture to wok; cook until thickened. Divide mixture over hairy gourd halves and serve.   *Makes 4 to 6 servings*

WOK'S COOKING?

Cucumbers may be substituted for the hairy gourd.

Vegetable-Tofu Stir-Fry

⅓ **cup water**
4 **teaspoons reduced-sodium soy sauce**
1 **tablespoon rice wine or dry white wine**
2 **teaspoons cornstarch**
1½ **teaspoons sugar**
¼ **teaspoon chicken bouillon granules**
1 **package (10½ ounces) extra-firm tofu, drained**
3 **teaspoons vegetable oil, divided**
3 **cups sliced fresh mushrooms**
1 **cup sliced leek**
2 **cloves garlic, minced**
2 **teaspoons minced fresh ginger**
2 **cups diagonally sliced carrots**
3 **cups torn stemmed spinach**
4 **cups hot cooked rice**

Combine water, soy sauce, rice wine, cornstarch, sugar and bouillon granules in small bowl. Press tofu lightly between paper towels; cut into ¾-inch squares or triangles.

Spray wok or large skillet with nonstick cooking spray; heat over medium-high heat. Add 1 teaspoon oil. Add mushrooms, leek, garlic and ginger. Stir-fry 2 to 3 minutes or until vegetables are tender. Remove from wok.

Add remaining 2 teaspoons oil to wok; add carrots. Stir-fry 5 to 6 minutes or until crisp-tender. Add cornstarch mixture; stir-fry about 1 minute or until mixture boils and thickens. Stir in mushroom mixture, tofu and spinach. Cover; cook about 1 minute or until heated through. Serve over rice.

Makes 4 servings

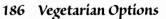

Vegetable-Tofu Stir-Fry

Acknowledgments

The publisher would like to thank the companies and organizations listed below for the use of their recipes and photographs in this publication.

Almond Board of California

Birds Eye®

Butterball® Turkey

California Tree Fruit Agreement

ConAgra Foods®

Del Monte Corporation

Dole Food Company, Inc.

Florida's Citrus Growers

The Golden Grain Company®

Hormel Foods, LLC

The Kingsford Products Company

Lee Kum Kee (USA) Inc.

McIlhenny Company
(TABASCO® brand Pepper Sauce)

Mushroom Council

National Chicken Council /
US Poultry & Egg Association

National Fisheries Institute

National Honey Board

National Pork Board

Norseland, Inc. / Lucini Italia Co.

North Dakota Beef Commission

Peanut Advisory Board

Pear Bureau Northwest

Reckitt Benckiser Inc.

Riviana Foods Inc.

The J.M. Smucker Company

StarKist® Seafood Company

The Sugar Association, Inc.

Tyson Foods, Inc.

Uncle Ben's Inc.

Unilever Bestfoods North America

USA Rice Federation

Index

METRIC CONVERSION CHART

VOLUME MEASUREMENTS (dry)

1/8 teaspoon = 0.5 mL
1/4 teaspoon = 1 mL
1/2 teaspoon = 2 mL
3/4 teaspoon = 4 mL
1 teaspoon = 5 mL
1 tablespoon = 15 mL
2 tablespoons = 30 mL
1/4 cup = 60 mL
1/3 cup = 75 mL
1/2 cup = 125 mL
2/3 cup = 150 mL
3/4 cup = 175 mL
1 cup = 250 mL
2 cups = 1 pint = 500 mL
3 cups = 750 mL
4 cups = 1 quart = 1 L

VOLUME MEASUREMENTS (fluid)

1 fluid ounce (2 tablespoons) = 30 mL
4 fluid ounces (1/2 cup) = 125 mL
8 fluid ounces (1 cup) = 250 mL
12 fluid ounces (1 1/2 cups) = 375 mL
16 fluid ounces (2 cups) = 500 mL

WEIGHTS (mass)

1/2 ounce = 15 g
1 ounce = 30 g
3 ounces = 90 g
4 ounces = 120 g
8 ounces = 225 g
10 ounces = 285 g
12 ounces = 360 g
16 ounces = 1 pound = 450 g

DIMENSIONS

1/16 inch = 2 mm
1/8 inch = 3 mm
1/4 inch = 6 mm
1/2 inch = 1.5 cm
3/4 inch = 2 cm
1 inch = 2.5 cm

OVEN TEMPERATURES

250°F = 120°C
275°F = 140°C
300°F = 150°C
325°F = 160°C
350°F = 180°C
375°F = 190°C
400°F = 200°C
425°F = 220°C
450°F = 230°C

BAKING PAN SIZES

Utensil	Size in Inches/Quarts	Metric Volume	Size in Centimeters
Baking or	8×8×2	2 L	20×20×5
Cake Pan	9×9×2	2.5 L	23×23×5
(square or	12×8×2	3 L	30×20×5
rectangular)	13×9×2	3.5 L	33×23×5
Loaf Pan	8×4×3	1.5 L	20×10×7
	9×5×3	2 L	23×13×7
Round Layer	8×1½	1.2 L	20×4
Cake Pan	9×1½	1.5 L	23×4
Pie Plate	8×1¼	750 mL	20×3
	9×1¼	1 L	23×3
Baking Dish	1 quart	1 L	—
or Casserole	1½ quart	1.5 L	—
	2 quart	2 L	—

Complicated Kris Northern

"This image illustrates some of the best qualities of fractals—infinity, reiteration, and self similarity."– **Kris Northern**

Investigations
IN NUMBER, DATA, AND SPACE®

PEARSON
Scott
Foresman
scottforesman.com

Editorial offices: Glenview, Illinois • Parsippany, New Jersey • New York, New York
Sales offices: Boston, Massachusetts • Duluth, Georgia
Glenview, Illinois • Coppell, Texas • Sacramento, California • Mesa, Arizona

T E R C

The Investigations curriculum was developed by TERC, Cambridge, MA.

This material is based on work supported by the National Science Foundation ("NSF") under Grant No. ESI-0095450. Any opinions, findings, and conclusions or recommendations expressed in this material are those of the author(s) and do not necessarily reflect the views of the National Science Foundation.

ISBN: 0-328-23742-6

ISBN: 978-0-328-23742-5

Second Edition Copyright © 2008 Pearson Education, Inc.
All Rights Reserved. Printed in the United States of America. This publication is protected by Copyright, and permission should be obtained from the publisher prior to any prohibited reproduction, storage in a retrieval system, or transmission in any form by any means, electronic, mechanical, photocopying, recording, or otherwise. For information regarding permission(s), write to: Permissions Department, Scott Foresman, 1900 East Lake Avenue, Glenview, Illinois 60025.

4 5 6 7 8 9 10-V003-15 14 13 12 11 10 09 08 07

CC:N1

T E R C

Co-Principal Investigators

Susan Jo Russell

Karen Economopoulos

Authors

Lucy Wittenberg
Director Grades 3–5

Karen Economopoulos
Director Grades K–2

Virginia Bastable
(SummerMath for Teachers,
Mt. Holyoke College)

Katie Hickey Bloomfield

Keith Cochran

Darrell Earnest

Arusha Hollister

Nancy Horowitz

Erin Leidl

Megan Murray

Young Oh

Beth W. Perry

Susan Jo Russell

Deborah Schifter
(Education
Development Center)

Kathy Sillman

Administrative Staff

Amy Taber
Project Manager

Beth Bergeron

Lorraine Brooks

Emi Fujiwara

Contributing Authors

Denise Baumann

Jennifer DiBrienza

Hollee Freeman

Paula Hooper

Jan Mokros

Stephen Monk
(University of Washington)

Mary Beth O'Connor

Judy Storeygard

Cornelia Tierney

Elizabeth Van Cleef

Carol Wright

Technology

Jim Hammerman

Classroom Field Work

Amy Appell

Rachel E. Davis

Traci Higgins

Julia Thompson

Collaborating Teachers

This group of dedicated teachers carried out extensive field testing in their classrooms, met regularly to discuss issues of teaching and learning mathematics, provided feedback to staff, welcomed staff into their classrooms to document students' work, and contributed both suggestions and written material that has been incorporated into the curriculum.

Bethany Altchek

Linda Amaral

Kimberly Beauregard

Barbara Bernard

Nancy Buell

Rose Christiansen

Chris Colbath-Hess

Lisette Colon

Kim Cook

Frances Cooper

Kathleen Drew

Rebeka Eston Salemi

Thomas Fisher

Michael Flynn

Holly Ghazey

Susan Gillis

Danielle Harrington

Elaine Herzog

Francine Hiller

Kirsten Lee Howard

Liliana Klass

Leslie Kramer

Melissa Lee Andrichak

Kelley Lee Sadowski

Jennifer Levitan

Mary Lou LoVecchio

Kristen McEnaney

Maura McGrail

Kathe Millett

Florence Molyneaux

Amy Monkiewicz

Elizabeth Monopoli

Carol Murray

Robyn Musser

Christine Norrman

Deborah O'Brien

Timothy O'Connor

Anne Marie O'Reilly

Mark Paige

Margaret Riddle

Karen Schweitzer

Elisabeth Seyferth

Susan Smith

Debra Sorvillo

Shoshanah Starr

Janice Szymaszek

Karen Tobin

JoAnn Trauschke

Ana Vaisenstein

Yvonne Watson

Michelle Woods

Mary Wright

Note: Unless otherwise noted, all contributors listed above were staff of the Education Research Collaborative at TERC during their work on the curriculum. Other affiliations during the time of development are listed.

Advisors

Deborah Lowenberg Ball,
University of Michigan

Hyman Bass, Professor of Mathematics and Mathematics Education
University of Michigan

Mary Canner, Principal, Natick Public Schools

Thomas Carpenter, Professor of Curriculum and Instruction,
University of Wisconsin-Madison

Janis Freckmann, Elementary Mathematics Coordinator,
Milwaukee Public Schools

Lynne Godfrey, Mathematics Coach,
Cambridge Public Schools

Ginger Hanlon, Instructional Specialist in Mathematics,
New York City Public Schools

DeAnn Huinker, Director, Center for Mathematics and
Science Education Research, University of Wisconsin-Milwaukee

James Kaput, Professor of Mathematics, University of
Massachusetts-Dartmouth

Kate Kline, Associate Professor, Department of Mathematics
and Statistics, Western Michigan University

Jim Lewis, Professor of Mathematics,
University of Nebraska-Lincoln

William McCallum, Professior of Mathematics,
University of Arizona

Harriet Pollatsek, Professor of Mathematics,
Mount Holyoke College

Debra Shein-Gerson, Elementary Mathematics Specialist,
Weston Public Schools

Gary Shevell, Assistant Principal,
New York City Public Schools

Liz Sweeney, Elementary Math Department,
Boston Public Schools

Lucy West, Consultant, Metamorphosis:
Teaching Learning Communities, Inc.

This revision of the curriculum was built on the work of the many authors who contributed to the first edition (published between 1994 and 1998). We acknowledge the critical contributions of these authors in developing the content and pedagogy of *Investigations*:

Authors

Joan Akers

Michael T. Battista

Douglas H. Clements

Karen Economopoulos

Marlene Kliman

Jan Mokros

Megan Murray

Ricardo Nemirovsky

Andee Rubin

Susan Jo Russell

Cornelia Tierney

Contributing Authors

Mary Berle-Carman

Rebecca B. Corwin

Rebeka Eston

Claryce Evans

Anne Goodrow

Cliff Konold

Chris Mainhart

Sue McMillen

Jerrie Moffet

Tracy Noble

Kim O'Neil

Mark Ogonowski

Julie Sarama

Amy Shulman Weinberg

Margie Singer

Virginia Woolley

Tracey Wright

Contents

UNIT 8

Partners, Teams, and Paper Clips

Investigations

C U R R I C U L U M

Overview of Program Components

FOR TEACHERS

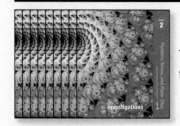

The **Curriculum Units** are the teaching guides. (See far right.)

Implementing Investigations in Grade 2 offers suggestions for implementing the curriculum. It also contains a comprehensive index.

The **Resources Binder** contains all the Resource Masters and Transparencies that support instruction. (Also available on CD) The binder also includes a student software CD.

FOR STUDENTS

The **Student Activity Book** contains the consumable student pages (Recording Sheets, Homework, Practice, and so on).

The **Student Math Handbook** contains Math Words and Ideas pages and Games directions.

The *Investigations* Curriculum

Investigations in Number, Data, and Space® is a K–5 mathematics curriculum designed to engage students in making sense of mathematical ideas. Six major goals guided the development of the *Investigations in Number, Data, and Space*® curriculum. The curriculum is designed to:

- Support students to make sense of mathematics and learn that they can be mathematical thinkers

- Focus on computational fluency with whole numbers as a major goal of the elementary grades

- Provide substantive work in important areas of mathematics—rational numbers, geometry, measurement, data, and early algebra—and connections among them

- Emphasize reasoning about mathematical ideas

- Communicate mathematics content and pedagogy to teachers

- Engage the range of learners in understanding mathematics

Underlying these goals are three guiding principles that are touchstones for the *Investigations* team as we approach both students and teachers as agents of their own learning:

1. *Students have mathematical ideas.* Students come to school with ideas about numbers, shapes, measurements, patterns, and data. If given the opportunity to learn in an environment that stresses making sense of mathematics, students build on the ideas they already have and learn about new mathematics they have never encountered. Students learn that they are capable of having mathematical ideas, applying what they know to new situations, and thinking and reasoning about unfamiliar problems.

2. *Teachers are engaged in ongoing learning* about mathematics content, pedagogy, and student learning. The curriculum provides material for professional development, to be used by teachers individually or in groups, that supports teachers' continued learning as they use the curriculum over several years. The *Investigations* curriculum materials are designed as much to be a dialogue with teachers as to be a core of content for students.

3. *Teachers collaborate with the students and curriculum materials* to create the curriculum as enacted in the classroom. The only way for a good curriculum to be used well is for teachers to be active participants in implementing it. Teachers use the curriculum to maintain a clear, focused, and coherent agenda for mathematics teaching. At the same time, they observe and listen carefully to students, try to understand how they are thinking, and make teaching decisions based on these observations.

Investigations is based on experience from research and practice, including field testing that involved documentation of thousands of hours in classrooms, observations of students, input from teachers, and analysis of student work. As a result, the curriculum addresses the learning needs of real students in a wide range of classrooms and communities. The investigations are carefully designed to invite all students into mathematics—girls and boys; members of diverse cultural, ethnic, and language groups; and students with a wide variety of strengths, needs, and interests.

Based on this extensive classroom testing, the curriculum takes seriously the time students need to develop a strong conceptual foundation and skills based on that foundation. Each curriculum unit focuses on an area of content in depth, providing time for students to develop and practice ideas across a variety of activities and contexts that build on each other. Daily guidelines for time spent on class sessions, Classroom Routines (K–3), and Ten-Minute Math (3–5) reflect the commitment to devoting adequate time to mathematics in each school day.

About This Curriculum Unit

This **Curriculum Unit** is one of nine teaching guides in Grade 2. The eighth unit in Grade 2 is *Partners, Teams, and Paper Clips*.

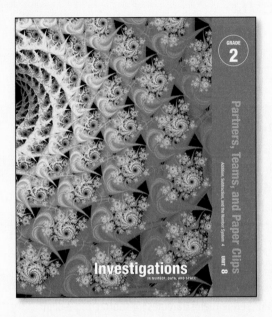

- The **Introduction and Overview** section organizes and presents the instructional materials, provides background information, and highlights important features specific to this unit.

- Each Curriculum Unit contains several **Investigations.** Each Investigation focuses on a set of related mathematical ideas.

- Investigations are divided into one-hour **Sessions,** or lessons.

- Sessions have a combination of these parts: **Activity, Discussion, Math Workshop, Assessment Activity,** and **Session Follow-Up.**

- Each session also has one or more **Classroom Routines** that are done outside of math time.

- At the back of the book is a collection of **Teacher Notes** and **Dialogue Boxes** that provide professional development related to the unit.

- Also included at the back of the book are the **Student Math Handbook** pages for this unit.

- The **Index** provides a way to look up important words or terms.

Overview

O F   T H I S   U N I T

Each *Investigations* session has some combination of these five parts: **Activity, Discussion, Math Workshop, Assessment Activity,** and **Session Follow-Up.** These session parts are indicated in the chart below. Each session also has one or more **Classroom Routines** that are done outside of math time.

Activity	Discussion	Math Workshop	Assessment Activity	Session Follow-Up
●●	●			●
●	●●			●
●	●	●		●
	●●	●		●
●●●	●			●
●	●	●		●
●	●	●		●
●●	●			●
	●	●		●
	●●	●		●
		●	●	●
●●	●			●
●	●●			●
●	●●			●
●	●			●
			●	●

Classroom Routines

Quick Images	Today's Number	How Many Pockets?	What Time Is It?
●			
●			
			●
		●	
●			
	●		
	●		
			●
	●		
			●
●			
●			
	●		
		●	
			●
●			

Mathematics

Partners, Teams, and Paper Clips is the eighth of nine units in the Grade 2 sequence and the last of four units in the Grade 2 number and operations strand of *Investigations*. These units develop ideas about counting and quantity, the composition of numbers, including work with place value and the structure of the base-ten number system, and the operations of addition and subtraction. The mathematical focus of this unit is on making generalizations about what happens when you add even and odd numbers, developing fluency with the remaining addition combinations, developing and refining strategies for adding and subtracting 2-digit numbers, and recording such work.

LOOKING BACK

This unit builds on the work students did in *Counting, Coins, and Combinations; Stickers, Number Strings, and Story Problems;* and *How Many Tens? How Many Ones?* Much of that work focused on developing an understanding of place value and our number system and on making sense of the operations of addition and subtraction. All of this work helped students develop strategies for solving addition and subtraction problems.

This unit focuses on 4 Mathematical Emphases:

1 Whole Number Operations Adding even and odd numbers

Math Focus Points

◆ Characterizing even and odd numbers as those that do or do not make groups of two (partners) and two equal groups (teams)

◆ Investigating what happens with partners and teams when two groups are combined

◆ Making and testing conjectures about adding even and odd numbers

◆ Finding combinations of odd and even numbers that make given numbers or determining that these combinations are not possible

◆ Making and justifying generalizations about adding even and odd numbers

In *Stickers, Number Strings, and Story Problems,* students worked to develop definitions of odd and even numbers in the context of partners (groups of two) and teams (two equal groups). This unit builds on that work as students investigate what happens when you add two even numbers, two odd numbers, and an even and an odd number. Students use the definitions developed in *Stickers, Number Strings, and Story Problems* to make and test conjectures about what happens when you add even and odd numbers. In Grade 2, many students' reasoning depends on testing several examples. This unit pushes them to think more generally about any two even numbers and to use reasoning based on partners, teams, and leftovers to explain those generalizations.

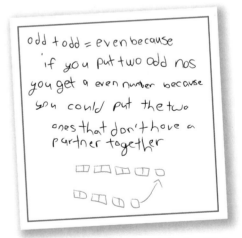

Sample Student Work

2 Computational Fluency Knowing addition combinations to 10 + 10

Math Focus Points

◆ Relating unknown combinations to known combinations

◆ Developing and achieving fluency with the plus 9 and remaining combinations

In this unit, students are formally introduced to the plus 9 combinations (e.g., 2 + 9 and 9 + 7). Much of the instruction around these combinations focuses on their relationship to the plus 10 combinations, which students mastered by the end of *Stickers, Number Strings, and Story Problems.* Students use cubes, the number line, and stickers to compare what happens when you add 9 and 10 to any number.

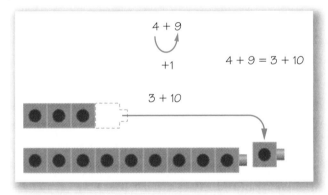

They are also introduced to the last set of addition combinations—the remaining combinations—which include all of the combinations that do not fall into one of the other categories. Students are expected to be fluent with these combinations and all of the addition combinations to 10 + 10 by the end of this unit, although they will benefit from continued practice during the last unit of the school year.

3 Whole Number Operations Making sense of and developing strategies to solve addition and subtraction problems with totals to 100

Math Focus Points

◆ Subtracting amounts from 100

◆ Visualizing, retelling, and modeling the action of addition and subtraction situations

◆ Developing efficient methods for adding, subtracting, and notating strategies

◆ Solving subtraction problems by subtracting in parts

◆ Solving subtraction problems by adding up or subtracting back to find the difference

◆ Comparing problems in which the amount subtracted differs by 1

◆ Adding 2-digit numbers by keeping one number whole

◆ Adding 2-digit numbers by adding tens and ones

◆ Noticing what happens to place value when two 2-digit numbers with a sum over 100 are combined

Students continue to develop and refine their strategies for subtraction. They consider and practice two strategies in particular—*subtracting in parts* and *adding up or subtracting back.* By the end of this unit, students are expected to have one strategy that they can use to accurately solve a subtraction problem. After studying two particular strategies for addition—*adding tens and ones* and *keeping one number whole*—students are expected to have at least one strategy that they can use to accurately and efficiently solve an addition problem. See **Teacher Notes:** Students' Subtraction Strategies, page 158, and Students' Addition Strategies, page 172.

Round 1: I pinched ___23___. Equation: ___100 − 23 = ▢___
There are ___77___ left in the box.

$$100 - 23 = ▢$$
$$100 - 10 = 90$$
$$90 - 10 = 80$$
$$80 - 3 = 77$$

Sample Student Work

$$46 + 58 = 104$$
$$40 + 6 \quad 50 + 8$$
$$40 + 50 = 90 \rightarrow 6 + 8 = 14 \rightarrow 90 + 10 = 100$$
$$100 + 4 = 104 \leftarrow \quad 10 + 4$$

Sample Student Work

As in all of the number work in Grade 2, there is a continued focus on making sense of the action of different types of problems and on developing efficient strategies for solving them and recording work.

4 **Whole Number Operations** **Using manipulatives, drawings, tools, and notation to show strategies and solutions**

Math Focus Points

◆ Using cubes and the number line to show how addition combinations are related

◆ Representing the action of subtraction and addition situations using notation ($-$, $+$, $=$)

Students are expected to be able to use standard notation to write an equation to represent an addition or subtraction problem. They are also expected to use sticker notation, equations, a number line, and the 100 chart—or some combination of these—for clearly showing their work.

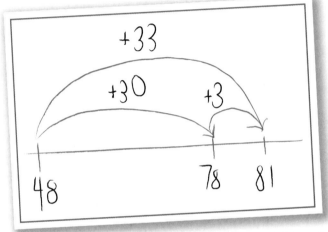

Carla's Work

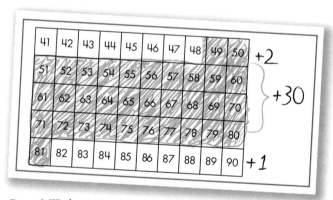

Darren's Work

Note that for many students, the equation that they write to show what a problem is asking does not necessarily match the strategy that they use to solve it.

Jake pinched 76 paper clips out of a box of 100. How many were still in the box?

Students may, for example, write 100 − 76 = _____ as an equation for the above problem—suggesting a strategy of removal—but solve the problem by adding up from 76 to 100 (represented by the equation 76 + _____ = 100). See **Teacher Notes:** Notating Subtraction Strategies, page 163, and Notating Addition Strategies, page 176.

This Unit also focuses on

◆ Counting a set of objects by equal groups

◆ Thinking about what happens if you subtract 1 more or 1 less

Classroom Routines focus on

◆ Generating equivalent expressions for a number

◆ Developing fluency with addition and subtraction

◆ Using standard notation (+, −, =) to record expressions and write equations

◆ Using clocks as tools for keeping track of and measuring time

◆ Naming, notating, and telling time to the hour, half hour, and quarter hour on digital and analog clocks

◆ Determining what time it will be when given start and elapsed times that are multiples of 15 minutes

◆ Developing and analyzing visual images for quantities

◆ Solving problems about an unknown change

◆ Adding or subtracting 10

◆ Noticing what happens to the tens place when a multiple of 10 is added or subtracted

◆ Making predictions about data

◆ Collecting, counting, representing, discussing, interpreting, and comparing data

◆ Counting by groups

◆ Counting a quantity in more than one way

◆ Developing strategies for solving addition problems with many addends

LOOKING FORWARD

In Grade 3, students extend their understanding of place value into 3-digit numbers. They work on adding and subtracting multiples of 10 and 100 and on using these "landmark" numbers in their strategies for computation. They continue to develop and examine strategies for addition with 2- and 3-digit numbers and use their fluency with the addition combinations to achieve fluency with their subtraction counterparts.

Assessment

IN THIS UNIT

ONGOING ASSESSMENT: Observing Students at Work

The following sessions provide **Ongoing Assessment: Observing Students at Work** opportunities:

- **Session 1.1, p. 29**
- **Session 1.3, pp. 39 and 40**
- **Session 2.1, pp. 57 and 57–58**
- **Session 2.2, p. 61**
- **Session 3.1, pp. 73–74 and 75**

- **Session 3.2, pp. 79–80 and 85–86**
- **Session 3.3, pp. 93 and 94**
- **Session 3.4, pp. 99–100**
- **Session 3.5, pp. 105–107**
- **Session 4.1, pp. 113–114 and 119–120**

- **Session 4.2, pp. 125–126**
- **Session 4.3, p. 133**
- **Session 4.4, p. 138–139**
- **Session 4.5, p. 148–149**

WRITING OPPORTUNITIES

The following sessions have **writing** opportunities for students to explain their mathematical thinking:

- **Session 1.3, pp. 38–40 and 42**
  Student Activity Book, pp. 7–11, 13–14

- **Session 3.4, p. 99**
  Student Activity Book, p. 36

- **Session 4.2, pp. 125 and 129**
  Student Activity Book, p. 48 and 50–51

- **Session 4.3, p. 133**
  Student Activity Book, p. 52

- **Session 4.4, p. 139**
  Student Activity Book, p. 58

- **Session 4.5, pp. 147–148**
  M41–M44, End-of-Unit Assessment

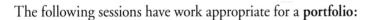

PORTFOLIO OPPORTUNITIES

The following sessions have work appropriate for a **portfolio:**

- **Sessions 1.3 and 1.4, pp. 39–40**
  Student Activity Book, pp. 9–11

- **Session 3.1, pp. 73–74**
  Student Activity Book, pp. 23–24

- **Session 3.2, pp. 79 and 84**
  Student Activity Book, pp. 27–28

- **Session 3.4, p. 99**
  Student Activity Book, pp. 35–36

- **Session 3.5, p. 105**
  M24, Assessment: Paper Clips and Cherries

- **Session 4.1, pp. 119–120**
  Student Activity Book, pp. 42–43

- **Session 4.2, pp. 123 and 125**
  M27, *Today's Number: 71* and
  Student Activity Book, pp. 47–48

- **Session 4.4, pp. 138–139**
  Student Activity Book, pp. 57–58

- **Session 4.5, pp. 147–148**
  M41–M45, End-of-Unit Assessment

Assessing the Benchmarks

Observing students as they engage in conversation about their ideas is a primary means to assess their mathematical understanding. Consider all of your students' work, not just the written assessments. See the chart below for suggestions about key activities to observe.

 Checklist Available

Benchmarks in This Unit	Key Activities to Observe	Assessment
1. Subtract 2-digit numbers.	**Sessions 3.1, 3.3, 3.4:** Pinching Paper Clips **Sessions 3.1, 3.2, 3.3, 3.4:** Story Problems	**Session 3.5: Assessment:** Paper Clips and Cherries
2. Reason about partners, teams, and leftovers to make and justify generalizations about what happens when even and odd numbers are added.	**Sessions 1.3, 1.4:** Can You Make . . . ? and What Happens When . . . ?	**Session 4.5: End-of-Unit Assessment:** Problems 1–3
3. Add two 2-digit numbers accurately and efficiently.	**Sessions 4.1, 4.2, 4.3, 4.4:** Story Problems	**Session 4.5: End-of-Unit Assessment:** Problems 4–5
4. Demonstrate fluency with addition combinations: plus 9 and remaining combinations.	**Sessions 2.1, 2.2:** *Plus 9 or 10 BINGO* **Sessions: 3.1, 3.3, 3.4, 3.5:** Addition Combinations Practice	**Session 4.5 End-of-Unit Assessment:** Problems 6A–6M ☑

Relating the Mathematical Emphases to the Benchmarks

Mathematical Emphases	Benchmarks
Whole Number Operations Adding even and odd numbers	2
Computational Fluency Knowing addition combinations to 10 + 10	4
Whole Number Operations Making sense of and developing strategies to solve addition and subtraction problems with totals to 100	1, 3
Whole Number Operations Using manipulatives, drawings, tools, and notation to show strategies and solutions	1, 3

This unit presents your students with opportunities to engage with ideas that lay a foundation for algebra. Seven- and eight-year-olds can and do think algebraically. Part of the work of Grade 2 is helping students learn to verbalize those thoughts and consider such questions as these: Is this statement always true? Does it work for all numbers? How can we know? Such discussions allow students to engage with generalizations about numbers and operations and help to establish a foundation for meaningful use of algebraic notation in the future.

This final number unit in Grade 2 provides students three kinds of opportunities to work on algebraic ideas: (1) formulating generalizations about adding even and odd numbers, (2) articulating generalizations about subtraction, and (3) applying generalizations that were discussed in earlier units.

The unit begins with an exploration of adding odd and even numbers: What kind of number do you get when you add two even numbers? Two odd numbers? An odd and an even? The emphasis in this investigation is not only to articulate the generalization, but to explain how you know it is true because, after all, you can never test all possible cases. This issue arises in the following vignette in which students are discussing this problem:

In Ms. Todd's class, there are 10 girls and 12 boys. Can everyone have a partner?

Carolina: I imagined the class lining up. If you have 10 girls and 10 boys, that's 10 pairs. Then there's 2 boys left over, but they are another pair.

Girls O O O O O O O O O O
Boys O O O O O O O O O O O O

Luis: I just thought 12 and 10 are both even numbers, so yes, they can have partners.

Travis: Yes, if 10 people make partners with no leftovers, and 12 people make partners with no leftover, then there's still no leftovers when you put them together.

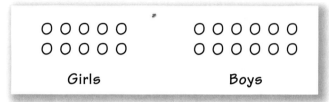

Girls   Boys

Teacher: Luis said he just thought, "12 and 10 are both even numbers, so everyone can have partners." If there are two other even numbers, will everyone still be able to have partners?

Travis: If the girls are an even number, they can all have partners. If the boys are an even number, they can all have partners. So when you add them together, everyone still has a partner.

In this vignette, the students use the definition of *even* as a number that can be grouped into pairs (partners), and they all offer good explanations for how they know that 10 + 12 will yield an even number. However, there are important differences among the arguments. Carolina's argument applies exclusively to the sum of 12 and 10. Luis applies a generalization that the sum of two even numbers is even, but he has not explained how he knows this to be the case. Travis offers a rationale for why the sum of two even numbers must always be even. Using the language of girls, boys, and partners, he argues that since the sum of two even numbers involves joining two sets of pairs, the joined set is itself a set of pairs.

In later years, students will learn how to represent even and odd numbers with algebraic notation, which will allow them to make proofs based on formal definitions and the distributive property. For more on this notation, and how second-grade students' ideas connect with it, see **Teacher Note:** Reasoning and Proof in Mathematics, page 153.

This unit also provides opportunities for students to articulate and apply generalizations about subtraction. It is very important to discuss generalizations about subtraction because students frequently lose sight of the fact that generalizations apply to a *particular operation*. So, for example, once they recognize that order does not matter when you add (e.g., $3 + 4 = 4 + 3$), they might assume that order does not matter when you subtract—though of course we know that $4 - 3 \neq 3 - 4$. Discussions about subtraction can focus students' attention on how subtraction behaves differently than addition.

For example, consider Roshaun's explanation for how he knows that $14 - 9 = 5$.

Roshaun: I know how to subtract 10: $14 - 10 = 4$. To do $14 - 9$, I took away 1 less, so I'm left with 1 more. $4 + 1 = 5$.

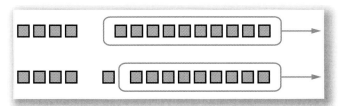

Although Roshaun is working to solve a particular problem, his explanation includes an important generalization: If you subtract 1 *less,* the result is 1 *more.* His demonstration represents subtraction as removing a set of tiles: No matter how many tiles you start with, if you first subtract some amount, and then subtract 1 less, you are left with 1 more.

Note the contrast between this generalization for subtraction and a similar one for addition: If you add 1 to either addend, the total is 1 more.

In later years, students will learn to represent these generalizations algebraically. For example, to express Roshaun's idea, they might write: If $a - b = c$, then $a - (b - 1) = c + 1$. This can be represented more concisely as $a - (b - 1) = (a - b) + 1$.

The unit also provides opportunities for students to apply generalizations they have worked on in earlier units. Many students use generalizations about addition to help them remember their addition combinations. For example, students make statements like these:

"I know $3 + 5 = 4 + 4$ because I can take 1 from one addend and add it to the other addend and the total is the same."

"I know $6 + 9$ is 1 less than $6 + 10$ because if I subtract 1 from an addend, the total is 1 less."

Similarly, students use generalizations as they devise efficient strategies for adding 2-digit numbers. For example:

"$27 + 32$ is the same as $20 + 7 + 30 + 2$ and then, because I can change the order with any number of addends, I can add $20 + 30$ and then $7 + 2$ and get the answer, 59."

For most adults, the use of algebraic notation (variables, operations, and equal signs) is the chief identifying feature of algebra. Underlying such notation, however, are ways of reasoning about how the operations work. This reasoning about how numbers can be put together and taken apart under different operations—not the notation—is the work of elementary students in algebra. *Investigations* students are encouraged to verbalize the generalizations they see about numbers and operations, and to explain and justify them using materials and tools, such as cubes. These discussions are not so much about finding an answer to a particular problem, but about describing a way to find answers to a whole class of problems. They are not exclusively about, for example, how to find $14 - 9$, but about the result of changing the number you subtract in *any* subtraction problem.

Note: *In the text for the sessions, you will find Algebra Notes that identify where these early algebra discussions are likely to arise. Some of the* **Teacher Notes** *and* **Dialogue Boxes** *further elaborate the ideas and illustrate students' conversations about them.*

Classroom Routines

Classroom Routines offer practice and review of key concepts for this grade level. These daily activities, to be done in ten minutes outside of math class, occur in a regular rotation every 4–5 days. Specific directions for the day's routine are provided in each session. For the full description and variations of each classroom routine, see *Implementing Investigations in Grade 2*.

Today's Number

Students use addition and subtraction to generate *Today's Number*. In one variation, *Today's Number* is represented by a set of counters. After some counters are covered, students use the number of counters showing to figure out how many are hidden.

Math Focus Points

◆ Generating equivalent expressions for a number

◆ Developing fluency with addition and subtraction

◆ Using standard notation (+, −, =) to record expressions and write equations

What Time Is It?

Students practice telling time to the hour, half hour, and quarter hour. They determine what time it will be in 15-, 30-, and 45-minute intervals and practice naming and notating those times.

Math Focus Points

◆ Using clocks as tools for keeping track of and measuring time

◆ Naming, notating, and telling time to the hour, half hour, and quarter hour on digital and analog clocks

◆ Determining what time it will be when given start and elapsed times that are multiples of 15 minutes

Quick Images: Cover Up with Tens and Ones

Students view an image of sticker strips and singles and determine the total number of stickers. Then, after some are covered, they figure out how many are hidden, given the number showing.

Math Focus Points

◆ Developing and analyzing visual images for quantities

◆ Solving problems about an unknown change

◆ Adding or subtracting 10

◆ Noticing what happens to the tens place when a multiple of 10 is added or subtracted

How Many Pockets?

Students build individual cube towers to represent their pockets. The class orders the towers, records the data, and calculates the total number of pockets. Later, students compare these data with the data from another class (collected by the teacher ahead of time).

Math Focus Points

◆ Making predictions about data

◆ Collecting, counting, representing, discussing, interpreting, and comparing data

◆ Counting by groups

◆ Counting a quantity in more than one way

◆ Developing strategies for solving addition problems with many addends

Practice and Review

Practice and review play a critical role in the *Investigations* program. The following components and features are available to provide regular reinforcement of key mathematical concepts and procedures.

Books	Features	In This Unit ...
Curriculum Unit	**Classroom Routines** offer practice and review of key concepts for this grade level. These daily activities, to be done in ten minutes outside of math class, occur in a regular rotation every 4–5 days. Specific directions for the day's routine are provided in each session. For the full description and variations of each classroom routine see *Implementing Investigations in Grade 2*.	• **All sessions**
Student Activity Book	**Daily Practice** pages in the *Student Activity Book* provide one of three types of written practice: **reinforcement** of the content of the unit, **ongoing review,** or **enrichment** opportunities. Some Daily Practice pages will also have Ongoing Review items with multiple-choice problems similar to those on standardized tests.	• **All sessions**
	Homework pages in the *Student Activity Book* are an extension of the work done in class. At times they help students prepare for upcoming activities.	• **Session 1.2** • **Session 3.4** • **Session 1.3** • **Session 4.1** • **Session 2.1** • **Session 4.2** • **Session 2.2** • **Session 4.3** • **Session 3.1** • **Session 4.4** • **Session 3.3**
Student Math Handbook	**Math Words and Ideas** in the *Student Math Handbook* are pages that summarize key words and ideas. Most Words and Ideas pages have at least one exercise.	• **Student Math Handbook, pp. 35–36, 41–42, 51–53, 59–75**
	Games pages are found in a section of the *Student Math Handbook*.	• **Student Math Handbook, p. G11**

Supporting the Range of Learners

Sessions	1.1	1.2	1.3	1.4	2.1	2.2	3.1	3.2	3.3	3.4	4.1	4.2	4.3	4.4	4.5
Intervention	•	•	•		•	•	•	•	•	•	•	•	•	•	
Extension		•		•	•			•	•	•	•	•	•		
ELL	•				•		•								•

Intervention

Suggestions are made to support and engage students who are having difficulty with a particular idea, activity, or problem.

Extension

Suggestions are made to support and engage students who finish early or may be ready for additional challenge.

English Language Learners (ELL)

As English Language Learners work through *Partners, Teams, and Paper Clips,* they will encounter words that have more than one meaning in English, such as *odd, even, record,* and *leftovers.* They will also encounter words such as *sum* (sounds like *some*), *pair* (sounds like *pear*), and *whole* (sounds like *hole*). To minimize confusion, use visual examples and modeling of the mathematical meanings as these words come up in your classroom discussions.

Throughout this unit, continue to provide opportunities for English Language Learners to practice the English names of numbers. Remind them to refer to the Numbers chart in the *Student Math Handbook* (or the Numbers chart you created at the beginning of the school year) when additional support is needed.

As you observe students at work or meet with them in small groups, continue to model the language needed to describe strategies for addition and subtraction as you have done in the other Grade 2 units on addition, subtraction, and the number system.

Working with the Range of Learners is a set of episodes written by teachers that focuses on meeting the needs of the range of learners in the classroom. In the first section, *Setting up the Mathematical Community,* teachers write about how they create a supportive and productive learning environment in their classrooms. In the next section, *Accommodations for Learning,* teachers focus on specific modifications they make to meet the needs of some of their learners. In the last section, *Language and Representation,* teachers share how they help students use representations and develop language to investigate and express mathematical ideas. The questions at the end of each case provide a starting point for your own reflection or for discussion with colleagues. See *Implementing Investigations in Grade 2* for this set of episodes.

Mathematical Emphasis

Whole Number Operations Adding even and odd numbers

Math Focus Points

◆ Characterizing even and odd numbers as those that do or do not make groups of two (partners) and two equal groups (teams)

◆ Investigating what happens with partners and teams when two groups are combined

◆ Making and testing conjectures about adding even and odd numbers

◆ Finding combinations of odd and even numbers that make given numbers or determining that these combinations are not possible

◆ Making and justifying generalizations about adding even and odd numbers

Adding Even and Odd Numbers

	Student Activity Book	Student Math Handbook	Professional Development: Read Ahead of Time	
SESSION 1.1 p. 24				
Partners and Teams with Two Groups Students review the definitions of even and odd numbers that they generated earlier in the year. They solve problems about combining two groups of children and consider whether everyone can have a partner or whether two equal teams can be made.	1–3	41–42	• **Mathematics in This Unit,** p. 10 • **Algebra Connections in This Unit,** p. 16 • **Teacher Note:** Defining Even and Odd, p. 151	
SESSION 1.2 p. 31				
More Partners and Teams with Two Groups Students solve and discuss problems about partners and teams when combining two groups of children, setting the stage for an investigation about adding even and odd numbers.	1–2, 4–6	41–42	• **Teacher Note:** Reasoning and Proof in Mathematics, p. 153	
SESSION 1.3 p. 37				
Adding Even and Odd Numbers Students investigate what happens when you add even and odd numbers. Class discussions focus on making and justifying generalizations about adding two odd numbers.	7–14	41–42, 65–66	• **Dialogue Boxes:** Two Leftovers Will Always Equal Another Pair, p. 190; Adding Two Evens or Two Odds, p. 192	
SESSION 1.4 p. 43				
More Adding Even and Odd Numbers Class work and discussion continue to focus on making and justifying generalizations about adding even and odd numbers.	7–11, 13–15	41–42		

Quick Images: Cover Up with Tens and Ones

- T38–T39, **Stickers: Strips and Singles** 🖨 Cut apart the images.

What Time Is It?

- **Student clocks** (1 per pair)

How Many Pockets?

- **Connecting cubes** (class set)

Materials to Gather	Materials to Prepare
• **T78, Problems About Two Small Groups** 🖨 (optional) • **Charts of even and odd definitions** Locate and post the charts of your students' definitions for even numbers and odd numbers from Unit 3, *Stickers, Number Strings, and Story Problems,* or prepare chart paper to make new ones. • **Chart paper** (as needed) • **Connecting cubes** (in towers of 10) • **Class 100 chart** (posted)	• **M2, Problems About Two Small Groups** Make copies. (as needed) • **M3–M4, Family Letter** Make copies. (1 per student)
• **M2, Problems About Two Small Groups** (from Session 1.1) • **Connecting cubes** (as needed) • **Charts of even and odd definitions** (from Session 1.1)	• **M5, Problems About Two Big Groups** Make copies. (as needed)
• **Chart paper** (optional) • **Connecting cubes**	
• **Connecting cubes**	

🖨 Overhead Transparency

Partners and Teams with Two Groups

Math Focus Points

◆ Characterizing even and odd numbers as those that do or do not make groups of two (partners) and two equal groups (teams)

◆ Investigating what happens with partners and teams when two groups are combined

Vocabulary

even
odd

Today's Plan		Materials
1 DISCUSSION **Reviewing Even and Odd Numbers**	15 MIN CLASS	• Charts: "Even Numbers" and "Odd Numbers" (prepared in Unit 3); chart paper; connecting cubes; class 100 chart
2 ACTIVITY **Introducing Two Groups**	15 MIN CLASS	• Connecting cubes; class 100 chart
3 ACTIVITY **Two Groups**	30 MIN INDIVIDUALS PAIRS	• *Student Activity Book*, pp. 1–2 • M2*; T78 (optional) • Connecting cubes (as needed)
4 SESSION FOLLOW-UP **Daily Practice**		• *Student Activity Book*, p. 3 • M3–M4*, Family Letter • *Student Math Handbook*, pp. 41–42

*See *Materials to Prepare*, p. 23.

Classroom Routines

Quick Images: Cover Up with Tens and Ones Using Stickers: Strips and Singles (T38–T39), display the number 24 with two strips and four singles. Follow the basic *Quick Images* activity. After students determine the total, cover 12 stickers (one strip and two singles) with a sheet of paper. Students use the number still showing (12) to determine how many are covered. Discuss and model students' strategies.

DISCUSSION

1 Reviewing Even and Odd Numbers

15 MIN   CLASS

Math Focus Points for Discussion

◆ Characterizing even and odd numbers as those that do or do not make groups of two (partners) and two equal groups (teams)

Begin by reminding students about the work they did with partners and teams in Unit 3, *Stickers, Number Strings, and Story Problems*. If you still have the posters from that unit on which you listed students' ideas about even and odd numbers, post them for reference during this discussion. You may also use this discussion to create new posters.

Earlier this year we thought about what happens when you put different numbers of people into partners or onto two teams. What do you remember? What did we find out?❶

Students might say:

"Some numbers make two equal teams (or partners) with no leftovers, but others have one leftover."

"If a number makes two equal teams, it also makes partners with no leftovers."

"Numbers that 'work' are even, and those that don't are odd. Evens are the 'counting by two' numbers. They end in 0, 2, 4, 6, and 8."

Model students' ideas with cubes, drawings, and the 100 chart. Point out related definitions on your existing posters, or record students' ideas on chart paper.❷

❶ **Teacher Note:** Defining Even and Odd, p. 151

Differentiation

❷ **English Language Learners** During this and all other discussions, encourage English Language Learners to contribute their ideas. Pairing these students with native English speakers during games and activities will help them develop their mathematical vocabulary before whole-class discussions. You may also wish to meet with English Language Learners before some discussions to preview the questions you plan to ask. By giving students the chance to formulate and practice answers ahead of time, you can assess their understanding of the math content and provide them with the language they may require. During discussions, allow students to respond to your questions not only with words, but also by demonstrating their thinking with manipulatives, drawings, and other representations.

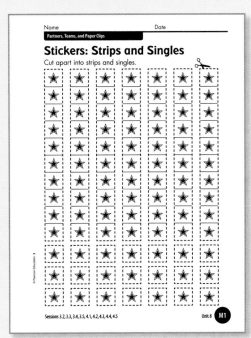

▲ Resource Masters, M1; T38–T39

Things We Think or Know About Even Numbers	
Our Ideas	Examples/Illustrations
Even numbers can go in 2s.	XX XX XX XX XX XX
When you (start at 0 or 2 and) count by 2s, you say the even numbers.	2, 4, 6, 8, 10, 12
Evens always come after an odd and before an odd.	1 2 3 4 5 6 7 8 9 10 11 12
If there is an even number in the ones place—if the number ends in 2, 4, 6, 8, or 0—the whole number is even.	2 is even, so 12 and 102 are even.
If a number is even, then you can make 2 equal teams (with no leftovers).	12 kids make 2 teams of 6. XXXXXX XXXXXX
Doubles facts make even numbers.	$2 + 2 = 4 \ldots 10 + 10 = 20$ $3 + 3 = 6 \ldots 11 + 11 = 22$

Things We Think or Know About Odd Numbers	
Our Ideas	Examples/Illustrations
If a number is odd, you cannot make partners, so there is always one person left alone.	XX XX XX XX XX X
Every other number is odd.	1, 2, 3, 4, 5, 6, 7, 8, 9, 10, 11
If you take 1 away from an odd number, you get an even number.	11 is odd. $11 - 1 = 10$ 10 is even.
If there is an odd number in the ones place, the whole number is odd.	1 is odd, so 11 and 101 are odd.
Odd is not a team because two against one is not good. Odd numbers do not make 2 equal or fair teams (with the same number on each team). There is always 1 leftover.	Half of 11 is 5 and a half. One team would have 5, the other would have 6. XXXXX XXXXX X
Odd numbers have a middle.	XXXXX X XXXXX

Imagine a group of 12 students. Can they make two equal teams? How do you know? Can they make partners with no one left over? How do you know? What about a group of 13 students?

Again use cubes, drawings, numbers, equations, and the 100 chart to model students' strategies. Record them on an existing chart or on a new sheet of chart paper.

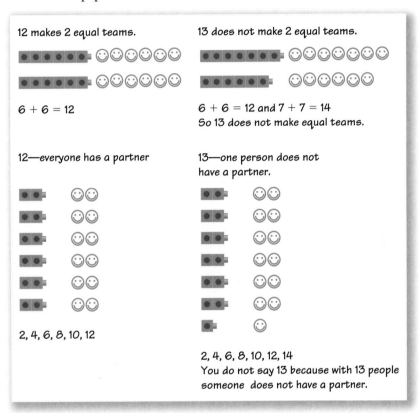

12 makes 2 equal teams.

6 + 6 = 12

12—everyone has a partner

2, 4, 6, 8, 10, 12

13 does not make 2 equal teams.

6 + 6 = 12 and 7 + 7 = 14
So 13 does not make equal teams.

13—one person does not have a partner.

2, 4, 6, 8, 10, 12, 14
You do not say 13 because with 13 people someone does not have a partner.

ACTIVITY

15 MIN   CLASS

2 Introducing Two Groups

Let's think about what happens when you put two groups together. Think about this problem: In Ms. Ortega's class, there are 4 students in the blue group and 6 students in the yellow group. If we put the two groups together, could everyone in the two groups have a partner? How many pairs would there be?

Give students a minute to think about and solve the problem. Then ask a few students to share how they solved it while you use cubes to model it for the class. Some students add 4 and 6, and then determine whether

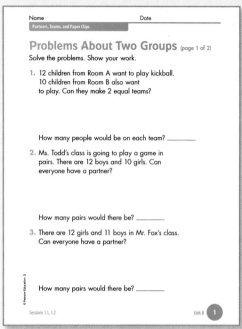

▲ **Student Activity Book, p. 1**

Name _____ Date _____
Partners, Teams, and Paper Clips

Problems About Two Groups (page 1 of 2)
Solve the problems. Show your work.

1. 12 children from Room A want to play kickball.
   10 children from Room B also want
   to play. Can they make 2 equal teams?

   How many people would be on each team? _____

2. Ms. Todd's class is going to play a game in
   pairs. There are 12 boys and 10 girls. Can
   everyone have a partner?

   How many pairs would there be? _____

3. There are 12 girls and 11 boys in Mr. Fox's class.
   Can everyone have a partner?

   How many pairs would there be? _____

Sessions 1.1, 1.2   Unit 8 1

▲ **Student Activity Book, p. 2**

Name _____ Date _____
Partners, Teams, and Paper Clips

Problems About Two Groups (page 2 of 2)
Solve the problems. Show your work.

4. 16 children from Room A want to play soccer.
   11 children from Room B also want to play.
   Can they make 2 equal teams?

   How many people would be on each team? _____

5. At recess 17 girls want to play baseball. 13 boys
   want to play, too. Can they make 2 equal teams?

   How many people would be on each team? _____

6. Ms. Ortega's class has 15 girls and 15 boys.
   Can everyone have a partner?

   How many pairs would there be? _____

2 Unit 8   Sessions 1.1, 1.2

the number 10 results in partners. Others think about whether each number works individually (e.g., if 4 results in everyone's having a partner and 6 results in everyone's having a partner, then everyone still has a partner when you combine the two groups).

What about equal teams? If you combined the blue and yellow groups, could you have two equal teams? How many people would be on each team?

Again, ask for strategies and model them for the class.

Some students reason that if you take one from the six and give it to the four, you have two equal teams of five.

Some students "just know" that they make two equal teams because they already made partners, and if something works for partners, then it also works for teams.

30 MIN INDIVIDUALS PAIRS

ACTIVITY

③ Two Groups

Students begin work on *Student Activity Book* pages 1–2, which focus on what happens with partners and teams when you combine two groups of students. They will continue to work on these pages in the next session.

As you are working, think about whether these problems make you want to change or add anything to our charts of **even** and **odd** number definitions.

ONGOING ASSESSMENT: Observing Students at Work

Students think about what happens with partners and teams when two groups are combined.

- **How do students model the problems?** Do they use cubes or pictures? Do they work mentally?

- **How do students solve the problems?** Do they figure out whether the sum makes partners or teams? Do they figure out whether each addend makes partners or teams? Do they change the numbers to create equivalent problems (e.g., "6 + 4 = 5 + 5, so you can make equal teams")?❸

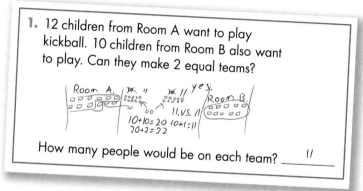

Sample Student Work

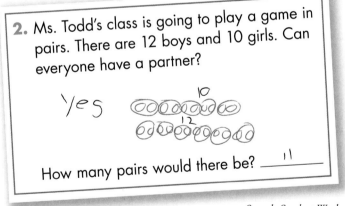

Sample Student Work

Algebra Note

❸ **Using Generalizations** Students who create equivalent problems may be applying a generalization—a general claim that you can make about the way numbers or operations work—that was discussed earlier in the year. If you subtract 1 from one addend and add 1 to the other, the total remains the same.

▲ Resource Masters, M2; T78

Problems About Two Small Groups

Solve the problems. Show your work.

1. 6 boys want to play soccer. 8 girls want to play, too. Can they make two equal teams?

How many people would be on each team? _____

2. There are 7 girls and 8 boys in Mr. Frank's class. Can everyone have a partner?

How many pairs would there be? _____

3. There are 11 boys in Ms. Singer's class. There are 9 girls. Can everyone have a partner?

How many pairs would there be? _____

At the Amusement Park

Solve each problem. Show your work.

NOTE Students determine which numbers can and cannot make equal groups of 2 or 2 equal teams.

1. 6 girls and 7 boys want to ride the Python roller coaster together. Can everyone have a partner to ride with?

How many pairs would there be? _____

2. Two groups can go into the Haunted House at one time. There are 26 children in line. Can they make two equal groups?

How many people would be in each group? _____

Ongoing Review

3. David has 13 pets. Some of them are mice, and some of them are hamsters. How many of David's 13 pets could be mice?

Which answer could **not** be correct?

(A) 12   (B) 11   (C) 1   (D) 0

Session 1.1   Unit 8 3

▲ Student Activity Book, p. 3

DIFFERENTIATION: Supporting the Range of Learners

Intervention Some students may benefit from solving problems with smaller numbers, such as those on Problems About Two Small Groups (M2). Encourage them to model the problems with cubes or pictures.

Some students' written work, although correct, may not provide enough information to get a sense of what students truly understand about even and odd numbers. Ask these students to explain how they know that 22 is even or how they figured out that there would be 11 on each team, and have them tie their explanations to the context of partners and teams.

1. 12 children from Room A want to play kickball. 10 children from Room B also want to play. Can they make 2 equal teams? Yes

22 is a Even number

How many people would be on each team? 11 for both teams,

Sample Student Work

SESSION FOLLOW-UP
4 Daily Practice

Daily Practice: For reinforcement of this unit's content, have students complete *Student Activity Book* page 3.

Family Letter: Send home copies of the Family Letter (M3–M4).

Student Math Handbook: Students and families may use *Student Math Handbook* pages 41–42 for reference and review. See pages 205–211 in the back of this unit.

More Partners and Teams with Two Groups

Math Focus Points

◈ Investigating what happens with partners and teams when two groups are combined

◈ Making and testing conjectures about adding even and odd numbers

Vocabulary

conjecture

Today's Plan		Materials
DISCUSSION **①Partners and Teams with Two Groups, Part 1**	🕐 15 MIN CLASS	• *Student Activity Book,* pp. 1–2 (from Session 1.1) • Connecting cubes (class set)
ACTIVITY **②Two Groups**	🕐 30 MIN INDIVIDUALS PAIRS	• *Student Activity Book,* pp. 1–2 • M2; M5* • Connecting cubes; charts: "Even Numbers" and "Odd Numbers"
DISCUSSION **③Partners and Teams with Two Groups, Part 2**	🕐 15 MIN CLASS	• *Student Activity Book,* pp. 1–2
SESSION FOLLOW-UP **④Daily Practice and Homework**		• *Student Activity Book,* pp. 4–6 • *Student Math Handbook,* pp. 41–42

*See *Materials to Prepare,* p. 23.

Classroom Routines

Quick Images: Cover Up with Tens and Ones Using Stickers: Strips and Singles (T38–T39), display 33 with three strips and three singles. Follow the basic *Quick Images* activity. After students determine the total, cover 11 (one strip and one single) with a sheet of paper. Students use the number of stickers showing (22) to determine how many are covered. Discuss and model students' strategies. Then, keeping the total at 33, cover 12. Discuss strategies, including any that use the first problem to solve the new problem. For example, "There is 1 fewer showing, so you must have hidden 1 more."

15 MIN   CLASS

Partners and Teams with Two Groups, Part 1

Math Focus Points for Discussion

◆ Investigating what happens with partners and teams when two groups are combined

◆ Making and testing conjectures about adding even and odd numbers

Begin this session with a discussion about the problems on *Student Activity Book* page 1.

Students typically approach these problems in one of two ways.

- Some add 12 and 10 and then decide whether 22 makes two equal teams. They may divide 22 into two groups, split 22 in half, or turn 12 + 10 into 11 + 11 by taking 1 from the 12 and giving it to the 10.

- Others think about whether each group makes equal teams and then reason about what would happen if the groups are combined.

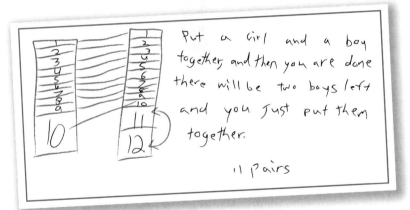

Sample Student Work

Did anyone know that the two groups would make equal teams *before*—or *without*—adding the two numbers together? How did you know?

As students share their strategies, model them with cubes, drawings, numbers, and equations. Some students solve the second problem by relating it to how they solved the first.

Students might say:

"The numbers are the same, and if it works for partners, it works for teams."

"Both problems are about 22. An even number's an even number—partners and teams are just two ways to figure it out."

Encourage students to find ways to explain and show why this is true.

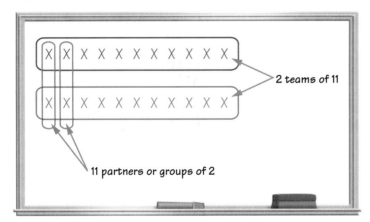

2 teams of 11

11 partners or groups of 2

Many students may start to make conjectures.❶ Pose questions that help students discuss and expand on these ideas.

[Juan] said that these problems made him think that when you add an even number and an even number, you get an even number. [Juan] has made a conjecture—an idea that we still need to prove. Let's think about [Juan]'s idea.

Both of these problems were about $10 + 12 = 22$. Is 10 odd or even? What about 12? 22? We added an even number to an even number in these problems, and we got an even number as our answer. I wonder why that happens and whether it always happens.❷

Encourage students to keep what you have been talking about in this discussion in mind as they continue working on *Student Activity Book* pages 1–2.

Algebra Note

❷ **Beyond Specific Examples** Encourage students to clearly state their conjectures about what happens when you add *any* two even numbers, *any* two odd numbers, or *any* even and *any* odd numbers.

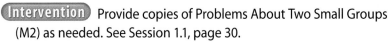

Name _____ Date _____

Partners, Teams, and Paper Clips

Problems About Two Big Groups

Solve the problems. Show your work.

1. Mr. Murphy has 27 students in his class. Mrs. Janner has 22 students. If the two classes play a game in partners, would every student have a partner?

How many pairs would there be? _____

2. In the second grade, there are 34 girls and 28 boys. Could there be two equal teams?

How many students would be on each team? _____

3. Ms. Chun has 33 students in her class. Mr. Fox has 25. If the two classes play a game in partners, will every student have a partner?

How many pairs would there be? _____

Session 1.2   Unit 8 **M5**

▲ Resource Masters, M5

② ACTIVITY
Two Groups

30 MIN   INDIVIDUALS   PAIRS

Students continue to work on Problems About Two Groups on *Student Activity Book* pages 1–2. For a full description of this activity, see Session 1.1, pages 27–30. Additionally, you may want to consider the following notes.

DIFFERENTIATION: Supporting the Range of Learners

Intervention Provide copies of Problems About Two Small Groups (M2) as needed. See Session 1.1, page 30.

Extension Students who finish the *Student Activity Book* pages can look for patterns or new ideas to add to the class charts about even and odd numbers. Students who are ready for more challenging work can solve the problems on Problems About Two Big Groups (M5).

③ DISCUSSION
Partners and Teams with Two Groups, Part 2

15 MIN   CLASS

Math Focus Points for Discussion

◆ Investigating what happens with partners and teams when two groups are combined

◆ Making and testing conjectures about adding even and odd numbers

When students have completed *Student Activity Book* pages 1–2, end the session with a discussion about Problem 3 (an even plus an odd) and Problem 5 (an odd plus an odd). This conversation should be quite similar to the one at the beginning of this session.

Encourage students to think about the kinds of numbers they have been adding in these problems and to comment on any patterns they are seeing. Explain that students will have more time to think about and explore similar questions in the next few sessions as they try to prove conjectures about adding even and odd numbers.

3. There are 12 girls and 11 boys in Mr. Fox's class.
Can everyone have a partner?

no

There are 6 2's in a 12.
There is 5 2's and a 1 in a 11.
5+b=11 1+0=1 and a 1

How many pairs would there be? _____ 11

---

5. At recess 17 girls want to play baseball. 13 boys
want to play, too. Can they make 2 equal teams?

10+10=20   tcam a   team b
3+7= 10   10   10
17+ 13= 30⁵   5

How many people would be on each team? ___ 15

---

5. At recess 17 girls want to play baseball. 13 boys
want to play, too. Can they make 2 equal teams?

yes

10+10=20
5+5=10
15+15 = 30
15. vs. 15

How many people would be on each team? ___ 15A 15B

Sample Student Work

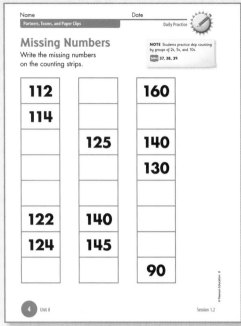

Missing Numbers
Write the missing numbers
on the counting strips.

NOTE Students practice skip counting
by groups of 2s, 5s, and 10s.
SMH 37, 38, 39

112		160
114		
	125	140
		130
122	140	
124	145	
		90

4 Unit 8   Session 1.2

▲ **Student Activity Book, p. 4**

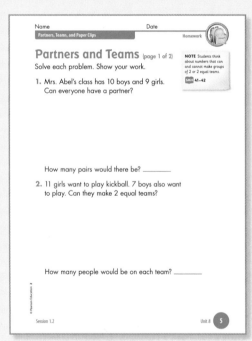

Partners and Teams (page 1 of 2)
Solve each problem. Show your work.

NOTE Students think about numbers that can and cannot make groups of 2 or 2 equal teams.
SMH 41–42

1. Mrs. Abel's class has 10 boys and 9 girls.
Can everyone have a partner?

How many pairs would there be? _____

2. 11 girls want to play kickball. 7 boys also want
to play. Can they make 2 equal teams?

How many people would be on each team? _____

Session 1.2   Unit 8 5

▲ **Student Activity Book, p. 5**

 SESSION FOLLOW-UP

Daily Practice and Homework

 Daily Practice: For ongoing review, have students complete *Student Activity Book* page 4.

Homework: Students solve more problems about partners and teams with two groups and record their work on *Student Activity Book* pages 5–6.

Student Math Handbook: Students and families may use *Student Math Handbook* pages 41–42 for reference and review. See pages 205–211 in the back of this unit.

Partners and Teams (page 2 of 2)
Solve each problem. Show your work.

3. Mr. Yoshi has 9 girls and 7 boys in his class.
Can everyone have a partner?

How many pairs would there be? _____

4. There are 8 boys and 11 girls who want to play
soccer. Can they make 2 equal teams?

How many people would be on each team? _____

6 Unit 8   Session 1.2

▲ **Student Activity Book, p. 6**

Adding Even and Odd Numbers

Math Focus Points

◆ Finding combinations of odd and even numbers that make given numbers or determining that these combinations are not possible

◆ Making and testing conjectures about adding even and odd numbers

◆ Making and justifying generalizations about adding even and odd numbers

Today's Plan		Materials
ACTIVITY **① Introducing Adding Even and Odd Numbers**	🕐 10 MIN 👥 CLASS	• *Student Activity Book,* pp. 7–11 • Chart paper (optional)
MATH WORKSHOP **② Adding Even and Odd Numbers** ② Can You Make . . . ? ② What Happens When . . . ?	🕐 30 MIN	2Ⓐ • *Student Activity Book,* pp. 7–8 • Connecting cubes (as needed) 2Ⓑ • *Student Activity Book,* pp. 9–11 • Connecting cubes (as needed)
DISCUSSION **③ Adding Two Odd Numbers**	🕐 20 MIN 👥 CLASS	• Connecting cubes
SESSION FOLLOW-UP **④ Daily Practice and Homework**		• *Student Activity Book,* pp. 12–14 • *Student Math Handbook,* pp. 41–42, 65–66

Classroom Routines

What Time Is It? Write these times on the board: 5:15, 5:30, and 5:45. Pairs work together setting their clocks to these times. Then partners take turns writing a time in digital format (e.g., 3:15) and setting their clock to that time.

ACTIVITY

10 MIN   CLASS

1 Introducing Adding Even and Odd Numbers

For the last two days, we have been thinking about what happens with partners and teams when there are two groups. People have been making some interesting observations. For example, [Juan] said that if you add an even number and an even number, you get an even number.

Today and tomorrow you are going to investigate statements, or conjectures, just like [Juan]'s. Here are the questions you will be thinking about:

- What happens when you add two even numbers?
- What happens when you add two odd numbers?
- What happens when you add an odd number and an even number?

Record the following on the board or on chart paper:

> **even + even**
>
> **odd + odd**
>
> **even + odd OR odd + even**

Students will explore and answer these questions as they work on the following two Math Workshop activities. The activities will push students toward making generalizations about adding odd and even numbers.

Read aloud *Student Activity Book* pages 7–8. Explain that students are to look for ways to make 24 and then 23 with two even numbers, with two odd numbers, and with one even and one odd number. Explain that some of the problems have no solution (that is, 24 or 23 cannot be made with the given combination of evens and/or odds). If students think they cannot make 24 or 23 in a particular case, they should explain why in the space provided.

Next, read aloud *Student Activity Book* pages 9–11. Explain that on each page, students will solve several problems, generate several problems of their own, and then write about what they notice. On the last page, students make generalizations about adding even and odd numbers and try to justify their ideas.

Can You Make . . . ? (page 1 of 2)

Today's Number is 24.

1. Is 24 even or odd? _____

2. Can you make 24 with two EVEN numbers?

   _____ + _____ = 24   _____ + _____ = 24

   If you think you cannot, explain why:
   _____
   _____

3. Can you make 24 with two ODD numbers?

   _____ + _____ = 24   _____ + _____ = 24

   If you think you cannot, explain why:
   _____
   _____

4. Can you make 24 with an EVEN and an ODD number?

   _____ + _____ = 24   _____ + _____ = 24

   If you think you cannot, explain why:
   _____
   _____

Sessions 1.3, 1.4   Unit 8   7

▲ **Student Activity Book, p. 7**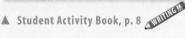

Can You Make . . . ? (page 2 of 2)

Today's Number is 23.

5. Is 23 even or odd? _____

6. Can you make 23 with two EVEN numbers?

   _____ + _____ = 23   _____ + _____ = 23

   If you think you cannot, explain why:
   _____
   _____

7. Can you make 23 with two ODD numbers?

   _____ + _____ = 23   _____ + _____ = 23

   If you think you cannot, explain why:
   _____
   _____

8. Can you make 23 with an EVEN and an ODD number?

   _____ + _____ = 23   _____ + _____ = 23

   If you think you cannot, explain why:
   _____
   _____

8   Unit 8   Sessions 1.3, 1.4

▲ **Student Activity Book, p. 8**

Professional Development

❶ **Teacher Note:** Reasoning and Proof in Mathematics, p. 153

❷ **Dialogue Box:** Two Leftovers Will Always Equal Another Pair, p. 190

❸ **Dialogue Box:** Adding Two Evens or Two Odds, p. 192

MATH WORKSHOP

② Adding Even and Odd Numbers

30 MIN

For much of this and the next session, students will work on the two sets of *Student Activity Book* pages you have just introduced.

②A Can You Make . . . ?

INDIVIDUALS   PAIRS

Students work on *Student Activity Book* pages 7–8, looking for combinations of odd and even numbers to make 24 and 23.❶ ❷

ONGOING ASSESSMENT: Observing Students at Work

Students work toward making general statements about adding even and odd numbers.❸

- **Can students find pairs of numbers that work?**

- **Can students reason about pairs of numbers that do not work?** How do they prove that a given example is not possible?

- **Do they work systematically?**

- **Do they suggest that even numbers have no leftovers and odd numbers do?**

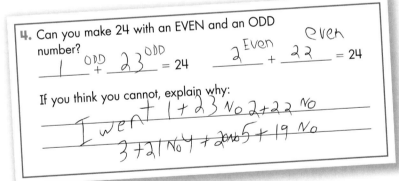

Sample Student Work

DIFFERENTIATION: Supporting the Range of Learners

Intervention If there are students who think that two even numbers cannot add to 23, challenge them to prove it to you by using words, pictures, cubes, or other models.

- Why do you think you cannot find two even numbers that add to 23?

- Can you find two even numbers that add to 25? Why not? What about 27?

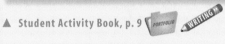

Name _____ Date _____
Partners, Teams, and Paper Clips

What Happens When . . . ? (page 1 of 3)
What happens when you add
two ODD numbers together?

1. Try these:

   9 + 9 = _____   Is the answer even or odd? _____

   11 + 7 = _____   Is the answer even or odd? _____

   15 + 23 = _____   Is the answer even or odd? _____

2. Now try some of your own:

   ___ + ___ = ___   Is the answer even or odd? _____

   ___ + ___ = ___   Is the answer even or odd? _____

   ___ + ___ = ___   Is the answer even or odd? _____

3. What do you get when you add two ODD numbers together?

   _____

4. Do you think this is **always** true? _____

5. Why do you think so? _____

   _____

Sessions 1.3, 1.4   Unit 8   9

▲ **Student Activity Book, p. 9**

Name _____ Date _____

Partners, Teams, and Paper Clips

What Happens When . . . ? (page 2 of 3)

What happens when you add
two EVEN numbers together?

6. Try these:

8 + 8 = _____   Is the answer even or odd? _____

12 + 6 = _____   Is the answer even or odd? _____

14 + 20 = _____   Is the answer even or odd? _____

7. Now try some of your own:

____ + ____ = ____   Is the answer even or odd? _____

____ + ____ = ____   Is the answer even or odd? _____

____ + ____ = ____   Is the answer even or odd? _____

8. What do you get when you add two EVEN numbers together?
_____

9. Do you think this is **always** true? _____

10. Why do you think so? _____
_____
_____

10   Unit 8   Sessions 1.3, 1.4

▲ Student Activity Book, p. 10

Name _____ Date _____

Partners, Teams, and Paper Clips

What Happens When . . . ? (page 3 of 3)

What happens when you add an EVEN
number and an ODD number?

11. Try these:

8 + 7 = _____   Is the answer even or odd? _____

11 + 6 = _____   Is the answer even or odd? _____

14 + 23 = _____   Is the answer even or odd? _____

12. Now try some of your own:

____ + ____ = ____   Is the answer even or odd? _____

____ + ____ = ____   Is the answer even or odd? _____

____ + ____ = ____   Is the answer even or odd? _____

13. What do you get when you add an EVEN
number and an ODD number?
_____

14. Do you think this is **always** true? _____

15. Why do you think so? _____
_____
_____

Sessions 1.3, 1.4   Unit 8   11

▲ Student Activity Book, p. 11

Note whether students solve each question you pose to see whether
they really know and believe that it will not work for *any* odd number.

2B What Happens When . . . ?

INDIVIDUALS   PAIRS

Students continue to investigate odds and evens through their work on
Student Activity Book pages 9–11.

ONGOING ASSESSMENT: Observing Students at Work

Students consider evidence, develop ideas based on evidence, and test
ideas by looking at examples and counterexamples.

- **What numbers do students test?** Are students accurate in their work?

- **What do students notice about what happens when you add
  even and odd numbers?** Do they make any general claims? Do
  they offer evidence?

DIFFERENTIATION: Supporting the Range of Learners

Intervention Encourage students whose explanations are "because I
tried a bunch of numbers" to try to explain—using words, pictures,
cubes, or other models—*why* something is or is not true.

How would you explain to our principal or the teacher next door why
you think an odd plus an odd is *always* even?

DISCUSSION

3 Adding Two Odd Numbers

20 MIN   CLASS

Math Focus Points for Discussion

◆ Making and testing conjectures about adding odd numbers

◆ Making and justifying generalizations about adding odd numbers

Before you began to investigate these problems, what did you think
would happen when you added two odd numbers? What made you
think so?

Everyone seems to agree that, for the examples you tried, an odd
number plus an odd number is an even number. Why do you think
that happens? Can you explain it?

Ground the discussion in a particular example, such as 7 + 9. Build two cube towers, each with an odd number of cubes. Establish that 7 and 9 are both odd numbers and that the sum, 16, is an even number.

Can someone use the cubes to show us that when two odd numbers are combined, the sum is an even number?

Some students break the cubes into groups of 2 (or partners). Others split them into two equal groups (or teams). As you discuss these strategies, ask questions that help you assess whether students believe that when added together, *any* two odd numbers will *always* equal an even number.❹

Do you think that this is true for all *numbers? In other words, when added together, will* any *two odd numbers* always *equal an even number?*

Some students say that they cannot know for sure; after all, they cannot test *all* of the odd numbers, and in fact, there are numbers they do not know about yet (very large numbers, negative numbers, and so on). Other students seem quite sure. Encourage these students to explain why they think so.❺

Why are you so sure that when two odd numbers are added, they will always *equal an even number? Can you prove it to us? How would you prove it to the teacher next door?*

Some students believe that an odd plus an odd is always an even because they tried several or even many examples. Others make more general statements, arguing that an odd number always has one leftover and so, if you combine two odd numbers, the two leftovers become partners. Any number that makes groups of 2 (partners) is an even number, so the sum of two odd numbers is an even number.

Students might say:

 "An odd number has one leftover. So two odd numbers each have one leftover. The two leftovers become partners."

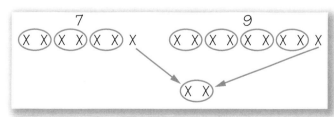

Teaching Note

❹ **Ideas May Be Revised** Initially, some students expect that adding two odds will make an odd. Remind them that people often revise their thinking based on new evidence.

Algebra Note

❺ **Is It True for *All* Numbers?** Some students think that, because all the examples they have tested come out one way, then problems must *always* work that way. They have not yet considered that there may be numbers they have not checked that will contradict their conjecture. Others think that because it is impossible to test all numbers, they can *never* make a claim about all numbers. This is an important idea to discuss, as is the reasoning of students who recognize that it is possible to reason about *all* even numbers and *all* odd numbers even though it is impossible to test them all.

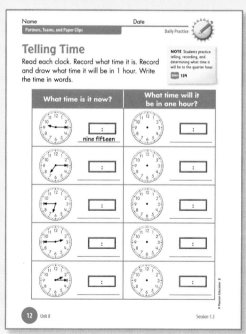

▲ **Student Activity Book, p. 12**

Algebra Note

Are You Convinced? To explain why a generalization must hold for *all* cases, discuss with students the difference between accepting a generalization on the basis of testing a few cases and reasoning from the definition of an even number as a number that can be made into pairs or an odd number as a number that can be made into pairs with one leftover.

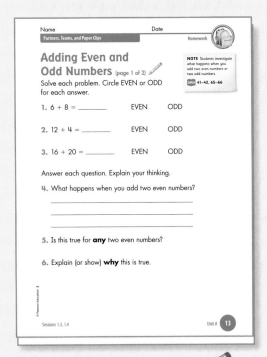

 "If you take one from the team of 9 and give it to the team with 7, you have two equal teams of 8."

Team A has 7: XXXXXXX

Team B has 9: XXXXXXX(X)

Push for these kinds of arguments, encouraging students to use cubes or drawings like the following to model why two odds *always* make an even. ⑥

9 + 9 = 18   It's even because the two persons that did not have a partner you could put them together.

Sample Student Work

▲ **Student Activity Book, pp. 13–14**

SESSION FOLLOW-UP

4 Daily Practice and Homework

Daily Practice: For ongoing review, have students complete *Student Activity Book* page 12.

Homework: Students continue their work adding even and odd numbers on *Student Activity Book* pages 13–14.

Student Math Handbook: Students and families may use *Student Math Handbook* pages 41–42 for reference and review. See pages 205–211 in the back of this unit.

More Adding Even and Odd Numbers

Math Focus Points

- Finding combinations of odd and even numbers that make given numbers or determining that these combinations are not possible
- Making and testing conjectures about adding even and odd numbers
- Making and justifying generalizations about adding even and odd numbers

Today's Plan		Materials
DISCUSSION **① Adding Evens**	10 MIN CLASS	• *Student Activity Book,* pp. 13–14 (completed homework) • Connecting cubes
MATH WORKSHOP **② Adding Even and Odd Numbers** **②A Can You Make . . . ?** **②B What Happens When . . . ?**	30 MIN	②A • *Student Activity Book,* pp. 7–8 (from Session 1.3) ②B • *Student Activity Book,* pp. 9–11 (from Session 1.3)
DISCUSSION **③ Adding an Even and an Odd**	20 MIN CLASS	• Connecting cubes
SESSION FOLLOW-UP **④ Daily Practice**		• *Student Activity Book,* p. 15 • *Student Math Handbook,* pp. 41–42

Classroom Routines

How Many Pockets? Represent the Data Each student takes one cube for each pocket he or she is wearing and builds a tower. Ask students with zero pockets (then 1, 2, 3 pockets, and so on) to put their towers in a central place. Record the information on a chart, posing questions such as these:

- Two people have two pockets. How many pockets is that?

After the data have been collected for each number of pockets, students determine the total number of pockets. Save this number (with other pocket data) for use in Session 4.3.

DISCUSSION

① Adding Evens

10 MIN   CLASS

Math Focus Points for Discussion

◆ Making and justifying generalizations about adding even numbers

Begin this session by discussing the questions that students answered for homework on *Student Activity Book* pages 13–14. This discussion should be quite similar to the one at the end of Session 1.3 but is likely to need less time because you already discussed adding two evens in the context of partners and teams in Session 1.2.

What did you find out about adding two even numbers? Why do you think that two even numbers make an even number?

Again, use two cube towers to ground the discussion in a particular example, but push students to consider whether their arguments apply to *all* even numbers and to explain why they think so.

Do you think that this is true for *all* numbers? In other words, when added together, will *any* two even numbers *always* equal an even number? Why do you think so? How would you show or prove it?

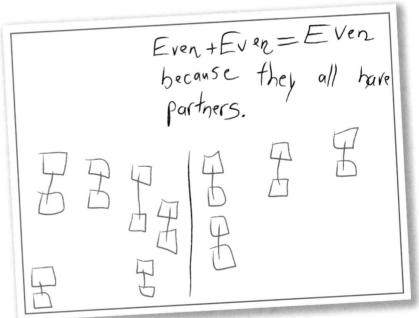

Sample Student Work

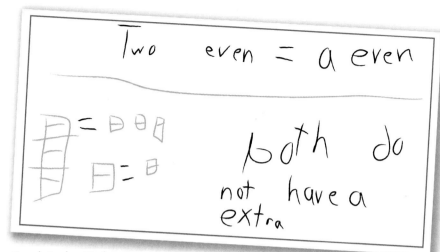

Sample Student Work

Students who are convinced argue that an even number makes partners or teams with no leftovers. Therefore, there are no leftovers when you combine two—or any number of—even numbers. So, the sum of two or more even numbers is always an even number.

MATH WORKSHOP

30 MIN

2 Adding Even and Odd Numbers

Students continue working on Can You Make . . . ? and What Happens When . . . ? from the previous session.

2A Can You Make . . . ?

INDIVIDUALS PAIRS

Students continue to work on *Student Activity Book* pages 7–8. For complete details about this activity, see Session 1.3, pages 39–40.

DIFFERENTIATION: Supporting the Range of Learners

Extension Students ready for more of a challenge can try to find all the possible solutions to one or more of the problems on *Student Activity Book* pages 7–8.

2B What Happens When . . . ?

INDIVIDUALS PAIRS

Students continue to work on *Student Activity Book* pages 9–11. For complete details about this activity, see Session 1.3, page 40.

Algebra Note

 Using a Generalization Some students call on a familiar generalization—the total remains the same when you switch the order of addends—to explain how they know that if an even plus an odd makes an odd, then an odd plus an even must also make an odd.

DIFFERENTIATION: Supporting the Range of Learners

Extension Some students may be interested in exploring what happens when you add the following:

- Three or four even numbers—an odd number of evens or an even number of evens (e.g., $2 + 4 + 6$)

- Three or four odd numbers—an odd number of odds or an even number of odds (e.g., $9 + 7 + 5$)

- Different combinations of odd and even numbers—two odds and an even or two evens and an odd

Some students may also be interested in exploring what happens when you subtract the following:

- An even number from an even number (e.g., $6 - 2$)

- An odd number from an odd number (e.g., $9 - 5$)

- An odd number from an even number (e.g., $12 - 3$)

- An even number from an odd number (e.g., $9 - 6$)

DISCUSSION

3 Adding an Even and an Odd

20 MIN   CLASS

Math Focus Points for Discussion

◆ Making and justifying generalizations about adding even and odd numbers

Base this discussion on the one at the end of Session 1.2 (odd + odd) and the activity at the beginning of Session 1.3 (even + even), but focus on what happens when you add an even and an odd.

*What did you find out about adding an even number and an odd number? [Alberto] said that an even number and an odd number make an odd number. What about an odd number plus an even number?*❶

Why do you think that when added, an even number and an odd number make an odd number?

Again, use cube towers to ground the discussion in a particular example, but push students to consider whether their arguments apply to *all* numbers and to explain and show why they think so.

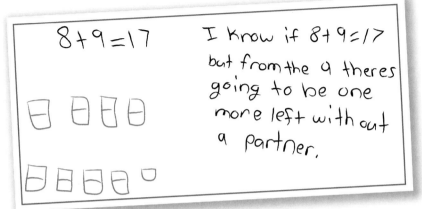

Sample Student Work

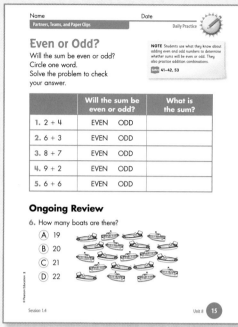

▲ **Student Activity Book, p. 15**

Students who are convinced argue that an even number never has a leftover and an odd number always has 1 leftover. Therefore, if you combine an even number and an odd number, you end up with 1 leftover, which makes the sum an odd number.

SESSION FOLLOW-UP

4 Daily Practice

 Daily Practice: For reinforcement of this unit's content, have students complete *Student Activity Book* page 15.

 Student Math Handbook: Students and families may use *Student Math Handbook* pages 41–42 for reference and review. See pages 205–211 in the back of this unit.

INVESTIGATION 2

Mathematical Emphases

Computational Fluency Knowing addition combinations to 10 + 10

Math Focus Points

◆ Relating unknown combinations to known combinations

◆ Developing fluency with the plus 9 and remaining combinations

Whole Number Operations Using manipulatives, drawings, tools, and notation to show strategies and solutions

Math Focus Points

◆ Using cubes and the number line to show how addition combinations are related

Remaining Addition Combinations

	Student Activity Book	Student Math Handbook	Professional Development: Read Ahead of Time	
SESSION 2.1 p. 52				
Plus 9 or 10 BINGO Students solve related problems that help them think about the relationship between adding 9 and adding 10 to any single-digit number. They then learn and play a variation of BINGO to practice their Plus 9 and Plus 10 combinations. Students receive and sort the set of Plus 9 combinations.	16–17	51, 52; G11	• **Teacher Note:** Strategies for Learning the Addition Combinations, p. 156 • **Dialogue Box:** Adding Nine, p. 194	
SESSION 2.2 p. 59				
The Remaining Combinations Students receive and sort the set of remaining combinations. Math Workshop continues to focus on practice with addition combinations. The session ends with a discussion about clues for remembering the remaining combinations.	19, 21–22	51, 52, 53; G11		

Materials to Gather	Materials to Prepare
• **T3–T6, Primary Number Cards** 🖳 • **T79, *Plus 9 or 10 BINGO* Gameboard** 🖳 • **Connecting cubes** • **Counters of two kinds, such as coins, buttons, or beans** (25 total per pair) • **Envelopes of "Combinations I Know" and "Combinations I'm Still Working On"** (1 of each per student; from previous units) • **Transparent counters**	• **M6–M9, Primary Number Cards** Students need their sets of cards from previous units. If new sets are needed, make copies on cardstock and cut apart. (1 deck per pair, as needed; 1 deck per student to send home) • **M10, *Plus 9 or 10 BINGO*** Make copies. (6–7 for the class) • **M11, *Plus 9 or 10 BINGO* Gameboard** Make copies. (1 per pair) • **M12, Addition Cards Set 5: Plus 9 Combinations** Make copies on cardstock or heavy paper and cut apart. (1 set per student)
• **Materials for *Plus 9 or 10 BINGO*** See Session 2.1. • **Envelopes of "Combinations I Know" and "Combinations I'm Still Working On"** (from Session 2.1) • **Connecting cubes** (as needed)	• **M13, Addition Cards Set 6: Remaining Combinations** Make copies on cardstock or heavy paper and cut out cards. (1 set per student) • **Chart paper** Write the eight pairs of remaining facts from Addition Cards Set 6: Remaining Combinations (M13) on a sheet of chart paper and title it "Remaining Combinations."

🖳 Overhead Transparency

Plus 9 or 10 BINGO

Math Focus Points

◆ Relating unknown combinations to known combinations

◆ Using cubes and the number line to show how addition combinations are related

◆ Developing fluency with the plus 9 and remaining combinations

Vocabulary

vertical
horizontal
diagonal
sum

Today's Plan		Materials
1 DISCUSSION **Related Problems**	10 MIN CLASS	• Connecting cubes
2 ACTIVITY **Introducing** *Plus 9 or 10 BINGO*	10 MIN CLASS	• T3–T6; T79 • Transparent counters
3 ACTIVITY **Playing** *Plus 9 or 10 BINGO*	30 MIN PAIRS GROUPS	• M6–M9*; M10*; M11* • Counters of two kinds
4 ACTIVITY **Addition Cards: Plus 9 Combinations**	10 MIN PAIRS CLASS	• M12* • Students' "Combinations" envelopes
5 SESSION FOLLOW-UP **Daily Practice and Homework**		• *Student Activity Book*, pp. 16–17 • M6–M9*; M10* • *Student Math Handbook*, pp. 51, 52; G11

*See *Materials to Prepare*, p. 51.

Classroom Routines

Quick Images: Cover Up with Tens and Ones Using Stickers: Strips and Singles (T38–T39), display 38 with three strips and eight singles. Follow the basic *Quick Images* activity. After students determine the total, cover 15 (one strip, five singles) with a sheet of paper. Students use the number showing (23) to determine how many are covered. Discuss and model students' strategies. Then, keeping the total at 38, cover 5. Discuss strategies, including any that used the first problem to solve the new one. For example, Last time there were *twenty*-three showing. This time there are *thirty*-three showing. That's 10 more, so you must have hidden 10 fewer.

DISCUSSION

Related Problems

10 MIN   CLASS

Math Focus Points for Discussion

◈ Relating unknown combinations to known combinations

◈ Using cubes and the number line to show how addition combinations are related

Begin by asking students to solve the problem $4 + 10$. Most students should "just know" the Plus 10 combinations (assessed at the end of *Pockets, Teeth, and Favorite Things*). Encourage students to explain the pattern that helps make these combinations easy. Then pose a related problem and ask students to solve it mentally.

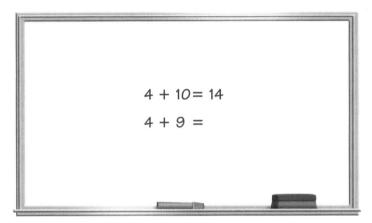

$$4 + 10 = 14$$
$$4 + 9 =$$

How can you use what you know about $4 + 10$ to help you solve $4 + 9$? ❶ ❷

Discuss students' strategies for solving $4 + 9$. Some students take 1 from the 4 and give it to the 9, changing the problem to $3 + 10$, which they "just know." Model this strategy with cubes.

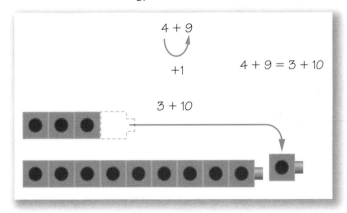

$4 + 9$

$+1$

$4 + 9 = 3 + 10$

$3 + 10$

Professional Development

❶ **Teacher Note:** Strategies for Learning the Addition Combinations, p. 156

Math Note

❷ **Related Problems** Solving pairs of related problems can help students see connections between combinations that are related, such as the Plus 10 and Plus 9 combinations.

Algebra Note

❸ **Generalizations About Addition** The relationship between 3 + 10 and 4 + 9 involves a generalization discussed earlier in the year: If you subtract 1 from one addend and add 1 to the other, the total remains the same. The relationship between 4 + 10 and 4 + 9 involves another generalization discussed earlier in the year: If you add 1 to an addend, the total increases by 1. If you subtract 1 from an addend, the total decreases by 1.

Professional Development

❹ **Dialogue Box:** Adding Nine, p. 194

Others use the first problem to solve the second.

Students might say:

"4 + 10 is 14. 4 + 9 is 1 less, so the answer is 1 less, or 13."

Model this strategy on the number line.❸

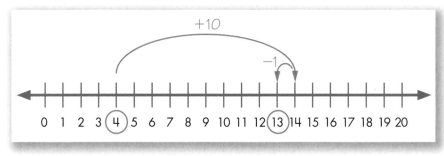

I see a plus 10 and a minus 1. But the problem is 4 plus 9. Where's the plus 9?

As students respond, highlight the 9 by drawing a dotted or different-colored line from 4 to 13 on the same number line.

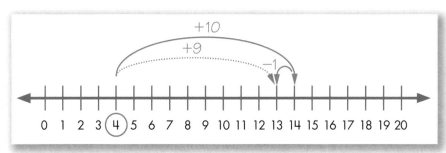

If any students counted on 9 from 4, ask them to demonstrate as well to reinforce that all of these strategies result in the same answer.❹

As time permits, present the following pairs of related problems:

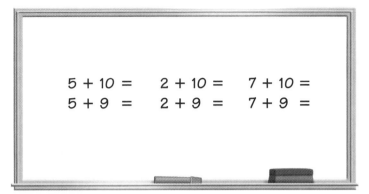

5 + 10 =   2 + 10 =   7 + 10 =
5 + 9 =   2 + 9 =   7 + 9 =

Algebra Note

❺ **Odd or Even?** Some students use generalizations about adding even and odd numbers to help remember addition combinations. For example, 7 + 9 must result in an even number because both 7 and 9 are odd, but 9 + 8 must be an odd number.

Math Note

❻ **Order Impacts Strategy** For some students, the reversal of the order changes the strategy they use to solve it. For example, they may use near-doubles for 9 + 8 or 9 + 1 + 5 for 9 + 6. This is fine as long as students recognize that because of the commutative property of addition, they *could* use the strategy that you have been discussing.

Continue to ask students about the relationship between the problems and their strategies for solving them. Use cubes and/or the number line to model students' thinking. The goal is for students to see that an easy way to add 9 to any number is to take 1 from one number and give it to the 9 (e.g., 5 + 9 = 4 + 10) or to add 10 and then subtract 1 (e.g., 5 + 9 = 5 + 10 − 1).❺ Finally, pose a problem set or two in which 10 and 9 are the first addends in pairs of equations.

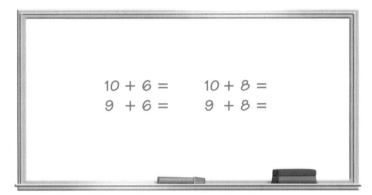

10 + 6 =   10 + 8 =
9 + 6 =   9 + 8 =

Discuss how students know the answer to the second problem in each pair, focusing on the relationship between the two problems in each set.❻

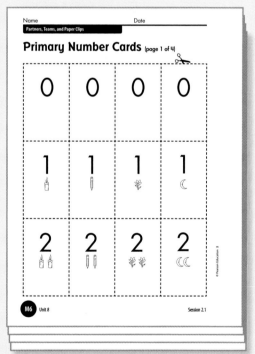

ACTIVITY
2 Introducing *Plus 9 or 10 BINGO*
10 MIN   CLASS

In this game, players take turns flipping over the top card from a deck of Primary Number Cards, adding either 9 or 10 to that number, and covering the sum on the gameboard. The object is to completely cover a vertical, horizontal, or diagonal row. Introduce the game by playing several rounds with the whole class at the overhead. Use transparencies for the Primary Number Cards (T3–T6) and *Plus 9 or 10 BINGO* Gameboard (T79) and transparent counters.

▲ **Resource Masters, M6–M9; T3–T6**

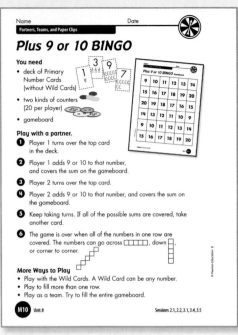

▲ Resource Masters, M10

▲ Student Activity Book, p. 17;
Resource Masters, M11; T79

Our first card is a 4. We can add either 9 or 10 to 4, and then cover the total—or **sum**—on the gameboard. What can we cover if we add 10? If we add 9?

Choose a sum, cover the number on your gameboard, and then record the move.

$$4 + 10 = 14$$

Our next card is a 7. What are the options? Which helps us get closer to covering one whole row?

Decide together on a move, place a counter on that number, and record this move below the first.

$$4 + 10 = 14$$
$$7 + [9 \text{ or } 10] = [16 \text{ or } 17]$$

Continue until students understand how to play. Explain what to do if one or both sums are all covered. For example, in the round above, if all the 16s are covered, cover 17 (or vice versa). If all of the 16s *and* 17s are covered, take a new card.

ACTIVITY

3 Playing *Plus 9 or 10 BINGO*

30 MIN   PAIRS   GROUPS

Students spend the rest of the session playing *Plus 9 or 10 BINGO*. Each pair will need a gameboard (M11), a deck of Primary Number Cards (M6–M9), and a set of 25 counters. Have available copies of *Plus 9 or 10 BINGO* (M10) as needed.

Students get repeated practice with addition combinations by playing Plus 9 or 10 BINGO.

ONGOING ASSESSMENT: Observing Students at Work

Students practice the Plus 9 and Plus 10 combinations.

- **How fluent are students in adding 9 and 10 to any single-digit number?** Do they use the relationship between adding 10 and adding 9 to solve plus 9 problems?

- **How do students decide whether to add 9 or 10?** Are they strategizing?

DIFFERENTIATION: Supporting the Range of Learners

Extension Students who call BINGO early can play to fill the entire board.

ELL Pair English Language Learners with English-proficient partners. Observe to ensure that both players contribute to the decision in choosing which number to use for a particular move.

ACTIVITY

4
Addition Cards: Plus 9 Combinations

10 MIN   PAIRS   CLASS

Show students several of the Addition Cards Set 5: Plus 9 Combinations (M12) and ask what category they think these combinations represent. Students should recognize these as the Plus 9 combinations. They are expected to be fluent with these combinations by the end of this unit.

Give each student a set of the Plus 9 Addition Cards. On the back of each card, students write their initials and the answer to the problems on the front of the card. Have pairs work together to figure out which problems they know and which ones they are still working on. Students should add this set of cards to their envelopes of "Combinations I Know" and "Combinations I'm Still Working On." Remind students to review the other combinations in the envelope that they are still working on as well.

ONGOING ASSESSMENT: Observing Students at Work

Students practice the Plus 9 combinations.

- **How fluent are students in adding 9 and 10 to any single-digit number?** Do they use what they know about adding 10 to solve Plus 9 problems?

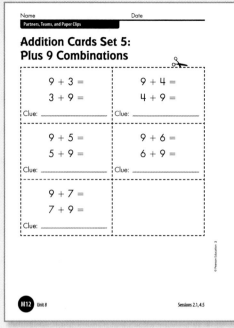

Name _____ Date _____

Partners, Teams, and Paper Clips

Addition Cards Set 5: Plus 9 Combinations

9 + 3 = 3 + 9 = Clue: _____	9 + 4 = 4 + 9 = Clue: _____
9 + 5 = 5 + 9 = Clue: _____	9 + 6 = 6 + 9 = Clue: _____
9 + 7 = 7 + 9 = Clue: _____	

M12 Unit 8   Sessions 2.1, 4.5

▲ Resource Masters, M12

Name _____ Date _____

Partners, Teams, and Paper Clips | Daily Practice

How Much Money?
How much money does each student have? How much more does each one need to make $1.00?

NOTE Students practice counting money and determining the difference between an amount and $1.00.
SMH 19, 20, 21

1.

Kira has _____.
She needs _____ to make $1.00.

2.

Franco has _____.
He needs _____ to make $1.00.

3.

Jake has _____.
He needs _____ to make $1.00.

4.

Sally has _____.
She needs _____ to make $1.00.

16 Unit 8   Session 2.1

▲ Student Activity Book, p. 16

• **Do students use what they know about adding even and odd numbers to reason about unknown combinations (e.g., "6 + 9 can't be 14 or 16 because an even plus an odd has to be an odd")?**

DIFFERENTIATION: Supporting the Range of Learners

Intervention Students often view the plus 9 combinations as particularly challenging. Encourage them to think about and model the relationship between the plus 9 and plus 10 combinations as they work to add clues to their cards. For many, an understanding of this relationship makes these combinations far easier.

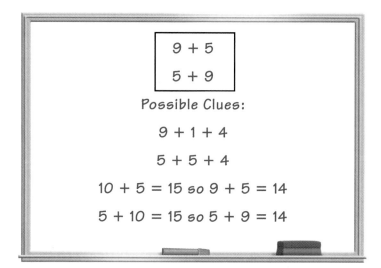

9 + 5
5 + 9

Possible Clues:

9 + 1 + 4

5 + 5 + 4

10 + 5 = 15 so 9 + 5 = 14

5 + 10 = 15 so 5 + 9 = 14

SESSION FOLLOW-UP

5 Daily Practice and Homework

 Daily Practice: For ongoing review, have students complete *Student Activity Book* page 16.

 Homework: Students play *Plus 9 or 10 BINGO* with someone outside school. They will need the gameboard on *Student Activity Book* page 17; a copy of *Plus 9 or 10 BINGO* (M10) or their *Student Math Handbook* page G11; and a deck of Primary Number Cards (M6–M9), which they should already have at home.

 Student Math Handbook: Students and families may use *Student Math Handbook* pages 51, 52 and G11 for reference and review. See pages 205–211 in the back of this unit.

The Remaining Combinations

Math Focus Points

- Relating unknown combinations to known combinations
- Using cubes and the number line to show how addition combinations are related
- Developing fluency with the plus 9 and remaining combinations

Today's Plan		Materials
ACTIVITY ① **Introducing the Remaining Combinations**	🕐 15 MIN 👥 PAIRS 👥 CLASS	• M13* • Students' "Combinations" envelopes; chart: "Remaining Combinations"*; connecting cubes
MATH WORKSHOP ② **Addition Combinations Practice** ②A Plus 9 and Remaining Combinations ②B *Plus 9 or 10 BINGO*	🕐 30 MIN	②A • M13* • Students' "Combinations" envelopes ②B • Materials from Session 2.1, p. 52
DISCUSSION ③ **Clues for the Remaining Combinations**	🕐 15 MIN 👥 CLASS	• Chart: "Remaining Combinations"
SESSION FOLLOW-UP ④ **Daily Practice and Homework**		• *Student Activity Book,* pp. 19, 21–22 • *Student Math Handbook,* pp. 51, 52, 53; G11

*See *Materials to Prepare,* p. 51.

Classroom Routines

Today's Number: Cover Up with 18 Explain that *Today's Number* is 18. At the overhead, count out 18 counters. Cover 5 of the counters. Students use the number of counters showing to figure out how many are covered. Discuss and model students' strategies. If time permits, repeat with the same total but covering 9 counters and then again covering 16 counters.

Teaching Note

❶ **Fluency with Addition Combinations** Students are expected to be fluent with the remaining combinations by the end of this unit.

Algebra Note

❷ **Generalizations About Addition** All of these strategies rely on the generalizations, or extensions of them, that were discussed earlier in the year. For example, students who think, "6 + 6 = 12, so 6 + 8 = 14" are making a familiar generalization and extending it: If you add 1 to an addend, the total increases by 1, *and* if you add 2 to an addend, the total increases by 2.

ACTIVITY

1 Introducing the Remaining Combinations

15 MIN PAIRS CLASS

Begin by asking students to flip through the collections of Addition Cards in their envelopes. Make a list of the combinations they have worked on so far this year.

plus 1	doubles
plus 2	doubles plus or minus 1
make 10	plus 10 plus 9

There are 47 combinations in these seven sets. There are only eight addition combinations that do not fall into any of these categories.

Remaining Combinations

3 + 5	3 + 6	3 + 8	4 + 7
5 + 3	6 + 3	8 + 3	7 + 4
4 + 8	5 + 7	5 + 8	6 + 8
8 + 4	7 + 5	8 + 5	8 + 6

Post the "Remaining Combinations" chart and direct students' attention to the eight pairs of problems. Choose one pair, such as 6 + 8 and 8 + 6, and ask the class to brainstorm strategies for remembering it.❶ ❷ Possible strategies include these:

- "6 + 6 is 12. You need 2 more to make 6 + 8, so it's 12 + 2 or 14." (doubles plus 2)

- "8 + 8 is 16, but that's 2 too many. 2 less makes 14." (doubles minus 2)

- "6 + 8 is the same as 6 + 4 + 4, which is 10 plus 4 more. 14." (make 10)

- "I know that $8 + 7 = 15$. $8 + 6$ is 1 less, so it's 14." (Use a known combination)

- "If you take 1 from the 8 and give it to the 6, you've got $7 + 7$. That's 14." (Create an equivalent problem)

Model these strategies with cubes and the number line, but keep this conversation brief. Students will have a more in-depth discussion of such strategies at the end of this session.

Give each student a set of the Addition Cards Set 6: Remaining Combinations (M13). On the back of each card, students write their initials and they can also lightly write the answer. Then they work with a partner to figure out which problems they know and which ones they are still working on. As usual, ask students about cards in the "Combinations I Know" envelope to check for fluency. Help them write clues for any they find difficult.

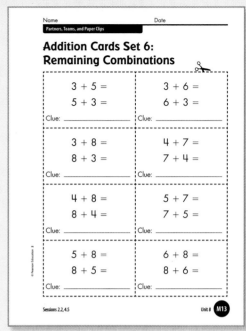

Addition Cards Set 6: Remaining Combinations

$3 + 5 =$ $5 + 3 =$ Clue: ___	$3 + 6 =$ $6 + 3 =$ Clue: ___
$3 + 8 =$ $8 + 3 =$ Clue: ___	$4 + 7 =$ $7 + 4 =$ Clue: ___
$4 + 8 =$ $8 + 4 =$ Clue: ___	$5 + 7 =$ $7 + 5 =$ Clue: ___
$5 + 8 =$ $8 + 5 =$ Clue: ___	$6 + 8 =$ $8 + 6 =$ Clue: ___

Sessions 2.2, 4.5   Unit 8   M13

▲ Resource Masters, M13

MATH WORKSHOP

Addition Combinations Practice

🕐 **30 MIN**

Students practice the Plus 9, Plus 10, and remaining combinations.

 Plus 9 and Remaining Combinations

👤 **INDIVIDUALS**

Students practice the combinations in their "Combinations I'm Still Working On" envelope, particularly the new Plus 9 and remaining combinations.

ONGOING ASSESSMENT: Observing Students at Work

Students practice the Plus 9 and remaining combinations.

- **How fluent are students in adding 9 and 10 to any single-digit number?** Do they use what they know about adding 10 to solve Plus 9 problems?

- **How fluent are students with the remaining combinations?** Do they use known combinations to help them remember combinations that are hard for them?

- **Do students use what they know about adding even and odd numbers to reason about unknown combinations?**

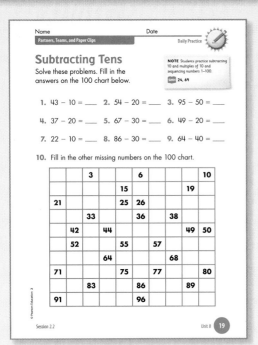

▲ **Student Activity Book, p. 19**

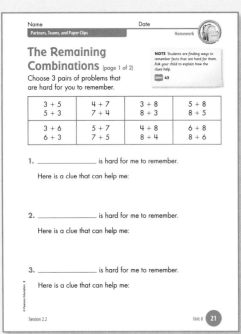

▲ **Student Activity Book, p. 21**

DIFFERENTIATION: Supporting the Range of Learners

Intervention For students who are having difficulty, help them write and understand clues that connect unknown combinations to ones that they already know. For example, for 8 + 3 and 3 + 8, a possible clue is "Think 8 + 2 is 10 and 1 more."

The number line can help students visualize combinations that are giving them trouble.

2B *Plus 9 or 10 BINGO*

PAIRS GROUPS

Students continue to play *Plus 9 or 10 BINGO*. For complete details, see Session 2.1, pages 55–57.

DISCUSSION

15 MIN CLASS

③ Clues for the Remaining Combinations

Math Focus Points for Discussion

◆ Relating unknown combinations to known combinations

Call attention once again to the "Remaining Combinations" chart.

Look through your "Combinations I'm Still Working On" envelopes and think about which of these remaining combinations you find the most challenging. Which ones are the hardest for you to remember?

Collect students' suggestions by placing a tally or check mark next to each problem that students mention. In the end, you will have a list of the problems that students find the most difficult to remember.

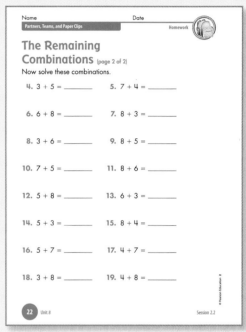

Remaining Combinations

3 + 5	3 + 6 ✓	3 + 8 ✓	4 + 7 ✓
5 + 3	6 + 3	8 + 3	7 + 4
4 + 8 ✓	5 + 7 ✓✓	5 + 8 ✓✓	6 + 8 ✓✓✓
8 + 4	7 + 5	8 + 5	8 + 6

Choose several of the problems with the most checks and collect strategies for quickly figuring out the sum, as you did in the discussion at the beginning of this session. Possible strategies will include using doubles and combinations of 10. ❸

Students should continue to practice these remaining addition combinations (as well as any others they are still working on in their envelopes) throughout this unit.

SESSION FOLLOW-UP

Daily Practice and Homework

 Daily Practice: For ongoing review, have students complete *Student Activity Book* page 19.

 Homework: Students write clues to help them remember the remaining combinations on *Student Activity Book* pages 21–22.

 Student Math Handbook: Students and families may use *Student Math Handbook* pages 51, 52, 53 and G11 for reference and review. See pages 205–211 in the back of this unit.

Algebra Note

❸ **Articulating Generalizations** Encourage students to articulate the generalizations behind their clues. For example, if a student suggests that $6 + 8 = 14$ because $6 + 6 = 12$, ask him or her to verbalize the underlying generalization: If you add 2 (or any amount) to an addend, the total increases by 2 (or that amount).

Name _____ Date _____
Partners, Teams, and Paper Clips   Homework

The Remaining Combinations (page 2 of 2)
Now solve these combinations.

4. 3 + 5 = _____   5. 7 + 4 = _____

6. 6 + 8 = _____   7. 8 + 3 = _____

8. 3 + 6 = _____   9. 8 + 5 = _____

10. 7 + 5 = _____   11. 8 + 6 = _____

12. 5 + 8 = _____   13. 6 + 3 = _____

14. 5 + 3 = _____   15. 8 + 4 = _____

16. 5 + 7 = _____   17. 4 + 7 = _____

18. 3 + 8 = _____   19. 4 + 8 = _____

22 Unit 8   Session 2.2

▲ **Student Activity Book, p. 22**

Mathematical Emphases

Computational Fluency Knowing addition combinations to 10 + 10

Math Focus Points

◆ Developing and achieving fluency with the plus 9 and remaining combinations

Whole Number Operations Making sense of and developing strategies to solve addition and subtraction problems with totals to 100

Math Focus Points

◆ Subtracting amounts from 100

◆ Visualizing, retelling, and modeling the action of subtraction situations

◆ Developing efficient methods for subtracting and notating strategies

◆ Solving subtraction problems by subtracting in parts

◆ Solving subtraction problems by adding up or subtracting back to find the difference

◆ Comparing problems in which the amount subtracted differs by 1

Whole Number Operations Using manipulatives, drawings, tools, and notation to show strategies and solutions

Math Focus Points

◆ Representing the action of subtraction situations using notation $(-, +, =)$

This Investigation also focuses on

◆ Counting a set of objects by equal groups
◆ Thinking about what happens if you subtract 1 more or 1 less

Subtraction

	Student Activity Book	Student Math Handbook	Professional Development: Read Ahead of Time	
SESSION 3.1 p. 70				
Pinching Paper Clips Students are introduced to and discuss Pinching Paper Clips, an activity that involves subtracting amounts from 100.	23–26	52, 79–80; G11	• **Teacher Notes:** Students' Subtraction Strategies, p. 158; Notating Subtraction Strategies, p. 163 • **Dialogue Boxes:** Modeling Students' Strategies for Pinching Paper Clips, p. 196; Subtraction Strategies, p. 200	
SESSION 3.2 p. 78				
Subtracting in Parts Students solve subtraction problems and record their work. Class discussion focuses on the strategy of subtracting in parts.	27–29	70, 71–72, 73–75		

Classroom Routines See page 18 for an overview.

Today's Number
- **Set of 21 counters**

What Time Is It?
- **Demonstration clock**
- **Student clocks** (1 per pair)

Quick Images: Cover Up with Tens and Ones
- **(T38–T39) Stickers: Strips and Singles** (from Investigation 1)

Materials to Gather	Materials to Prepare
• **T58, Pages in a Sticker Book** • **Paper clips** (1 box of 100 per student or pair) • **Connecting cubes** (in towers of 10) • **Materials for** *Plus 9 or 10 BINGO* See Session 2.1. • **Students' envelopes of "Combinations I Know" and "Combinations I'm Still Working On"** (from Session 2.2)	• **M14–M15, Pinching Paper Clips** Make copies. (1–2 per student) • **M16, Pages in a Sticker Book** Make copies. (1 per student, or as needed) • **M17, 100 Chart** Make copies. (1 per student, or as needed)
• **T38–T39, Stickers: Strips and Singles** (from Session 1.1) • **T33, 100 Chart** (optional) • **M17, 100 Chart** (as needed) • **Connecting cubes** (towers of 10)	• **M1, Stickers: Strips and Singles** Make copies on card stock of several different colors, two copies per color. Cut apart to make sets of paper stickers. Store each set (by color) in an envelope or resealable plastic bag. (as needed) • **M18–M19, Story Problems: Variations** Make copies. (as needed) • **M20–M21, Story Problems: Challenges** Make copies. (as needed) • **M25–M26, Family Letter** Make copies. (1 per student) • **Chart paper** Title a sheet of chart paper "Subtract in Parts."

Overhead Transparency

Subtraction, *continued*

SESSION 3.3 p. 87	Student Activity Book	Student Math Handbook	Professional Development: Read Ahead of Time	
Adding Up or Subtracting Back Class discussion focuses on the strategy of adding up or subtracting back to find the difference. Students continue to solve subtraction story problems.	23–24, 27–28, 30–34	69, 71–72, 73–75; G11		
SESSION 3.4 p. 96				
Story Problems The session begins with a discussion about what happens when you subtract 1 more or 1 less. Math Workshop continues, and the session ends with a discussion about strategies for subtracting 2-digit numbers.	33–38	52, 53, 69, 71–72, 73–75; G11		
SESSION 3.5 p. 104				
Assessment: Paper Clips and Cherries Students solve two subtraction problems and record their work. They continue to practice addition and subtraction combinations in Math Workshop.	23–24, 27–28, 30–31, 35–36, 39	53, 69, 73–75; G11	• **Teacher Note:** Assessment: Paper Clips and Cherries, p. 168	

Materials to Gather	Materials to Prepare
• T38–T39, Stickers: Strips and Singles • M16, Pages in a Sticker Book (from Session 3.1) • M17, 100 Chart (from Session 3.1) • M18–M19, Story Problems: Variations (from Session 3.2) • M20–M21, Story Problems: Challenges (from Session 3.2) • Connecting cubes (in towers of 10) • Sets of paper stickers (from Session 3.2) • Materials for Pinching Paper Clips See Session 3.1. • Materials for Plus 9 or 10 BINGO See Session 2.1. • Students' envelopes of "Combinations I Know" and "Combinations I'm Still Working On" (from Session 2.2) • Counters, such as pennies, buttons, or beans	• Chart paper Title a sheet of chart paper "Add Up or Subtract Back."
• Math Workshop materials (from Session 3.3)	• M22–M23, More Story Problems: Challenges Make copies. (as needed)
• Math Workshop materials (from Session 3.3)	• M24, Assessment: Paper Clips and Cherries Make copies. (1 per student)

Overhead Transparency

Pinching Paper Clips

Math Focus Points

◆ Counting a set of objects by equal groups

◆ Subtracting amounts from 100

◆ Developing and achieving fluency with the plus 9 and remaining combinations

Today's Plan		Materials
ACTIVITY **① Introducing Pinching Paper Clips**	10 MIN CLASS	• T58 🖥 • Paper clips
MATH WORKSHOP **② Subtraction and Addition Practice** **②Ⓐ** Pinching Paper Clips **②Ⓑ** Story Problems: Subtracting from 100 **②Ⓒ** Addition Combinations Practice	35 MIN	**②Ⓐ** • M14–M15*; M16*; M17* • Paper clips; connecting cubes **②Ⓑ** • *Student Activity Book,* pp. 23–24 • M16; M17 (as needed) • Connecting cubes (as needed) **②Ⓒ** • Materials for *Plus 9 or 10 BINGO* (from Session 2.1, p. 52) • Students' envelopes of "Combinations"
DISCUSSION **③ Pinching Paper Clips**	15 MIN CLASS	
SESSION FOLLOW-UP **④ Daily Practice and Homework**		• *Student Activity Book,* pp. 25–26 • *Student Math Handbook,* pp. 52, 53, 79–80; G11 • M17*

*See *Materials to Prepare,* p. 67.

Classroom Routines

Today's Number: Cover Up with 21 Explain that *Today's Number* is 21. At the overhead, count out 21 counters. Cover 11 of the counters. Students use the number of counters still showing to determine how many counters are covered. Discuss and model students' strategies. If time permits, repeat with the same total but covering 15 counters and then again covering 19 counters.

ACTIVITY

Introducing Pinching Paper Clips

10 MIN   **CLASS**

Show students a box of 100 paper clips as you introduce this activity before Math Workshop.

Paper clips come in boxes of 100. We're going to take a pinch of paper clips, count how many we pinched, and then figure out how many are left in the box.

Discuss what a "pinch" is as you demonstrate.❶ Ask a student to count how many paper clips you pinched. When there is agreement, record this number on the board.

There were 100 paper clips in the box. I pinched 17 paper clips. How many paper clips are still in the box?

Give students time to think. Remind them to visualize the action of the problem and to think about what is known and unknown.

There were 100 paper clips altogether, and then I took 17 out of the box. So we know the total amount and how many were removed. What are we trying to figure out? *(how many remain)* What equation would you write to represent this problem?❷ ❸

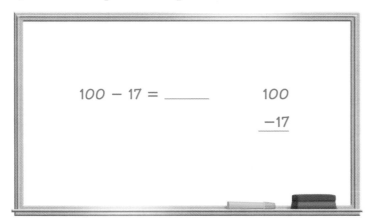

Ask several students to share how they would figure out how many paper clips are still in the box. As students suggest strategies, model them on

---

Teaching Notes

❶ **What's a Pinch?** Establishing a consistent pinch is not crucial; students may use a variety of methods. One class decided that a pinch should use only the thumb and forefinger. Another class agreed on the thumb, forefinger, and middle finger.

❷ **Vertical or Horizontal?** Throughout this Investigation, use both vertical and horizontal notation when you record equations that represent a problem. Emphasize that both methods mean the same thing and that the way a problem is written does not dictate how students must solve it. Use horizontal equations to record students' strategies.

Math Note

❸ **Different Ways to Visualize the Same Problem** Although most students see this problem as removing an amount from 100 ($100 - 17 =$ ____), some think about how much they need to add to get to 100 ($17 +$ ____ $= 100$) or how much they need to subtract to get to 17 ($100 -$ ____ $= 17$).

Professional Development

④ **Teacher Note:** Students' Subtraction Strategies, p. 158

⑤ **Teacher Note:** Notating Subtraction Strategies, p. 163

Algebra Note

⑥ **The Relationship Between Addition and Subtraction** If some students solve the problem by subtracting and others solve the same problem by finding a missing addend, take the opportunity to comment on the relationship between addition and subtraction. This idea will be highlighted in the next session. See Algebra Connections in This Unit, page 16, for more information.

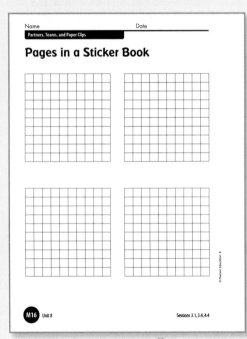

▲ Resource Masters, M16; T58

Pages in a Sticker Book (T58), on the class number line, or by recording on the board, as appropriate. Possibilities include the following: ④ ⑤

- **Representing the situation on 100 chart** (shade on T58 or use colored inserts with the class 100 chart)

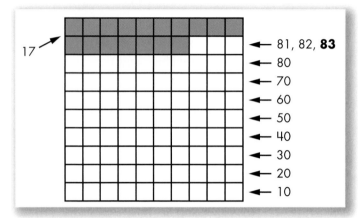

- **Counting back 17 from 100 or subtracting it in parts (e.g., subtract 10, then 7)**

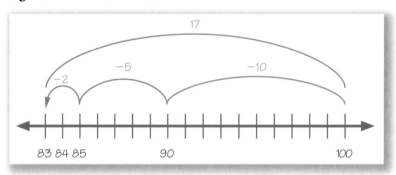

- **Finding the difference between 17 and 100 by adding up or subtracting back** ⑥

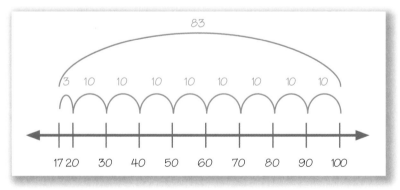

- **Relating the problem to a known combination**

$$20 + 80 = 100$$

$$17 + 83 = 100$$

One way we can double-check our work is to count the paper clips that are left in the box. How could we count these paper clips?

Organize the clips as students suggest—for example, in groups of ten—and then count them as a class.

Explain that when they are doing this activity during Math Workshop, students should put all of the paper clips back in the box after each round and repeat these steps:

1. Remove a pinch of paper clips and count them.

2. Figure out how many paper clips are still in the box.

3. Record their work.

4. Double-check by counting the paper clips that are left in the box.

5. Put all of the paper clips back in the box.

MATH WORKSHOP

35 MIN

2 Subtraction and Addition Practice

Students begin by completing three rounds of Pinching Paper Clips (M14–M15). Then they work on the Pennies and Paper Clips story problems on *Student Activity Book* pages 23–24. They will continue working on these problems in upcoming sessions.

Students also keep working on their addition combinations, as needed, for the rest of this unit. You can assign addition practice during Math Workshops, for homework, or at other times of the day.

2A Pinching Paper Clips

INDIVIDUALS PAIRS

Students do three rounds of Pinching Paper Clips. When they have finished with this activity, ask them to count the paper clips in the box before returning the box to make sure that there are exactly 100.

ONGOING ASSESSMENT: Observing Students at Work

Students subtract amounts from 100.

- **How accurate and efficient are students in their counting?**

- **What strategies do students use?** Do they count back? Add up by 1s or groups? Do they use information from previous rounds? Do they use different strategies depending on the number pinched?

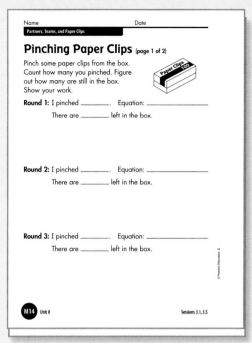

▲ Resource Masters, M14–M15

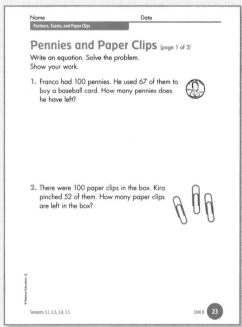

▲ Student Activity Book, p. 23

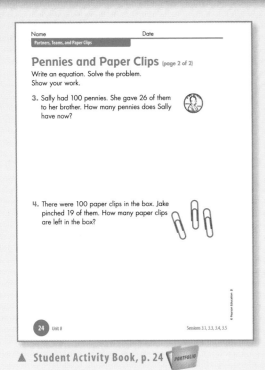

▲ Student Activity Book, p. 24

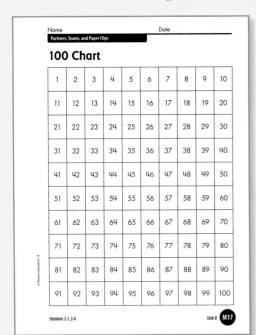

▲ Resource Masters, M17

- **What tools do students use?** Cubes? 100 chart? Pages in a sticker book? Number lines?

- **Do students' equations represent the situation?** Which operation do they use? Can they record their strategies clearly?

DIFFERENTIATION: Supporting the Range of Learners

Intervention Some students may benefit from working on this activity with you in a small group. Encourage them to model the situation with cubes in towers of 10, on Pages in a Sticker Book (M16), or on the 100 Chart (M17). Discuss how each square or cube represents one of the 100 paper clips. Then, students can cross out squares or take away cubes to show how many paper clips they pinched.

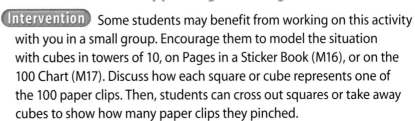

Sample Student Work

Sample Student Work

Round 1: I pinched __2 3__. Equation: __100-23 =____

There are __7 7__ left in the box.

I Know 20 + 80 = 100

So 77 + 23 must = 100

Sample Student Work

2B Story Problems: Subtracting from 100

INDIVIDUALS

Students work independently on *Student Activity Book* pages 23–24 to solve story problems about subtracting amounts of pennies and paper clips from 100. As necessary, briefly review the process for solving story problems.❼

ONGOING ASSESSMENT: Observing Students at Work

Students solve story problems about subtracting amounts from 100.

- **Can students write equations that represent the problems?** What operation do they use?

- **What strategies do students use?** Do they count back or add up? By ones or groups? Do they use different strategies depending on the number being subtracted? Do they use previous problems to help them?

- **What tools do students use?** Cubes? The 100 chart? The number line?

- **Can students record their strategies clearly?** How accurate are they in their use of standard notation?

DIFFERENTIATION: Supporting the Range of Learners

ELL Some English Language Learners may have difficulty with the language of the story problems in this and other activities in Investigation 3. To assess students' understanding, read the problems aloud and ask guiding questions to help students restate the problems in their own words. Ask questions such as, "What information do we know in this problem? What do we need to find out?"

Teaching Note

❼ **Story Problem Routine** Remind students of the established routine for story problems.
1. Read the story problem and visualize the action.
2. Identify what you know and do not know. Ask, "What am I trying to figure out?"
3. Write an equation that shows what the problem is asking.
4. Solve the problem and record your strategy.

Professional Development

⑧ **Dialogue Box:** Modeling Students' Strategies for Pinching Paper Clips, p. 196

Math Note

⑨ **Different Ways to Visualize the Same Problem**
Most students see this problem as removing 13 from 100, but some think, "How much do I need to add to 13 to get to 100?" or "How much do I need to subtract from 100 to get to 13?"

② Addition Combinations Practice

 PAIRS INDIVIDUALS

Students play *Plus 9 or 10 BINGO* (M10); for complete details, see Session 2.1, pages 55–57. They also continue to practice the Addition Cards in their "Combinations I'm Still Working On" envelopes.

DISCUSSION

③ Pinching Paper Clips

15 MIN   CLASS

Math Focus Points for Discussion

◆ Subtracting amounts from 100

Gather students for a brief discussion about strategies for subtracting amounts from 100. Be sure to highlight how strategies change depending on how many paper clips are pinched. First, pose a problem about pinching a small number of paper clips.

Let's say I pinched 13 paper clips. How many would still be in the box?

Ask students for an equation that represents the problem.

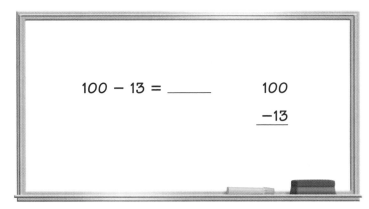

$$100 - 13 = \underline{\quad\quad}$$

$$\begin{array}{r} 100 \\ -13 \\ \hline \end{array}$$

Discuss and model students' strategies for figuring out how many paper clips are still in the box.⑧ When the number of paper clips pinched is small, many students count back 13 from 100 by 1s or by breaking 13 into useful parts (e.g., 10 and 3). Some students add up or subtract back to find the difference between 13 and 100. Still others reason about a combination they know (e.g., $10 + 90 = 100$ or $100 - 90 = 10$).⑨

What if I pinched 76 paper clips? How many would still be in the box? How do you know?

Again, ask students to generate an equation for this question about pinching a large number of paper clips. Discuss and model students' strategies for figuring out how many paper clips are still in the box. Some students will see this problem as they did the previous one and subtract 76 from 100 to solve it. Many others will count up when a large amount is pinched.

I noticed that when I pinched only 13, many of you subtracted. You started at 100 and counted back 13. But when I pinched 76 paper clips, many of you added. You started at 76 and counted up to 100. Why do you think that is?

This question provides an opportunity to discuss efficiency when there is a difference in strategy between subtracting a small number and subtracting a large number. Students who do this say that it is quicker (i.e., there are fewer steps) to count back when the number to be subtracted is small and quicker to count up when the number to be subtracted is large. This is true for students who are not yet adding and subtracting multiples of 10 (so, for example, they add 13 + 10 + 10 + 10 + 10 + 10 + 10 + 10 + 10 + 7), but there is often no difference between strategies when students add or subtract the largest multiple of ten possible. For example, $100 - 10 - 3 = 87$ takes the same number of steps as $13 + \underline{80} + \underline{7} = 100$.

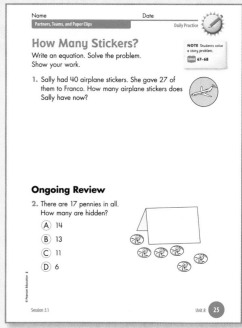

▲ Student Activity Book, p. 25

SESSION FOLLOW-UP

4 Daily Practice and Homework

 Daily Practice: For reinforcement of this unit's content, have students complete *Student Activity Book* page 25.

 Homework: Students collect 100 items, such as pennies, buttons, beans, or paper clips. Then they repeat the Pinching Paper Clips activity, using the 100 Chart (M17) and recording their work on *Student Activity Book* page 26.

 Student Math Handbook: Students and families may use *Student Math Handbook* pages 52, 53, 79–80 and G11 for reference and review. See pages 205–211 in the back of this unit.

▲ Student Activity Book, p. 26

Subtracting in Parts

Math Focus Points

◆ Visualizing, retelling, and modeling the action of subtraction situations

◆ Representing the action of subtraction situations using notation ($-$, $+$, $=$)

◆ Developing efficient methods for subtracting and notating strategies

◆ Solving subtraction problems by subtracting in parts

Today's Plan		Materials
ACTIVITY ❶ A Subtraction Problem	20 MIN INDIVIDUALS CLASS	• *Student Activity Book*, p. 27 • M1*; M17; T33 • Connecting cubes; paper stickers
DISCUSSION ❷ Strategies for Subtraction	20 MIN CLASS	• *Student Activity Book*, p. 27 • T38–T39 • Connecting cubes; chart: "Subtract in Parts"*
ACTIVITY ❸ More Subtraction Problems	20 MIN INDIVIDUALS CLASS	• *Student Activity Book*, pp. 27–28 • M17 (from Session 3.1); M18–M21* • Connecting cubes; paper stickers (from Activity 1)
SESSION FOLLOW-UP ❹ Daily Practice		• *Student Activity Book*, p. 29 • M25–M26*, Family Letter • *Student Math Handbook*, pp. 67, 68, 69, 70, 71–72, 73–75

*See *Materials to Prepare*, p. 67.

Classroom Routines

What Time Is It? What Time Will It Be? Set the demonstration clock to 6:00. Ask students to set their clocks to the time it will be in 30 minutes and to record that time in digital format (6:30). Repeat, varying the starting and elapsed times and keeping both times on whole, half, or quarter hours. Depending on your students, choose times that will cross into another hour. For example:

• If it is now 7:30, what time will it be in 45 minutes?

ACTIVITY

① A Subtraction Problem

20 MIN INDIVIDUALS CLASS

Read aloud Problem 1 on *Student Activity Book* page 27.

Franco had 45 pennies on the table. He put 27 of them in his piggy bank. How many were still on the table?

Ask several students to retell the story and predict whether there will be more or fewer pennies on the table at the end of the story.

Franco had 45 pennies altogether, and then he put 27 in his piggy bank. So we know the total amount, and we know how many are in the piggy bank. What are we trying to find out? (*how many are on the table*) What's an equation that shows what's happening in this problem?①

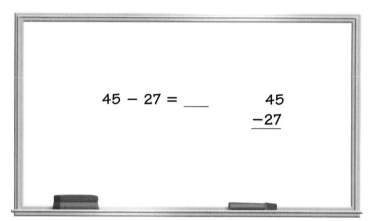

$$45 - 27 = \_\_\_ \qquad \begin{array}{r} 45 \\ -27 \\ \hline \end{array}$$

Students then work independently to solve the problem, showing their work in their *Student Activity Book*.

ONGOING ASSESSMENT: Observing Students at Work

Students solve a subtraction story problem and record their work.

- **What strategies do students use?** Do they subtract the 27 in parts? Do they add up or subtract back to find the difference? Are they working with ones or groups? Do they use another strategy?②

- **What tools, models, or representations do students use to solve the problem and record their work?** Cubes? Paper stickers? 100 chart? Number lines?

- **How do students communicate their thinking on paper?**

Math Note

① **Equations Versus Strategies** The equations that students write to represent a problem do not necessarily match the strategies that they use to solve the problem. For example, whereas most students suggest $45 - 27 = \_\_\_$ as an equation for this problem, $27 + \_\_\_ = 45$ and $45 - \_\_\_ = 27$ are also accurate. Students may actually add up ($27 + \_\_\_ = 45$) or subtract back ($45 - \_\_\_ = 25$) to solve it.

Professional Development

② **Teacher Note:** Students' Subtraction Strategies, p. 158

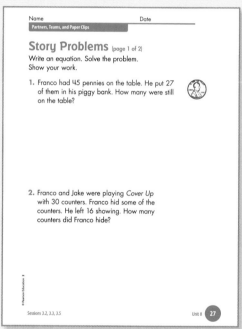

▲ **Student Activity Book, p. 27** **PORTFOLIO**

Look for students who subtract 27 from 45 to solve the problem, as in the samples shown, because the discussion that follows focuses on these strategies.

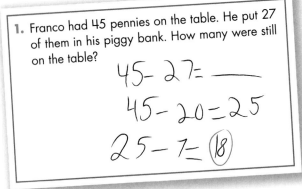

1. Franco had 45 pennies on the table. He put 27 of them in his piggy bank. How many were still on the table?

45- 27= ———
45- 20 =25
25 - 7 = ⑱

Sample Student Work

1. Franco had 45 pennies on the table. He put 27 of them in his piggy bank. How many were still on the table?

45 - 27 = ___18___

27 + ③ = 30
30 + ①0 = 40   40 + ⑤ = 45

Sample Student Work

DIFFERENTIATION: Supporting the Range of Learners

Intervention If students have difficulty getting started, encourage them to model the problem with cubes or paper stickers.

Extension Students who solve the problem quickly and accurately and who adequately show their work should find a different way to solve the same problem. They can also begin working on Problem 2.

DISCUSSION

2 Strategies for Subtraction

20 MIN   CLASS

Math Focus Points for Discussion

◆ Developing efficient methods for subtracting and notating strategies

Call students together to discuss their work on *Student Activity Book* page 27, Problem 1. Read the problem aloud and review students' equations.

Focus this discussion on the strategy of subtracting in parts. Post the "Subtract in Parts" chart you have started and as students suggest ways of recording, add them to the chart. Students who use this strategy subtract 27 from 45. Some use cubes (in towers of 10) or sets of paper stickers, and others use equations or the 100 chart and number lines.❸

[Amaya] used cubes to solve the problem. Her first step was to show the 45 pennies Franco started with. How many towers of 10 do I need to show that? How many single cubes?

Ask the class to help you model this strategy with cubes.

Franco had 45 pennies [gesture over the 45 cubes]. He put 27 in his piggy bank, so [Amaya] said she took away 27 cubes. First she took away 20 [remove two towers of 10]. How many do we still have to take away? *(seven)* How did she do that?

Some students may suggest first subtracting the 5 ones and then trading (or breaking up) a tower of 10 to subtract 2 more. Others may break up a tower of 10 first and then subtract 7.

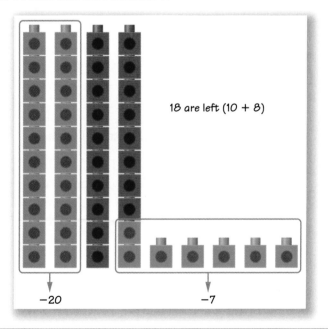

18 are left (10 + 8)

−20   −7

Teaching Note

❸ **Counting by Ones**   A few students may use the most basic version of this strategy: They count back by ones or draw 45 in a way that does not use groups and then cross out 27 and count those that remain. Counting by ones is time-consuming and prone to error, so these are not efficient ways to subtract 2-digit numbers. Work with such students to help them subtract tens, modeling with paper stickers or cubes, the 100 chart, or number lines. *Student Activity Book* pages 19 and 59 offer practice with subtracting 10 (and multiples of 10) from any number.

Teaching Note

④ **Sticker Notation** Students were introduced to a simple way to record stickers in Unit 6, *How Many Tens? How Many Ones?* Quickly review this notation as you represent 45 with four vertical lines (strips of ten) and five small dots or squares.

Use sticker notation to record Amaya's strategy on your "Subtract in Parts" chart, helping students see that sticker notation is a more efficient way to record than drawing 10-cube towers or individual pennies.④

Because drawings of stickers cannot be physically broken apart like cubes, be sure to model and talk through what happens to the strip of ten that, in this case, is broken into an 8 and a 2.

Franco had 45 pennies [draw 45 using sticker notation]. He put 27 in the bank. [Amaya] dealt with the 20 first. How can I show that? [circle two 10s] We still have to put 7 pennies in the bank. Here are 5 [circle the five singles]. Where can we get 2 more? [Leo] said to take 2 from one of these strips of 10. If I do that, how many will be left? *(8)*

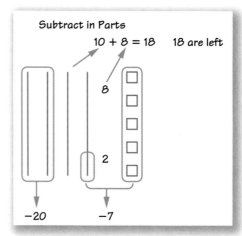

Next, ask students who worked numerically to share their strategies. Use equations to record their strategies on the "Subtract in Parts" chart; several possible approaches are shown below, varying in the way the 27 is broken apart.

$$45 - 27 = \underline{\hspace{1cm}}$$

$45 - 20 = 25$	$45 - 20 = 25$	$45 - 5 = 40$
$25 - 7 = 18$	$25 - 5 = 20$	$40 - 20 = 20$
	$20 - 2 = 18$	$20 - 2 = 18$

Encourage students to compare this strategy to the sticker recording.

[Juan] did 45 minus 20 and got 25. Then he still had 7 left to take away. How is that like [Amaya]'s way? [Amaya] used stickers and [Juan] used equations, but they both saw the problem as taking 27 away from 45. They broke the 27 into parts and subtracted 20 and then 7 from 45.

Rephrase students' strategies in your own words, and ask volunteers to do the same. Also consider what the strategy looks like when represented with different tools. Keep bringing students back to the context and focus on where you can *see* the 27 that is being subtracted.

Let's look at [Amaya]'s and [Juan]'s strategy on the 100 chart. Where are the pennies Franco started with? Where are the ones he put in the piggy bank? The ones left on the table? Where do we see the answer on the 100 chart?

The 18 pennies that are left

The 27¢ that Franco put in his bank

The total number of pennies that Franco started with

Professional Development

⑤ **Teacher Note:** Notating Subtraction Strategies, p. 163

Math Note

⑥ **Subtracting by Place** Because many students add 2-digit numbers by place, some may experiment with this strategy for subtraction. Subtracting by place is fairly straightforward when there are more ones in the total amount than in the number to be subtracted, as in $45 - 23$ ($40 - 20 = 20$, $5 - 3 = 2$, and $20 + 2 = 22$). However, when there are more ones in the number to be subtracted, as in $45 - 27$, students must think "$40 - 20 = 20$, $5 - 7 = -2$, and $20 + -2 = 18$" or "45 is the same as 30 and 15. $30 - 20 = 10$ and $15 - 7 = 8$."

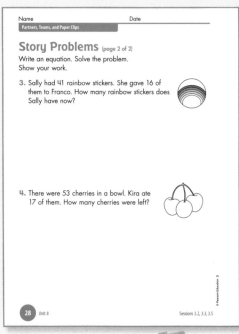

You may also demonstrate the same strategy on the number line.

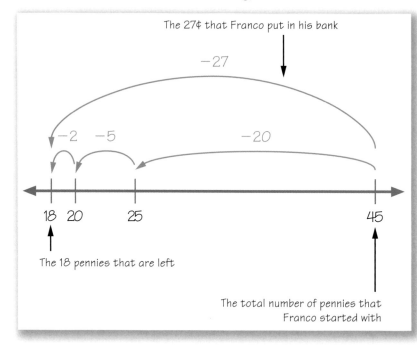

Finally, ask students about what is happening with this problem in terms of place value.

The problem was 45 minus 27. If you subtract the tens, you get 4 tens minus 2 tens, or 40 minus 20, and that's 2 tens or 20. Why wasn't our answer in the 20s?

Modeling the problem with sticker notation, as described above, can help students see that one of those tens must be broken up to subtract 7, leaving you with *less than* 2 tens.

Although the focus of this discussion is on subtracting in parts, acknowledge any other strategies students used.⑤ These may include the following:

• Adding up or subtracting back to find the difference between 27 and 45 (The discussion that starts Session 3.3 focuses on this strategy.)

• Using a known addition or subtraction problem (e.g., "$45 - 30 = 15$. But I subtracted 3 too many, so I have to add 3 and that's 18.")

• Subtracting by place⑥

• Using the U.S. standard algorithm for subtraction

ACTIVITY

3 More Subtraction Problems

20 MIN INDIVIDUALS CLASS

Students finish the problems on *Student Activity Book* pages 27–28. The discussion at the beginning of Session 3.3 will focus on Problem 2.

ONGOING ASSESSMENT: Observing Students at Work

Students practice solving subtraction story problems and recording their work.

- **Can students write equations that represent the problems?** Do they use addition or subtraction?

- **What strategies do students use to solve the problems?** Are they subtracting in parts? Adding up or subtracting back to find the difference? Using other strategies?

- **What tools, models, or representations do students use to solve the problems and record their work?** Cubes? Stickers? The 100 chart? The number line?

- **Can you tell from students' written work how they solved the problem?** How accurate are they in their use of standard notation?

Collect students' work to get a sense of the range of strategies that they are using to solve subtraction problems. In particular, look for students who solve Problem 2 by adding up or subtracting back to find the difference between 16 and 30, as seen in the sample student work. The discussion that starts Session 3.3 focuses on these strategies.

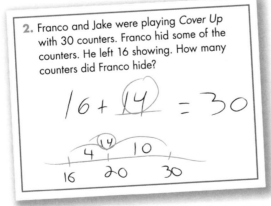

Sample Student Work

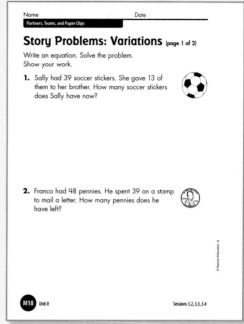

▲ **Resource Masters, M18**

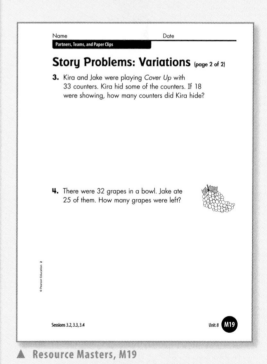

▲ **Resource Masters, M19**

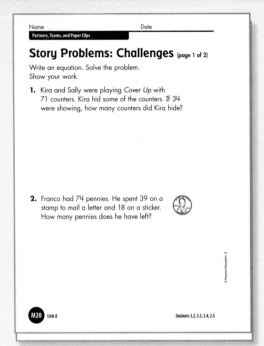

Name _____ Date _____

Partners, Teams, and Paper Clips

Story Problems: Challenges (page 1 of 2)

Write an equation. Solve the problem.
Show your work.

1. Kira and Sally were playing *Cover Up* with
71 counters. Kira hid some of the counters. If 34
were showing, how many counters did Kira hide?

2. Franco had 74 pennies. He spent 39 on a
stamp to mail a letter and 18 on a sticker.
How many pennies does he have left?

M20 Unit 8   Sessions 3.2, 3.3, 3.4, 3.5

▲ Resource Masters, M20–M21

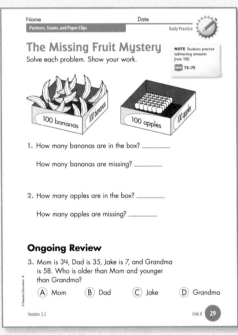

Name _____ Date _____

Partners, Teams, and Paper Clips   Daily Practice

The Missing Fruit Mystery

Solve each problem. Show your work.

NOTE Students practice
subtracting amounts
from 100.
SMH 73–75

100 bananas   100 apples

1. How many bananas are in the box? _____

How many bananas are missing? _____

2. How many apples are in the box? _____

How many apples are missing? _____

Ongoing Review

3. Mom is 34, Dad is 35, Jake is 7, and Grandma
is 58. Who is older than Mom and younger
than Grandma?

Ⓐ Mom   Ⓑ Dad   Ⓒ Jake   Ⓓ Grandma

Session 3.2   Unit 8   29

▲ Student Activity Book, p. 29

2. Franco and Jake were playing *Cover Up*
with 30 counters. Franco hid some of the
counters. He left 16 showing. How many
counters did Franco hide?

$$30 - \underline{14} = 16$$
I used a 100 chart
$$30 - 10 = 20$$
$$20 - 4 = 16$$

Sample Student Work

DIFFERENTIATION: Supporting the Range of Learners

Intervention Work in a small group with students who are using
inefficient strategies, particularly those who are counting by ones. As
usual, make sure that they can describe the action of the problems and
help them model the situation with cubes or paper stickers. Focus on
groups of 10 and amounts that get them to a multiple of 10. Some
students may benefit from work on problems with smaller numbers,
such as those on Story Problems: Variations (M18–M19).

Extension Students who finish quickly and adequately show
their work can solve the problems on Story Problems: Challenges
(M20–M21).

SESSION FOLLOW-UP

4 Daily Practice

 Daily Practice: For reinforcement of this unit's content, have
students complete *Student Activity Book* page 29.

 Family Letter: Send home copies of the Family Letter
(M25–M26).

 Student Math Handbook: Students and families may use
Student Math Handbook pages 70, 71–72, 73–75 for reference
and review. See pages 205–211 in the back of this unit.

Adding Up or Subtracting Back

Math Focus Points

◆ Solving subtraction problems by adding up or subtracting back to find the difference

◆ Developing efficient methods for subtracting and notating strategies

◆ Subtracting amounts from 100

Today's Plan		Materials
DISCUSSION **① Adding Up or Subtracting Back**	🕐 15 MIN 👥 CLASS	• *Student Activity Book,* p. 27 (students' completed work) • T38–T39 📄 • Connecting cubes; chart: "Add Up or Subtract Back"*

MATH WORKSHOP
② Subtraction and Addition Practice
②A Story Problems
②B Pinching Paper Clips
②C Addition Combinations Practice
②D *Cover Up*
	🕐 45 MIN	**②A** • *Student Activity Book,* pp. 23–24, 27–28, and 30–31
		   • M16; M17; M18–M19; M20–M21 (as needed; from Sessions 3.1–3.2)
		   • Connecting cubes; paper stickers
		②B • Materials from Session 3.1, p. 70
		②C • Materials from Session 2.2, p. 59
		②D • Counters, such as cubes, pennies, buttons, or beans

SESSION FOLLOW-UP **③ Daily Practice and Homework**		• *Student Activity Book,* pp. 32–34 • *Student Math Handbook,* pp. 71–72, 73–75; G11

*See *Materials to Prepare,* p. 69.

Classroom Routines

Today's Number: 45 Using Subtraction Individually, students generate expressions for 45 by using only subtraction and two numbers; for example, 50 − 5 and 65 − 20. Collect a number of examples on the board. Discuss one or two patterns, such as 55 − 10, 65 − 20, and 75 − 30 or 46 − 1, 47 − 2, and 48 − 3, as a whole class.

DISCUSSION
1 Adding Up or Subtracting Back

Math Focus Points for Discussion

◆ Solving subtraction problems by adding up or subtracting back to find the difference

Call students together to discuss their work on *Student Activity Book* page 27, Problem 2. Read it aloud and model the situation by hiding cubes under a sheet of paper.

Franco and Jake were playing *Cover Up* with 30 counters. Franco hid some of the counters. He left 16 showing. How many counters did Franco hide?

What equations did you write to represent this problem?

Students generally interpret this problem in several ways. Some write an addition equation, such as $16 + \underline{\quad} = 30$, whereas others suggest subtraction equations, such as $30 - 16 = \underline{\quad}$ or $30 - \underline{\quad} = 16$. Encourage each student to explain how his or her equation represents the problem.

Students might say:

"There were 30 counters, and then Franco hid some, so that's the blank, and then there were 16 left."

$$30 - \underline{\quad} = 16$$

When I was watching everyone solve this problem, I noticed that many of you started at 16 and added up. Would someone who used this strategy share it with us?

Students who add up to solve this problem may use the 100 chart, number line, or equations to figure out how much they need to add to 16 to get a total of 30. Help the class see how these students conceptualized the problem by rephrasing the strategy as you model it with cubes, starting with three towers of 10.

[Monisha] thought, "Franco and Jake started with 30. [Cover 14 of the 30 cubes.] If Franco left 16 showing [gesture over the 16], then 16 plus what's missing [gesture over the hidden 14] has to equal what we started with, 30."

Also model this strategy on the number line, asking why students chose the jumps they did and where the answer in each example can be found.

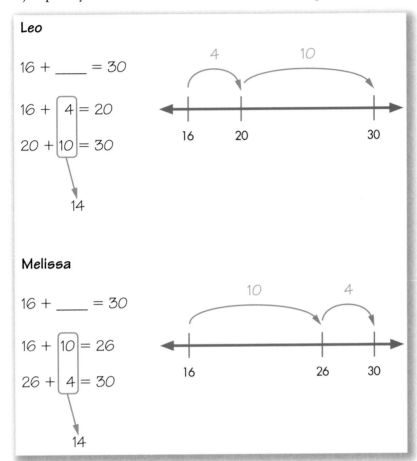

Leo

16 + ____ = 30

16 + [4] = 20

20 + [10] = 30

14

Melissa

16 + ____ = 30

16 + [10] = 26

26 + [4] = 30

14

Why do you think [Leo] chose to add 4 first? Where is [Leo]'s answer? What about [Melissa]? Why did she start by adding 10? Where is her answer?

If you have any students who subtracted back to find the difference, ask them to share their strategy now. Again, rephrase the strategy as you model it with cubes.

[Katrina] thought, "Jake and Franco started with 30 [show all 30 cubes, and then hide 14]. They took some away [gesture over the cubes under the paper] and then there were 16 [gesture over the cubes that are showing]. So, 30 minus however many they took away equals 16. I have to find out how many they subtracted."

Again, talk through the student's strategy on the number line and use equations to record it on the "Add Up or Subtract Back" chart.

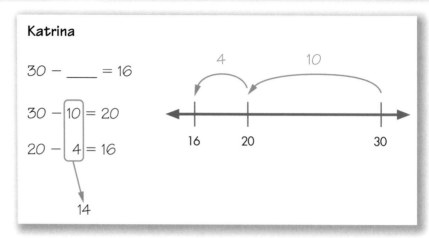

Katrina

$$30 - \underline{\quad} = 16$$

$$30 - \boxed{10} = 20$$

$$20 - \boxed{4} = 16$$

14

Encourage students to compare subtracting back and adding up, the strategies shared earlier. Students often notice on their own—particularly when the strategies are recorded on the number line—that Leo's and Katrina's jumps are the same, except that one started at 16 and added and the other started at 30 and subtracted.

Some students do not necessarily think about adding up or subtracting back. Instead, they locate the numbers on the number line, label the space between them, and combine those amounts to find the distance between them.

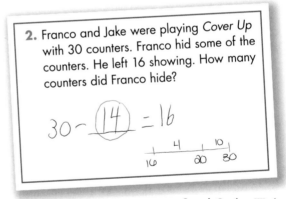

2. Franco and Jake were playing *Cover Up* with 30 counters. Franco hid some of the counters. He left 16 showing. How many counters did Franco hide?

$$30 - \boxed{14} = 16$$

Sample Student Work

Acknowledge any other strategies, including the following:

• Using cubes (in towers of 10) or paper stickers to show 30, separating out 16, and counting those that remain

• Subtracting 16 from 30 in parts

• Using a nearby addition or subtraction problem they know

> **2.** Franco and Jake were playing *Cover Up* with 30 counters. Franco hid some of the counters. He left 16 showing. How many counters did Franco hide?
>
> $30 - 16 = \boxed{14}$
>
> $\quad 14 \quad 16$
> $\cancel{15} + \cancel{15} = 30$

Sample Student Work

When you wrote equations to represent this problem, you suggested three different equations. One used addition. The other two used subtraction. The two that used subtraction were different from each other. But we all got the same answer. How can all of these equations represent the same problem? Why is the answer always 14?

$$16 + 14 = 30$$
$$30 - 16 = 14$$
$$30 - 14 = 16$$

Encourage students to consider the relationship among these equations by thinking about them in terms of the parts and whole of the situation and the information that was known and unknown; that is, each equation takes into account the 30 cubes altogether (the whole, which is known), the 16 visible cubes (one part, which is known), and the number of hidden cubes (the other part, which is unknown).❶❷

Teaching Note

❶ **Missing Part Problems** Problems that involve finding a missing part can be very challenging. Students who struggle to make sense of and solve problems of this type will benefit from playing *Cover Up* with small numbers.

Algebra Note

❷ **Relating Addition and Subtraction** The relationship between addition and subtraction—that one "undoes" the other and that either operation can be used to solve a given situation—has arisen in previous units. See the discussion in the algebra essay in *Stickers, Number Strings, and Story Problems*. Notice whether more students are able to recognize this relationship and verbalize the generalization.

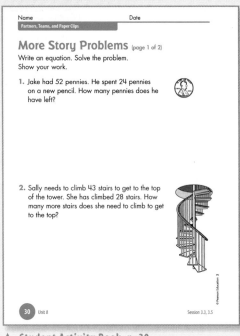

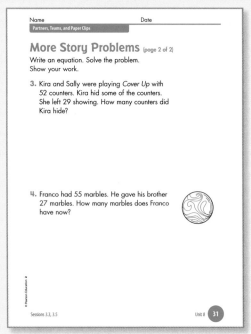

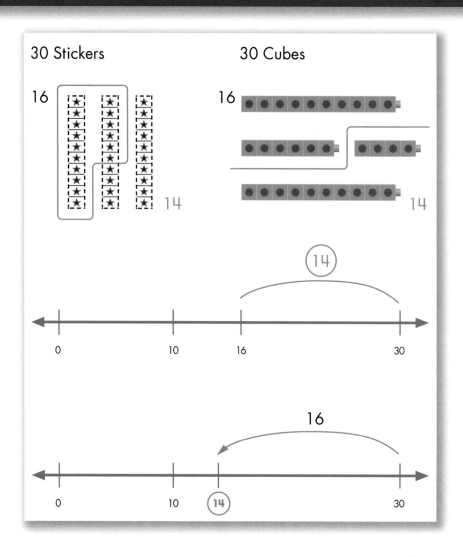

MATH WORKSHOP
2 Subtraction and Addition Practice

45 MIN

For the remainder of this session and much of the next two sessions, students practice solving addition and subtraction problems and recording their strategies in a set of Math Workshop activities. They will be working on story problems and practicing with their Addition Cards, and they may continue with Pinching Paper Clips. *Cover Up* is an optional activity.

2A Story Problems

INDIVIDUALS

Students continue working on Story Problems on *Student Activity Book* pages 27–28 and begin working on More Story Problems, pages 30–31. If any students have not finished Pennies and Paper Clips, pages 23–24, they should do so now.

ONGOING ASSESSMENT: Observing Students at Work

Professional Development

❸ **Teacher Note:** Students' Subtraction Strategies, p. 158

Students solve subtraction story problems and record their work.

- **Can students write equations that represent the problems?** Do they use addition or subtraction?

- **What strategies do students use?** Do they subtract in parts? Do they add up or subtract back to find the difference? Are they working with ones or groups? Do they use another strategy?❸

- **What tools, models, or representations do students use to solve the problems and record their work?** Cubes? Stickers? 100 chart? Number lines?

- **How do students communicate their thinking on paper?** Can you tell from their written work how they solved the problem? How accurate are they in their use of standard notation?

DIFFERENTIATION: Supporting the Range of Learners

Intervention Some students may benefit from working on story problems with you in a small group. Encourage students to think through the whole problem before they try to solve it and to visualize and model what is happening. Discourage approaches that rely on looking for words that signal a particular operation. If necessary, focus on problems with smaller numbers, such as Story Problems: Variations (M18–M19).

Extension Students ready for more challenge can work on Story Problems: Challenges (M20–M21).

2B Pinching Paper Clips

INDIVIDUALS PAIRS

For complete details about this activity, see Session 3.1, pages 71–75.

2C Addition Combinations Practice

INDIVIDUALS PAIRS

For ongoing practice with the addition combinations, students play *Plus 9* or *10 BINGO* (M10); see Session 2.1, pages 55–57. They may also review the cards in their "Combinations I Know" and "Combinations I'm Still Working On" envelopes; see Session 2.2, pages 61–62.

2D *Cover Up*

PAIRS

Cover Up is an optional activity for students who need more practice with "missing part" problems. They will be familiar with this simple game that was introduced in Unit 3, *Stickers, Number Strings, and Story Problems,* and is featured in the story problems they are working on.

Suggest that students begin with 18 counters. Players take turns hiding some of the counters under a piece of paper and using the number of counters still showing to figure out how many are hidden.

Playing Cover Up *gives students additional practice with "missing part" problems.*

ONGOING ASSESSMENT: Observing Students at Work

Students practice finding the missing part of a whole.

- **How do students figure out how many counters are hidden?** Do they count by ones? By groups? Do they count up or back? Do they reason about the quantities involved? Do they choose strategies depending on the situation? Can they explain their strategies?

DIFFERENTIATION: Supporting the Range of Learners

Intervention Help students adjust the total number of counters to create situations that are appropriately challenging. Some students may benefit from playing in a small group with you. They may need to work with smaller numbers and use cubes to model and solve the problem.

Extension Some students may be ready to play with larger amounts.

SESSION FOLLOW-UP

Daily Practice and Homework

 Daily Practice: For reinforcement of this unit's content, have students complete *Student Activity Book* page 32.

 Homework: Students solve related story problems and show their work on *Student Activity Book* pages 33–34.

 Student Math Handbook: Students and families may use *Student Math Handbook* pages 69, 71–72, 73–75 and G11 for reference and review. See pages 205–211 in the back of this unit.

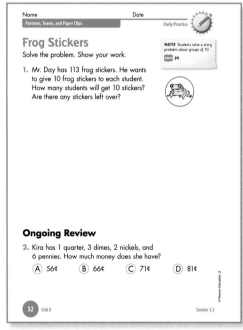

▲ Student Activity Book, p. 32

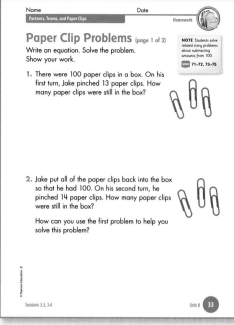

▲ Student Activity Book, p. 33

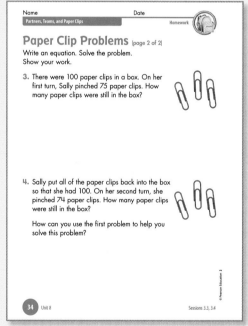

▲ Student Activity Book, p. 34

Story Problems

Math Focus Points

◆ Comparing problems in which the amount subtracted differs by 1

◆ Developing efficient methods for subtracting and notating strategies

◆ Developing and achieving fluency with the plus 9 and remaining combinations

Today's Plan		Materials
DISCUSSION **① Related Paper Clip Problems** 15 MIN · CLASS		• *Student Activity Book,* pp. 33–34 (students' completed work)
MATH WORKSHOP **② Subtraction and Addition Practice** **②A** Story Problems **②B** Pinching Paper Clips **②C** Addition Combinations Practice **②D** *Cover Up* 30 MIN		**②A** • *Student Activity Book,* pp. 35–36 • M22–M23* (as needed) • Connecting cubes; 100 charts; paper stickers **②B** • Materials from Session 3.1, p. 70 **②C** • Materials from Session 2.2, p. 59 **②D** • Counters, such as cubes, pennies, buttons, or beans
DISCUSSION **③ Subtraction Strategies** 15 MIN · CLASS		• *Student Activity Book,* p. 35 • Connecting cubes; paper stickers
SESSION FOLLOW-UP **④ Daily Practice and Homework**		• *Student Activity Book,* pp. 37–38 • *Student Math Handbook,* pp. 52, 53, 71–72, 79–80; G11

*See *Materials to Prepare,* p. 69.

Classroom Routines

What Time Is It? What Time Will It Be? Set the demonstration clock to 10:00. Ask students to set their clocks to the time it will be in 15 minutes and to record the time in digital format (10:15). Repeat, varying the starting and elapsed times and keeping both times on whole, half, or quarter hours. Depending on your students, choose times that will cross into another hour. For example:

• If it is now 11:45, what time will it be in 30 minutes?

DISCUSSION
① Related Paper Clip Problems

15 MIN   CLASS

Math Focus Points for Discussion

◆ Comparing problems in which the amount subtracted differs by 1

Begin class with a discussion about the homework on *Student Activity Book* page 33. Briefly look at Problem 1, but focus on students' strategies for Problem 2, particularly methods that used the first problem to help solve the second.

In Problem 1, Jake pinched 13 paper clips. In Problem 2, he pinched 14. How did you figure out how many paper clips were still in the box when Jake pinched 14?

Encourage students to articulate the relationship between the problems and to explain how the first problem helped them solve the second.① Model the relationship by comparing what each situation looks like with sticker notation or on the number line.

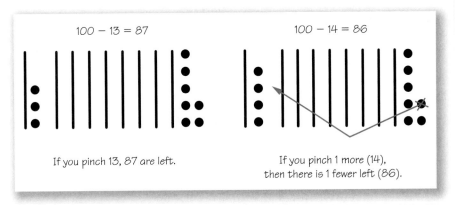

$100 - 13 = 87$

$100 - 14 = 86$

If you pinch 13, 87 are left.

If you pinch 1 more (14), then there is 1 fewer left (86).

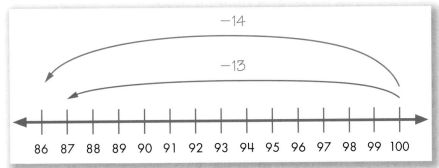

-14

-13

86 87 88 89 90 91 92 93 94 95 96 97 98 99 100

Ask students to use this strategy to think about how many would be in the box if you pinched one more time, or 15. Have them demonstrate what is happening with the stickers or on the number line.

What if I pinched 15? How many would still be in the box? How do you know?

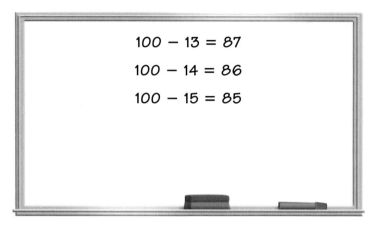

$$100 - 13 = 87$$
$$100 - 14 = 86$$
$$100 - 15 = 85$$

If students seem comfortable with this idea, challenge them to think about another related problem.

If I pinch 15, there are 85 left in the box. What if I pinched 25? How many would still be in the box? Can you use what we've done to help you solve it?

$$100 - 13 = 87$$
$$100 - 14 = 86$$
$$100 - 15 = 85$$

$$100 - 25 = 75$$

Again, encourage students to articulate the relationship between the problems: "You pinched 10 more than in the previous problem."

If time permits, discuss related Problems 3 and 4 on *Student Activity Book* page 34, in which 1 fewer paper clip was pinched.

MATH WORKSHOP

② Subtraction and Addition Practice

30 MIN

Students continue with the Math Workshop choices from the previous session. Everyone must do Activity 2A. When students have finished, they can continue working on story problems from previous sessions or choose one of the other three activities.

. . . .

2A Story Problems

INDIVIDUALS

All students need to work on Pennies and Stickers, *Student Activity Book* pages 35–36. The discussion at the end of this session will focus on Problem 1.

Explain that this work includes story problems as well as horizontal and vertical subtraction problems for which they will write matching story problems. Remind students that the way a problem is written does not change what it is asking or the strategies that they can use to solve it.

✓ ONGOING ASSESSMENT: Observing Students at Work

Students solve subtraction story problems and record their work.

- **Can students write equations that represent the problems?** Do they use addition or subtraction?

- **What strategies do students use?** Do they subtract in parts? Add up or subtract back to find the difference? Are they working with ones or groups? Do they use another strategy?

- **What tools, models, or representations do students use to solve the problems and record their work?** Cubes? Stickers? 100 chart? Number lines?

- **How do students communicate their thinking on paper?** Can you tell from their written work how they solved the problem? How accurate are they in their use of standard notation?

As you observe, note students' strategies for solving Problem 1. You will focus on two strategies in the discussion at the end of this session: (1) subtracting 58 from 72 in parts, and (2) adding up or subtracting back to find the difference between 58 and 72.

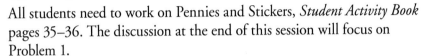

Name _____ Date _____

Partners, Teams, and Paper Clips

Pennies and Stickers (page 1 of 2)

Write an equation. Solve the problem.
Show your work.

1. Jake had 72 pennies. He spent 58 on a new pencil. How many pennies does he have left?

2. Kira had 86 sun stickers. She gave 53 of them to her sister. How many sun stickers does Kira have now?

Sessions 3.4, 3.5   Unit 8 35

▲ **Student Activity Book, p. 35** PORTFOLIO

Name _____ Date _____

Partners, Teams, and Paper Clips

Pennies and Stickers (page 2 of 2)

Write a story that matches the problem.
Solve the problem. Show your work.

3. $65 - 38 =$ _____

4. 62
   −45

36 Unit 8   Sessions 3.4, 3.5

▲ **Student Activity Book, p. 36** PORTFOLIO WRITING

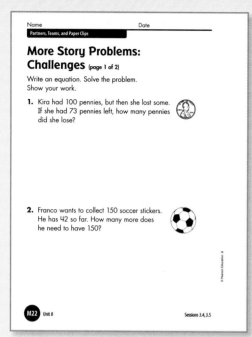

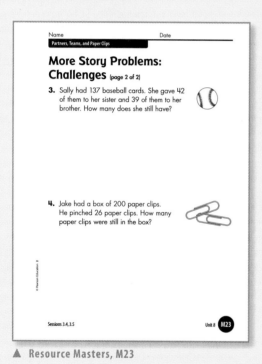

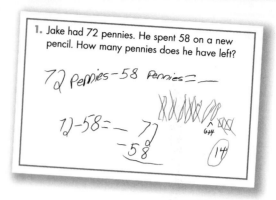

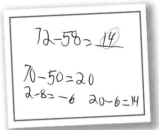

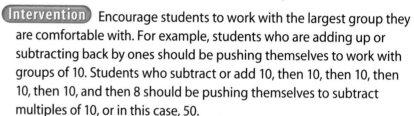

Sample Student Work

DIFFERENTIATION: Supporting the Range of Learners

Intervention Encourage students to work with the largest group they are comfortable with. For example, students who are adding up or subtracting back by ones should be pushing themselves to work with groups of 10. Students who subtract or add 10, then 10, then 10, then 10, then 10, and then 8 should be pushing themselves to subtract multiples of 10, or in this case, 50.

Extension Some students may be ready for More Story Problems: Challenges (M22–M23).

2B Pinching Paper Clips

INDIVIDUALS PAIRS

For complete details about this activity, see Session 3.1, pages 71–75.

2C Addition Combinations Practice

INDIVIDUALS PAIRS

Students play *Plus 9 or 10 BINGO* (M10) and practice with their Addition Cards. For complete details about this activity, see Session 2.1, pages 55–57, Session 2.2, pages 61–62 and Session 3.3, page 93.

2D *Cover Up*

PAIRS

For complete details about this activity, see Session 3.3, page 94.

DISCUSSION

③ Subtraction Strategies

15 MIN   CLASS

Math Focus Points for Discussion

◆ Developing efficient methods for subtracting and notating strategies

Gather students together to discuss their strategies for solving Problem 1 on *Student Activity Book* page 35.②

Students need to be able to see the 100 chart and number line and should have access to cubes and paper stickers to model their strategies. Throughout the discussion, encourage students to explain their own and others' strategies and to use a variety of tools to model, name, and compare them. They should think about how each strategy is similar to and different from their own.

Read the problem aloud and then ask students about the equation they wrote to represent the problem.

Jake had 72 pennies. He spent 58 on a new pencil. How many pennies does he have left?

$$72 - 58 = \underline{\qquad} \qquad \begin{array}{r} 72 \\ -\ 58 \\ \hline \end{array}$$

Discuss students' solution strategies, beginning with a student who used cubes or stickers to subtract the 58 in parts.③

[Darren] drew 72 stickers to solve this problem. How many strips of 10 is that? How many singles? [Draw 72 stickers.] To take away 58, he crossed out five strips of 10. [Cross them out.] How much was that? *(50)*

How many did he still have to subtract? *(8)* He took away the two singles and then six from one of the remaining strips of 10. [Cross them out.] How many did he have left? *(14)*

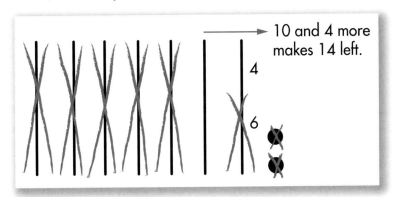

10 and 4 more makes 14 left.

Professional Development
❷ **Dialogue Box:** Subtraction Strategies, p. 200

Math Note
❸ **Different Ways to Visualize the Same Problem**
Although most students see the problem as removing 58 from 72, $58 + \underline{\qquad} = 72$ and $72 - \underline{\qquad} = 58$ are also accurate.

Next discuss the work of students who used equations, the 100 chart, or the number line to solve the problem and represent how they subtracted the 58 in parts.

$$72 - 58 = \underline{\quad}$$
$$72 - 50 = 22$$
$$22 - 8 = 14$$
(−2 to get to 20, then −6 more)

$$72 - 58 = \underline{\quad}$$
$$72 - 2 = 70$$
$$70 - 50 = 20$$
$$20 - 6 = 14$$

Throughout this discussion, rephrase strategies and ask students to do the same. Also, ask volunteers to model their strategies on different tools. For example, if a student used equations, ask another student to model the strategy on the number line. Encourage students to compare the strategies that are shared.

How is what [Paige] did with equations similar to what [Darren] did with stickers? They both saw the problem as taking 58 away from 72. They subtracted 50 and then they subtracted 8.

Next, ask a student who added up and/or subtracted back to find the difference between 58 and 72 to share. Rephrase the strategy and model it on the number line, focusing on why the student chose the jumps she did, and where you can see the answer.

[Holly] thought, "How many do I have to add to 58 to get to 72?" She started at 58 and added 10 and that got her to 68. Why do you think she added 10 first? Then she added 4 more to get to 72. Where is [Holly]'s answer?

$$58 + \underline{\quad} = 72$$
$$58 + \boxed{10} = 68$$
$$68 + \boxed{4} = 72$$

$$10 + 4 = 14$$

$$58 + \underline{\quad} = 72$$
$$58 + \boxed{2} = 60$$
$$60 + \boxed{10} = 70$$
$$70 + \boxed{2} = 72$$

$$2 + 10 + 2 = 14$$

[Leo] thought, "How many do I have to subtract from 72 to get to 58?" He started at 72 and subtracted 2. Why do you think he subtracted 2 first? Where is [Leo]'s answer?

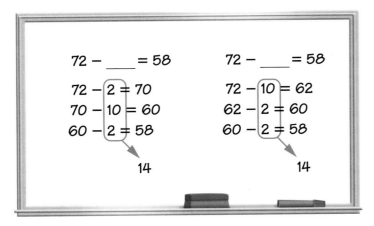

Acknowledge any other strategies students used. These may include using an addition or subtraction problem you know, such as 72 − 60, and then compensating or subtracting by place.

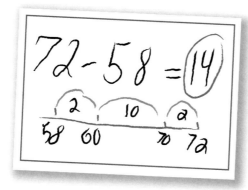

Sample Student Work

SESSION FOLLOW-UP
Daily Practice and Homework

 Daily Practice: For reinforcement of this unit's content, have students complete *Student Activity Book* page 37.

 Homework: Students solve two story problems and show their work on *Student Activity Book* page 38.

 Student Math Handbook: Students and families may use *Student Math Handbook* pages 52, 53, 71–72, 79–80 and G11 for reference and review. See pages 205–211 in the back of this unit.

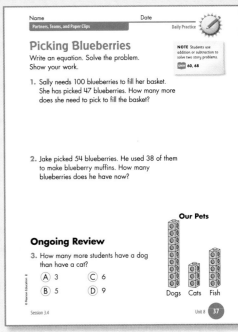

▲ **Student Activity Book, p. 37**

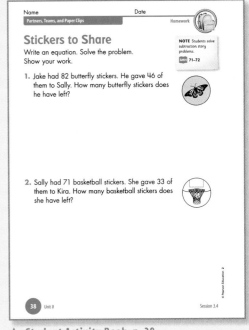

▲ **Student Activity Book, p. 38**

Assessment: Paper Clips and Cherries

Math Focus Points

◆ Developing efficient methods for subtracting and notating strategies

Today's Plan	Materials
ASSESSMENT ACTIVITY **①** **Paper Clips and Cherries** ✓ 🕐 30 MIN 👤 INDIVIDUALS	• M24* • Connecting cubes; paper stickers; 100 charts
MATH WORKSHOP **②** **Subtraction and Addition Practice** **2A** Story Problems **2B** Pinching Paper Clips **2C** Addition Combinations Practice **2D** *Cover Up* 🕐 30 MIN	**2A** • *Student Activity Book,* pp. 23–24, 27–28, 30–31, and 35–36 **2B** • Materials from Session 3.1, p. 70 **2C** • Materials from Session 2.2, p. 59 **2D** • Counters, such as cubes, pennies, buttons, or beans
SESSION FOLLOW-UP **③** **Daily Practice**	• *Student Activity Book,* p. 39 • *Student Math Handbook,* pp. 53, 79–80

*See *Materials to Prepare,* p. 69.

Classroom Routines

Quick Images: Cover Up with Tens and Ones Using Stickers: Strips and Singles (T38–T39), display 45 with four strips and five singles. Follow the basic *Quick Images* activity. After students determine the total, cover 23 (two strips, three singles) with a sheet of paper. Students use the number of stickers showing (22) to determine how many are covered. Discuss and model students' strategies. Then, keeping the total at 45, cover 33 stickers. Discuss strategies, including any that used the first problem to solve the new one. For example, "Last time there were 22 showing. This time there are 12. That's 10 fewer, so you must have hidden 10 more."

ASSESSMENT ACTIVITY

Paper Clips and Cherries

30 MIN INDIVIDUALS

This assessment addresses Benchmark 1: Subtract 2-digit numbers.❶

Introduce the assessment by explaining that you would like to get an idea of how each student is thinking about and solving story problems. For that reason, students will work independently on the two problems on Assessment: Paper Clips and Cherries (M24). Read each problem aloud to the class.

1. Sally started with 100 paper clips in the box. She pinched 36 paper clips. How many paper clips were still in the box?

2. There were 52 cherries in a bowl. Jake ate 14 of the cherries. How many cherries were left?

Explain that tools such as cubes, paper stickers, and 100 charts (M17) are always available and that if students use them, they should explain how they used them. Remind students what it means to show their work.

It is important to explain your thinking so that someone reading your paper can understand how you solved the problems.

ONGOING ASSESSMENT: Observing Students at Work

Students demonstrate their strategies for solving story problems and recording their work.

- **Can students write equations that accurately represent both situations?**

- **What strategies do students use?** Do they subtract one number in parts? Add up or subtract back to find the difference? Use a fact they know?

- **What tools do students use?** Cubes? Stickers? 100 chart? Number lines?

- **How do students communicate their thinking on paper?** Can you tell from their written work how they solved the problem? How accurate are they in their use of standard notation?

Professional Development

❶ **Teacher Note:** Assessment: Paper Clips and Cherries, p. 168

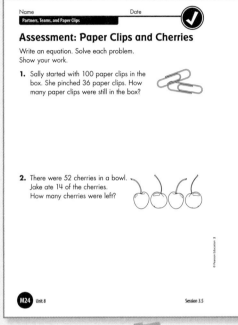

Name _____ Date _____

Partners, Teams, and Paper Clips

Assessment: Paper Clips and Cherries

Write an equation. Solve each problem. Show your work.

1. Sally started with 100 paper clips in the box. She pinched 36 paper clips. How many paper clips were still in the box?

2. There were 52 cherries in a bowl. Jake ate 14 of the cherries. How many cherries were left?

M24 Unit 8   Session 3.5

▲ **Resource Masters, M24**

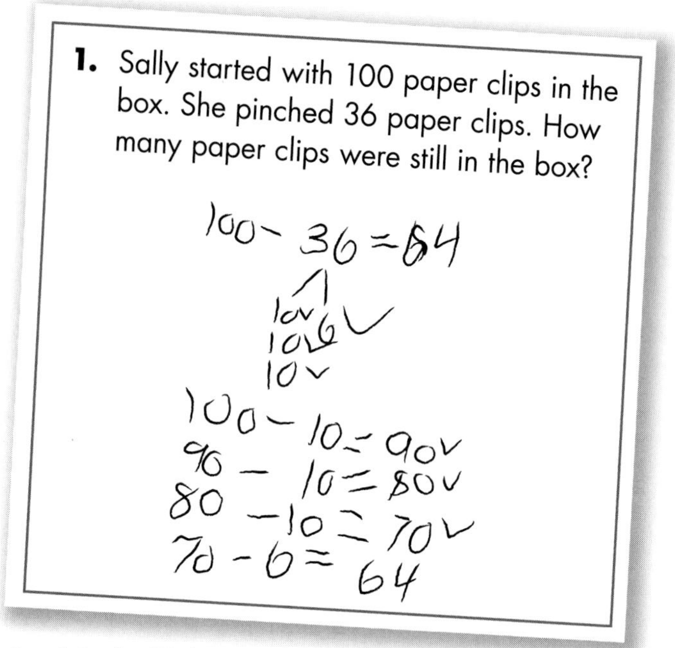

1. Sally started with 100 paper clips in the box. She pinched 36 paper clips. How many paper clips were still in the box?

$$100 - 36 = 64$$

10
10 6
10

$$100 - 10 = 90$$
$$90 - 10 = 80$$
$$80 - 10 = 70$$
$$70 - 6 = 64$$

Sample Student Work

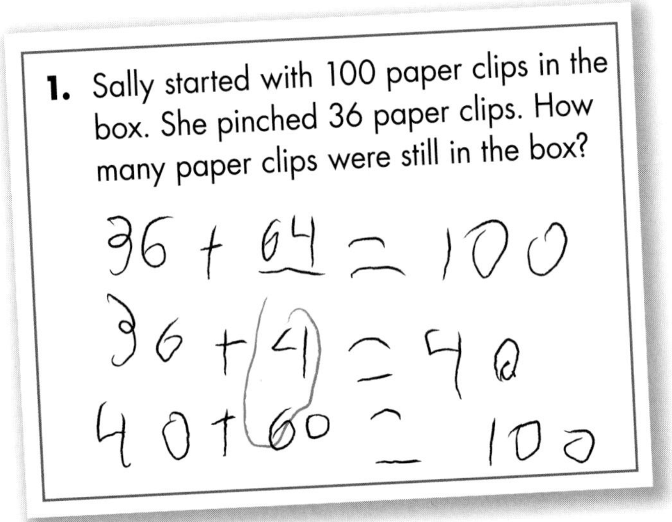

1. Sally started with 100 paper clips in the box. She pinched 36 paper clips. How many paper clips were still in the box?

$$36 + \underline{64} = 100$$
$$36 + 4 = 40$$
$$40 + 60 = 100$$

Sample Student Work

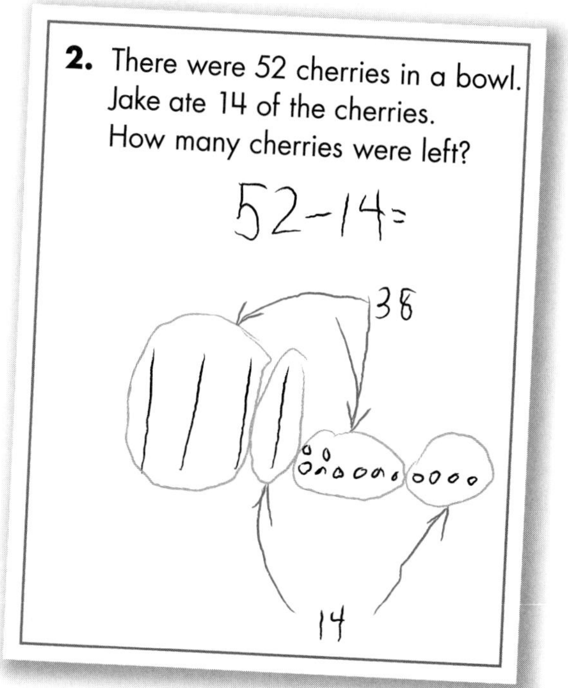
2. There were 52 cherries in a bowl.
Jake ate 14 of the cherries.
How many cherries were left?
52-14=
38
14

Sample Student Work

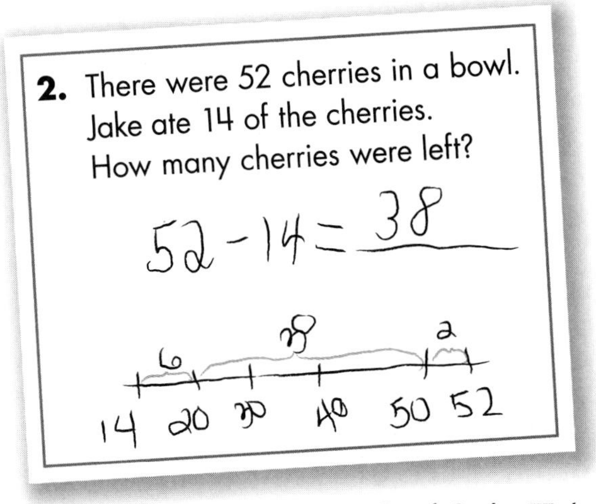
2. There were 52 cherries in a bowl.
Jake ate 14 of the cherries.
How many cherries were left?
52-14= 38
6
38
2
14 20 30 40 50 52

Sample Student Work

❷ Continued Practice with the Addition Combinations This Math Workshop is the last time this activity is formally suggested. These combinations will be assessed in the End-of-Unit Assessment. According to your observations of students, you need to decide how long to keep this activity available through the rest of the unit. You can also provide more practice for individual students by assigning these activities during other times of the day and for homework.

Name _____ Date _____
Partners, Teams, and Paper Clips   Daily Practice

What Is the Fraction?
What fraction of the flag is gray? Black? White? Write the fraction for each color.

NOTE Students use what they know about fractions to determine how much of a flag is shaded a certain color.
SMH 86, 87

1. Gray: _____

2. Gray: _____
   Black: _____
   White: _____

3. Black: _____
   White: _____

4. Black: _____
   White: _____
   Gray: _____

5. White: _____
   Gray: _____

Session 3.5   Unit 8   39

▲ **Student Activity Book, p. 39**

MATH WORKSHOP

② Subtraction and Addition Practice

30 MIN

As students complete the assessment, they can return to any of the Math Workshop activities from the past two sessions.

2A Story Problems

INDIVIDUALS

Students work independently on story problems from their *Student Activity Book* that remain unfinished. These include Pennies and Paper Clips, pages 23–24; Story Problems, pages 27–28; More Story Problems, pages 30–31; and Pennies and Stickers, pages 35–36; as well as any variations or challenges you have provided during this Investigation.

2B Pinching Paper Clips

INDIVIDUALS   PAIRS

For complete details about this activity, see Session 3.1, pages 71–73.

2C Addition Combinations Practice

INDIVIDUALS   PAIRS

Students play *Plus 9 or 10 BINGO* (M10) and practice with their Addition Cards. For complete details about this activity, see Session 2.1, pages 55–57; Session 2.2, pages 61–62; and Session 3.3, page 93.❷

2D *Cover Up*

PAIRS

For complete details about this activity, see Session 3.3, page 94.

SESSION FOLLOW-UP

③ Daily Practice

Daily Practice: For ongoing review, have students complete *Student Activity Book* page 39.

Student Math Handbook: Students and families may use *Student Math Handbook* pages 53, 69, 73–75 and G11 for reference and review. See pages 205–211 in the back of this unit.

Mathematical Emphases

Whole Number Operations Adding even and odd numbers

Math Focus Points

◆ Making and justifying generalizations about adding even and odd numbers

Computational Fluency Knowing addition combinations to 10 + 10

Math Focus Points

◆ Developing and achieving fluency with the Plus 9 and remaining combinations

Whole Number Operations Making sense of and developing strategies to solve addition and subtraction problems with totals to 100

Math Focus Points

◆ Visualizing, retelling, and modeling the action of addition situations

◆ Developing efficient methods for adding and notating strategies

◆ Adding 2-digit numbers by keeping one number whole

◆ Adding 2-digit numbers by adding tens and ones

◆ Noticing what happens to place value when two 2-digit numbers with a sum over 100 are combined

Whole Number Operations Using manipulatives, drawings, tools, and notation to show strategies and solutions

Math Focus Points

◆ Representing the action of addition situations using notation ($+$, $=$)

Addition

	Student Activity Book	Student Math Handbook	Professional Development: Read Ahead of Time	
SESSION 4.1 p. 112				
Strategies for Addition Students solve addition problems and record their work. Class discussion focuses on strategies for adding 2-digit numbers.	40–46	62, 63–64, 65–66	• **Teacher Notes:** Students' Addition Strategies, p. 172; Notating Addition Strategies, p. 176 • **Dialogue Box:** Addition Strategies, p. 202	
SESSION 4.2 p. 122				
Keeping One Number Whole Students discuss the strategy of keeping one number whole and then practice using it to solve addition problems.	45, 47–51	63–64, 65–66		
SESSION 4.3 p. 130				
Adding Tens and Ones Students discuss the strategy of adding tens and ones and then practice using it to solve addition problems.	50, 52–56	63–64, 65–66		
SESSION 4.4 p. 137				
Adding 2-Digit Numbers Students practice solving addition problems. Class discussion focuses on strategies for adding.	57–61	63–64, 65–66		
SESSION 4.5 p. 146				
End-of-Unit Assessment Students explain what they know about adding even and odd numbers. They also demonstrate fluency with the plus 9 and remaining addition combinations and with adding 2-digit numbers.	63–64	41–42, 52, 53, 63–64, 65–66	• Assessment in This Unit, pp. 14–15 • **Teacher Note:** End-of-Unit Assessment, p. 181	

Classroom Routines See page 18 for an overview.

Quick Images
- T38–T39, Stickers: Strips and Singles 🖳
  (from Session 1.1)

Today's Number
- M27, *Today's Number: 71* Make copies.
  (1 per student)

How Many Pockets?
- **Connecting cubes** (class set)
- **Pocket data from another class**
- **Class list written on chart paper**

What Time Is It?
- **Demonstration clock**
- **Student clocks** (1 per pair)

Materials to Gather	Materials to Prepare
• **M16, Pages in a Sticker Book** (from Session 3.1) • **M17, 100 Chart** (from Session 3.1) • **Connecting cubes** (in towers of 10) • **Sets of paper stickers** (from Session 3.2)	• **Chart paper** Title one sheet "Adding Tens and Ones" and a second sheet "Keeping One Number Whole."
• **M17, 100 Chart** (from Session 3.1) • **Connecting cubes** (in towers of 10) • **Sets of paper stickers** (from Session 3.2) • **Chart: "Keeping One Number Whole"** (from Session 4.1) • **Chart paper** (as needed)	• **M28–M29, Addition Problems, Set 3: Variations** Make copies. (as needed) • **M30–M31, Addition Problems, Set 3: Challenges** Make copies. (as needed)
• **Chart: "Adding Tens and Ones"** (from Session 4.1) • **Chart paper** (1 sheet; optional) • **Connecting cubes** (in towers of 10) • **Sets of paper stickers** (from Session 3.2)	• **M32–M33, Addition Problems, Set 4: Variations** Make copies. (as needed) • **M34–M35, Addition Problems, Set 4: Challenges** Make copies. (as needed)
• **M16, Pages in a Sticker Book** (from Session 3.1) • **M17, 100 Chart** (from Session 3.1) • **T81, Stickers: Sheet of 100** 🖳 • **Connecting cubes** (in towers of 10) • **Sets of paper stickers** (from Session 3.2)	• **M36–M37, Addition Problems, Set 5: Variations** Make copies. (as needed) • **M38–M39, Addition Problems, Set 5: Challenges** Make copies. (as needed)
• **M17, 100 Chart** (from Session 3.1) • **Connecting cubes** (in towers of 10) • **Sets of paper stickers** (from Session 3.2)	• **M41–M45, End-of-Unit Assessment** Make copies. (1 per student) • **M46, Assessment Checklist: Assessing the Plus 9 and Remaining Combinations** Make copies. (as needed) ☑ • **Alternative to M45: Use M12, Addition Cards Set 6: Plus 9 Combinations** and **M13, Addition Cards Set 7: Remaining Combinations** Make 1 copy on card stock or heavy paper and cut out cards. Do not add clues. (1 set)

🖳 Overhead Transparency   ☑ Checklist Available

Strategies for Addition

Math Focus Points

◆ Visualizing, retelling, and modeling the action of addition situations

◆ Representing the action of addition situations using notation ($+$, $=$)

◆ Developing efficient methods for adding and notating strategies

Today's Plan		Materials
ACTIVITY **❶ An Addition Problem** 20 MIN · INDIVIDUALS · CLASS		• *Student Activity Book,* pp. 40–41 • M16 (as needed)* • Connecting cubes; 100 charts; paper stickers
DISCUSSION **❷ Strategies for Addition** 20 MIN · CLASS		• *Student Activity Book,* p. 40 • Charts: "Adding Tens and Ones"; and "Keeping One Number Whole"*; connecting cubes
ACTIVITY **❸ More Addition Problems** 20 MIN · INDIVIDUALS · CLASS		• *Student Activity Book,* pp. 42–43 • Connecting cubes; 100 charts; paper stickers
SESSION FOLLOW-UP **❹ Daily Practice and Homework**		• *Student Activity Book,* pp. 44–46 • *Student Math Handbook,* pp. 62, 63–64, 65–66

* See *Materials to Prepare,* p. 111.

Classroom Routines

Quick Images: Cover Up with Tens and Ones Using Stickers: Strips and Singles (T38–T39), display 58 with five strips and eight singles. Follow the basic *Quick Images* activity. After students determine the total, cover 27 (two strips, seven singles) with a sheet of paper. Students use the number showing (31) to determine how many are covered. Discuss and model students' strategies. Then, keeping the total at 58, cover 17. Discuss strategies, including any that used the first problem to solve the new one. For example, "Last time there were 31 showing. This time there are 41. That's 10 more, so you must have hidden 10 fewer."

ACTIVITY

① An Addition Problem

20 MIN INDIVIDUALS CLASS

Explain to students that for the rest of this unit, they will find and practice ways to add that are both efficient and accurate.❶

Read aloud Problem 1 on *Student Activity Book* page 40.

Kira had 48 balloons. Jake gave her 33 more balloons. How many balloons does Kira have now?

Ask several students to retell the story and predict whether there will be more or fewer balloons at the end of the story. Students then work individually on *Student Activity Book* page 40 to write an equation that represents the problem and to solve the problem, being sure to show their work.

ONGOING ASSESSMENT: Observing Students at Work

Students add 2-digit numbers and record their work.

- **Can students accurately write an equation that represents the problem?**

- **What strategies do students use to solve the problem?** Keeping one number whole? Adding tens and ones? Another strategy?

- **What tools, models, or representations do students use to solve the problem?** Cubes? Stickers? 100 chart? Number lines?

- **How do students show their work?** Can you tell how they solved the problem? Are they using standard notation accurately?

Professional Development

❶ **Teacher Note:** Students' Addition Strategies, p. 172

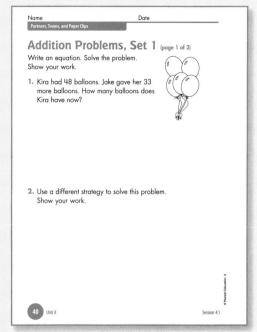

Name _____ Date _____

Partners, Teams, and Paper Clips

Addition Problems, Set 1 (page 1 of 2)

Write an equation. Solve the problem. Show your work.

1. Kira had 48 balloons. Jake gave her 33 more balloons. How many balloons does Kira have now?

2. Use a different strategy to solve this problem. Show your work.

40 Unit 8   Session 4.1

▲ Student Activity Book, p. 40

Make note of particular students who are keeping one number whole and adding the other in parts and also of those who are adding by place. You will be calling on them in the discussion that follows.

Name _____ **Date** _____

Partners, Teams, and Paper Clips

Addition Problems, Set 1 (page 2 of 2)

Write a story that matches the equation. Solve the problem. Show your work.

3. 44 + 26 = _____

_____
_____
_____

4. Use a different strategy to solve this problem. Show your work.

Session 4.1   Unit 8   **41**

▲ **Student Activity Book, p. 41**

---

1. Kira had 48 balloons. Jake gave her 33 more balloons. How many balloons does Kira have now?

48 + 33 = 81

48 + 2 = 50
50 + 30 = 80
80 + 1 = 81

---

1. Kira had 48 balloons. Jake gave her 33 more balloons. How many balloons does Kira have now?

48
+33
_____
70 + 11 = 81

Sample Student Work

DIFFERENTIATION: Supporting the Range of Learners

Intervention Encourage students who have difficulty getting started to use cubes in towers of 10 or paper stickers to model the problem.

Extension Students who solve this problem quickly and accurately and who adequately show their work should find a different way to solve the same problem. They can also begin work on *Student Activity Book* page 41.

DISCUSSION

② Strategies for Addition

20 MIN   CLASS

Math Focus Points for Discussion

◆ Developing efficient methods for adding and notating strategies

When all students have solved the problem on *Student Activity Book* page 40, call them together to discuss their strategies. The goal of this conversation is to discuss two strategies in particular: keeping one number whole and adding tens and ones. Students will be practicing these two strategies throughout Investigation 4. ❷ ❸

Begin by asking students about the equations they wrote to show what the problem was asking. There are two equations that could represent this problem and two ways to write each equation. Record them on the board or on chart paper. ❹ ❺

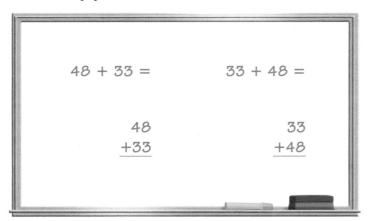

$$48 + 33 = \qquad 33 + 48 =$$

$$\begin{array}{r} 48 \\ +33 \\ \hline \end{array} \qquad \begin{array}{r} 33 \\ +48 \\ \hline \end{array}$$

From your observations of student work in the first activity, call on students who kept one number whole and added on the other to share their solution strategies. Begin with a student who broke the 33 into tens and ones to add it on to the 48. Use equations to record the strategy on the "Keeping One Number Whole" chart. You can also model it with vertical notation if you have seen students using this in their work. ❻

Algebra Note

❷ **Order Does Not Matter** All of the strategies in this discussion involve breaking apart one or both addends and combining the parts in a different order. The ideas behind this are discussed in Unit 6, *How Many Tens? How Many Ones?* In particular, see the algebra essay in that unit and **Dialogue Box: Does Order Matter?** (also in Unit 6).

Professional Development

❸ **Dialogue Box:** Addition Strategies, p. 202

❹ **Teacher Note:** Notating Addition Strategies, p. 176

Math Notes

❺ **Vertical or Horizontal?** Throughout this investigation, use both vertical and horizontal notation, emphasizing that both methods mean the same thing and that the way a problem is written does not dictate how students must solve it.

❻ **Understanding Vertical Notation** Some students use vertical notation to record. As you model their strategies, add horizontal equations that show what was added (e.g., 48 + 30 =) to help students make sense of both the strategy and the notation. Emphasize that you are doing this for demonstration purposes. Students who use vertical notation do not need to write these extra equations when they record.

Math Note

7 Efficiency Some students break the 30 into 3 tens and add $48 + 10 + 10 + 10 + 3$. Help them compare this strategy with $48 + 30 + 3$. Students should be working toward increasingly efficient strategies. Thus, students who are counting by ones should try adding groups of 10, and students who can easily add tens should try adding multiples of 10.

[Juan] kept the 48 whole and added on the 33. He used tens and ones to add on the 33.

$$48 + 33 =$$

$$48 + 30 = 78$$
$$78 + 3 = 81$$

$$48 + 30 = \quad \begin{array}{r} 48 \\ +30 \\ \hline 78 \\ +3 \\ \hline 81 \end{array}$$

Juan's Work

Ask another student to model the strategy on the number line.

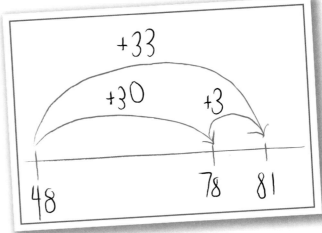

Carla's Work

As you discuss this strategy, focus the discussion on how students choose to add on the 33 (or the 48 if they kept the 33 whole) and how you can "see" the 33 in the strategy.**7**

Where is the 33 in [Juan]'s equations? Where can we see the 33 in what [Carla] drew on the number line?

Some students feel more comfortable adding on to a number that is a multiple of 10. Whether they use the 100 chart, number line, or equations, these students solve this problem by adding $48 + 2 + 30 + 1$. If there are students who used this strategy, discuss and record it, again focusing on how students added the 33 and how they can *see* the 33 in their strategy.

[Leo] kept the 48 whole, too, but he added on the 33 differently. [Leo], why did you start by adding 2?

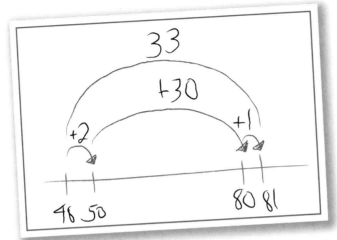

Leo's Work

The problem was 48 + 33. Where is the 33 in [Leo]'s equations? [Darren] showed us [Leo]'s strategy on the 100 chart. Where can we see the 33 there?

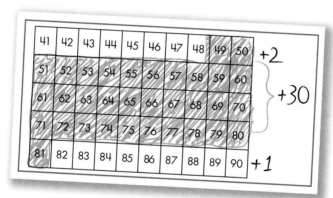

Darren's Work

When you have several variations of this strategy recorded on the "Keeping One Number Whole" chart, ask students to look at their work and decide whether they used this strategy. If they did, ask them to consider which example most closely matches their work.

Next, call on a student who added by place to solve the problem. As the student shares, record the strategy on the "Adding Tens and Ones" chart.

[Juan] and [Leo] broke up one of the numbers, the 33. [Paige] broke up both numbers. She broke 48 into 40 + 8 and 33 into 30 + 3. She broke the numbers into tens and ones.

$$48 + 33 = ?$$
$$40 + 8 + 30 + 3 = ?$$

⑧ **How Are They the Same?** Most students begin with 40 + 30 or 30 + 40. Their second steps will vary (e.g., 8 + 3 = 11, 70 + 8 = 78, or 70 + 3 = 73), as will the ways they carry out these subproblems (e.g., adding 11 as a whole vs. breaking it into 10 and 1). Focus students' attention on the first step (40 + 30) to help them see what is the same in each of these methods and to understand why they are all considered "adding tens and ones."

First [Paige] added the 10s, and then she added the 1s. What did [Paige] still have left to do? *(combine the subtotals, 70 and 11)*

$$40 + 30 = 70$$
$$8 + 3 = 11$$
$$70 + 11 = 81 \ \ (\text{or}, 70 + 10 + 1 = 81)$$

Also discuss how the same information can be recorded vertically.

$$
\begin{array}{r}
48 \\
+33 \\
\hline
40 + 30 = \quad 70 \\
8 + \ \ 3 = \quad +11 \\
\hline
81
\end{array}
$$

Ask another student to use sticker notation to model the strategy for the class, or ask the class to help you do so. Be sure to demonstrate how the 11 singles can be represented as, or traded in for, one strip of ten and one single.

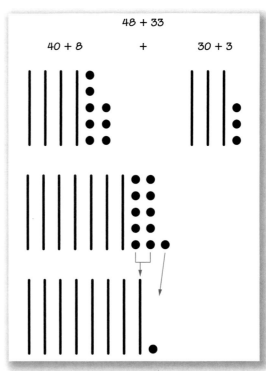

If you have students who used another version of adding tens and ones, ask one of them to share.⑧

You may have students who add the ones first and then the tens. Some may do this in their own way, and others may be using the steps and notation of the U.S. standard algorithm for addition. Help students see that this, too, is adding tens and ones. Although the strategies are similar, the shorthand notation used to record the standard algorithm often presents confusion for young students.

After you have recorded one or two strategies on your "Adding Tens and Ones" chart, ask students to look at their work and decide whether they used this strategy. Ask students which strategy more closely matches what they did.

Finally, ask students to consider what is happening with the tens and ones in this problem.

The problem was 48 + 33. If you add the tens, you get 4 tens plus 3 tens or 40 plus 30, and that's 7 tens or 70. Why wasn't our answer in the 70s?

Modeling the problem with paper stickers or sticker notation, as described above, can help students see that there is another ten in the 11 ones. That makes 8 tens, which puts the answer in the 80s.

ACTIVITY

3 More Addition Problems

20 MIN INDIVIDUALS CLASS

Students finish Addition Problems, Set 1 on *Student Activity Book* pages 40–41 and continue with Addition Problems, Set 2 on pages 42–43. Explain that these pages include story problems as well as horizontal and vertical addition problems for which they will write matching story problems. Remind students that the way a problem is written does not change what it is asking or the strategies that they can use to solve it.

These pages ask students to solve each problem in two ways. Encourage students to use whatever strategy they are most comfortable with first and then to try using one of the strategies just discussed.

ONGOING ASSESSMENT: Observing Students at Work

Students add 2-digit numbers and record their work.

- **Can students accurately write an equation or a story problem that represents the problem?**

- **What strategies do students use to solve the problem?** Are they using the ideas and strategies just discussed? Other strategies?

- **What tools, models, or representations do students use to solve the problem?** Cubes? Stickers? The 100 chart? The number line?

- **How do students show their work?** Can you tell how they solved the problem? Are they using equations accurately?

Math Note

⑨ **Other Strategies** Be sure to acknowledge other strategies used to solve the problem. For example, some students create an equivalent problem, reasoning, "I can take 2 from the 33 and give it to the 48. That's 50 plus 31, and that's 81." Others add a nearby "friendly" or "landmark" number and then compensate, thinking, "33 + 50 would be 83. I added 2 too many, so take 2 away from 83, and it's 81."

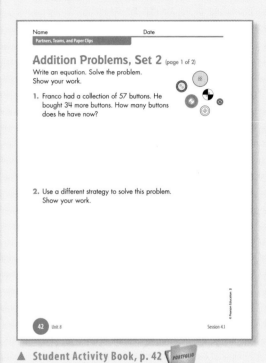

▲ Student Activity Book, p. 42

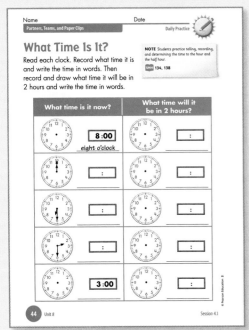

▲ **Student Activity Book, p. 43**

▲ **Student Activity Book, p. 44**

Collect students' work to get a sense of the range of strategies they are using to solve addition problems.

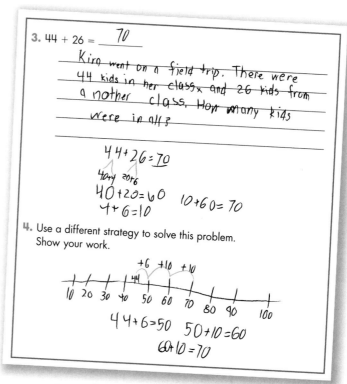

Sample Student Work

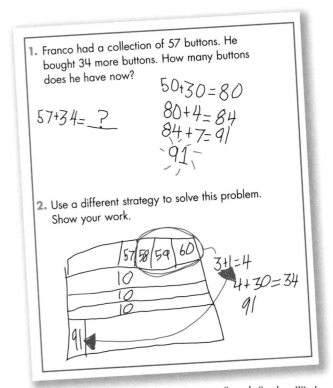

Sample Student Work

DIFFERENTIATION: Supporting the Range of Learners

Intervention Work in a small group with students who need more support. Make sure that they can describe and model the action of the problems. Encourage students who count all, use a faulty strategy, or do not have a strategy to model the situation with cubes or paper stickers. Work together to use sticker notation, numbers, and equations to show their strategy.

Use cubes, the 100 chart, or the number line to help students who count on by ones to think about how they could use groups.

The problem is 44 + 26. [Show these two numbers with cubes.] Would you keep the 44 whole and count on by ones? Let's try it. [Together, count the 26 cubes by ones.] That's a lot to count and keep track of! What if we kept the 44 whole and added one whole tower of 10? How many would we have then?

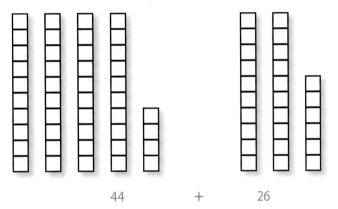

44 + 26

SESSION FOLLOW-UP

4 Daily Practice and Homework

 Daily Practice: For ongoing review, have students complete *Student Activity Book* page 44.

 Homework: Students solve two addition problems and show their work on *Student Activity Book* pages 45–46.

 Student Math Handbook: Students and families may use *Student Math Handbook* pages 62, 63–64, 65–66 for reference and review. See pages 205–211 in the back of this unit.

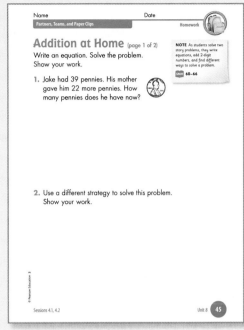

Name _____ Date _____

Partners, Teams, and Paper Clips   Homework

Addition at Home (page 1 of 2)

NOTE As students solve two story problems, they write equations, add 2-digit numbers, and find different ways to solve a problem. *SMH* 60–66

Write an equation. Solve the problem.
Show your work.

1. Jake had 39 pennies. His mother gave him 22 more pennies. How many pennies does he have now?

2. Use a different strategy to solve this problem. Show your work.

Sessions 4.1, 4.2   Unit 8   45

▲ **Student Activity Book, p. 45**

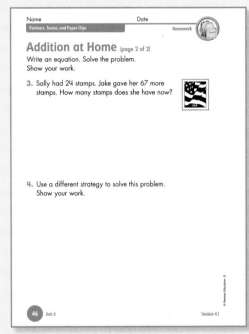

Name _____ Date _____

Partners, Teams, and Paper Clips   Homework

Addition at Home (page 2 of 2)

Write an equation. Solve the problem.
Show your work.

3. Sally had 24 stamps. Jake gave her 67 more stamps. How many stamps does she have now?

4. Use a different strategy to solve this problem. Show your work.

46   Unit 8   Session 4.1

▲ **Student Activity Book, p. 46**

Keeping One Number Whole

Math Focus Points

◆ Adding 2-digit numbers by keeping one number whole

◆ Developing efficient methods for adding and notating strategies

Today's Plan			Materials
DISCUSSION **❶ Keeping One Number Whole**	15 MIN	CLASS	• *Student Activity Book,* p. 45 • Chart: "Keeping One Number Whole"; chart paper
ACTIVITY **❷ Practicing Keeping One Number Whole**	30 MIN	INDIVIDUALS	• *Student Activity Book,* pp. 47–48 • M28–M31* (as needed) • Connecting cubes; paper stickers; 100 charts
DISCUSSION **❸ Keeping One Number Whole**	15 MIN	CLASS	• *Student Activity Book,* pp. 47–48 • Paper stickers or cubes
SESSION FOLLOW-UP **❹ Daily Practice and Homework**			• *Student Activity Book,* pp. 49–51 • *Student Math Handbook,* pp. 63–64, 65–66

*See *Materials to Prepare,* p. 111.

Classroom Routines

Today's Number: 71 Students individually generate at least ten expressions for the number 71, five using addition and five using subtraction. They record their work on *Today's Number: 71* (M27). This work, the eighth in a series of work samples for this activity, will provide information about how students are understanding and working with *Today's Number.*

DISCUSSION

(1) Keeping One Number Whole

15 MIN   CLASS

Math Focus Points for Discussion

◆ Adding 2-digit numbers by keeping one number whole

Start this session with a discussion of the homework, focusing on the strategy of keeping one number whole and adding the other in parts. Call attention to the list you made on the "Keeping One Number Whole" chart in Session 4.1. Point out examples of breaking one number into useful parts, such as an amount that gets you to a multiple of 10 or an amount that gives you a problem you can easily solve.

For homework last night, you solved this problem: Jake had 39 pennies. His mother gave him 22 more pennies. How many pennies does he have now?

Ask students to help you write an equation that represents what the problem is asking. Record the equations at the top of a piece of chart paper.

$$39 + 22 = \qquad\qquad \begin{array}{r} 39 \\ + 22 \\ \hline \end{array}$$

On your homework, some of you kept one number whole, some of you added tens and ones, and some of you used another strategy. But right now I want everyone to think about this: How could you solve this problem by keeping one number whole and adding the other one in parts?

Give students a few minutes to think about this question and discuss it with a partner. Encourage students for whom this question is difficult to think about the first step.

Let's say that we keep 39 whole. How could we think about adding on the 22?

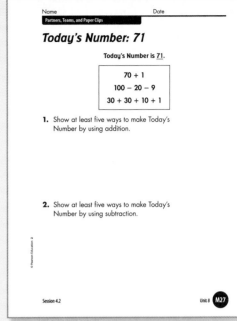

▲ Resource Masters, M27; T80   PORTFOLIO

Algebra Note

❶ **The Associative Property** Keeping one number whole and adding the other number in parts is an application of the associative property of addition.

$39 + 22 = 39 + (20 + 2) = (39 + 20) + 2 = 59 + 2$

$39 + 22 = 39 + (1 + 21) = (39 + 1) + 21 = 40 + 21$

Second graders are not expected to know and use such terminology as *associative property*, but they can recognize that when they break up the number 22, they have a new problem with multiple addends that they can add in any order.

As you did in Session 4.1, use equations to record the strategies that students suggest, and ask students to model them. The number line and 100 chart can be particularly useful for modeling the strategy of keeping one number whole. Focus on where you can see the 22 that is being added in each strategy and on each representation.❶

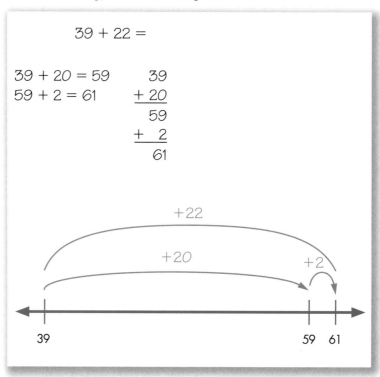

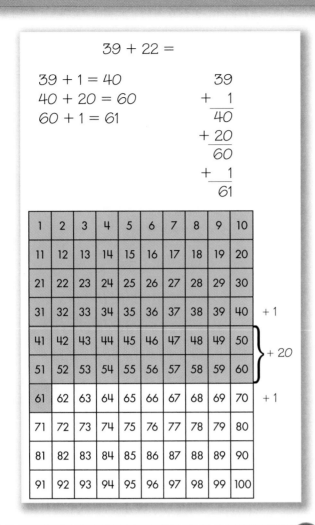

$$39 + 22 =$$

$$39 + 1 = 40$$
$$40 + 20 = 60$$
$$60 + 1 = 61$$

```
   39
 +  1
 ‾‾‾‾
   40
 + 20
 ‾‾‾‾
   60
 +  1
 ‾‾‾‾
   61
```

1	2	3	4	5	6	7	8	9	10
11	12	13	14	15	16	17	18	19	20
21	22	23	24	25	26	27	28	29	30
31	32	33	34	35	36	37	38	39	40
41	42	43	44	45	46	47	48	49	50
51	52	53	54	55	56	57	58	59	60
61	62	63	64	65	66	67	68	69	70
71	72	73	74	75	76	77	78	79	80
81	82	83	84	85	86	87	88	89	90
91	92	93	94	95	96	97	98	99	100

+ 1

+ 20

+ 1

ACTIVITY

30 MIN INDIVIDUALS

2 Practicing Keeping One Number Whole

Students use the strategy of keeping one number whole as they solve Addition Problems, Set 3 on *Student Activity Book* pages 47–48.

ONGOING ASSESSMENT: Observing Students at Work

Students practice using the strategy of keeping one number whole to solve addition problems.

- **Can students accurately write an equation or a story problem that represents the problem?**

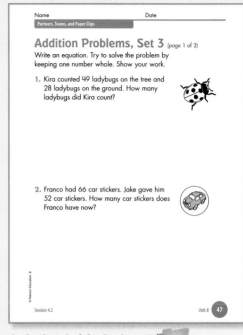

Name _____ Date _____

Partners, Teams, and Paper Clips

Addition Problems, Set 3 (page 1 of 2)
Write an equation. Try to solve the problem by keeping one number whole. Show your work.

1. Kira counted 49 ladybugs on the tree and 28 ladybugs on the ground. How many ladybugs did Kira count?

2. Franco had 66 car stickers. Jake gave him 52 car stickers. How many car stickers does Franco have now?

Session 4.2   Unit 8   47

▲ Student Activity Book, p. 47 PORTFOLIO

Name _____ Date _____

Partners, Teams, and Paper Clips

Addition Problems, Set 3 (page 2 of 2)
Write a story that matches each problem.
Solve the problems. Show your work.

3.   55
   +36

_____
_____
_____
_____

4. 17 + 62 = _____

_____
_____
_____
_____
_____

48   Unit 8   Session 4.2

▲ Student Activity Book, p. 48 PORTFOLIO WRITING

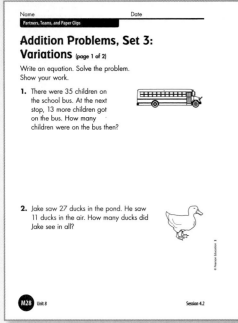

▲ Resource Masters, M28

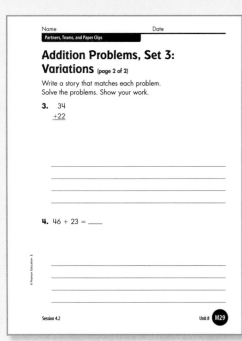

▲ Resource Masters, M29

- **Are students able to keep one number whole and add on the other?** How do they add on? Do they use 1s? 10s and then 1s? Other useful chunks? How do they keep track? What tools, models, or representations do they use? Do they get the right answer?

- **How do students record their work?** Are they using standard notation accurately?

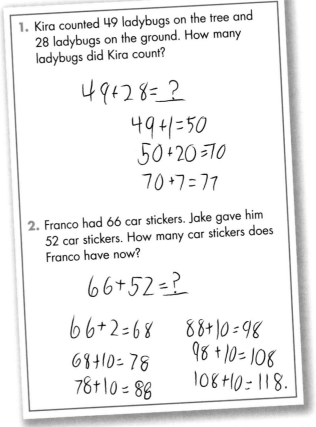

Sample Student Work

DIFFERENTIATION: Supporting the Range of Learners

Intervention Some students may benefit from first working on the easier problems on Addition Problems, Set 3: Variations (M28–M29).

If students are ready for *Student Activity Book* page 47, consider working with a small group. Have them retell the problem and identify the action. Some students may find cubes or paper stickers more helpful than the 100 chart or number lines. Ask questions to help them focus on the strategy of keeping one number whole.

I see that you have 49 cubes and 28 cubes. Which number are you going to keep whole? (49) How will you add 28 in parts? What if you add 10 of the 28 onto the 49? [Move one tower of 10 cubes.] Can you add another 10? Now how many do you have left to add?

Help students use sticker notation and/or equations to record their work.

Extension For students who are ready for more challenge, provide copies of Addition Problems, Set 3: Challenges (M30–M31).

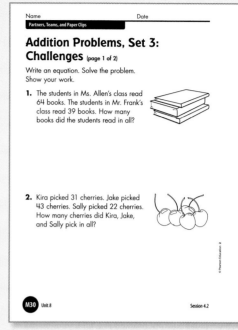

▲ Resource Masters, M30

DISCUSSION

3 Keeping One Number Whole

 15 MIN CLASS

Math Focus Points for Discussion

◆ Adding 2-digit numbers by keeping one number whole

◆ Developing efficient methods for adding and notating strategies

Begin by asking students about the experience of trying to use a particular strategy to solve a set of problems. Ask if it was difficult or whether it made the problems easier to solve.

Choose one problem from Addition Problems, Set 3, pages 47–48, for the focus of this discussion. Gather equations that represent what the problem is asking, and then discuss different ways to solve it by keeping one number whole—just as you did at the beginning of this session. Use equations to record students' strategies and have students model the strategies on the number line or 100 chart and/or with cubes or paper stickers.

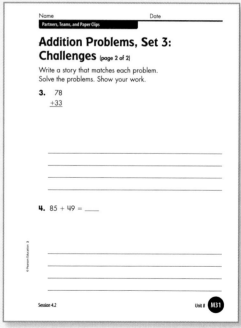

▲ Resource Masters, M31

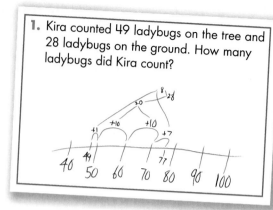

Yama's Work

Yama used the number line to add 28 onto 49. She added 1 to get to 50, then two 10s, and then the remaining 7. She also showed how she knew that she added 28 in all.

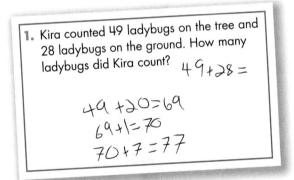

Monisha's Work

Roshaun's Work

Monisha and Roshaun both used equations. They broke the 28 apart by place to add it on to the 49. Can you see the 28 in each of their solutions?

SESSION FOLLOW-UP

④ Daily Practice and Homework

 Daily Practice: For reinforcement of this unit's content, have students complete *Student Activity Book* page 49.

 Homework: Students write story situations for two given addition problems and solve them, showing their work on *Student Activity Book* pages 50–51.

 Student Math Handbook: Students and families may use *Student Math Handbook* pages 63–64, 65–66 for reference and review. See pages 205–211 in the back of this unit.

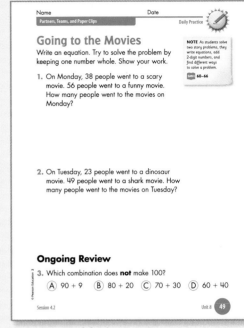

Name _____ Date _____
Partners, Teams, and Paper Clips   Daily Practice

Going to the Movies

Write an equation. Try to solve the problem by keeping one number whole. Show your work.

NOTE As students solve two story problems, they write equations, add 2-digit numbers, and find different ways to solve a problem.
SMH 60–66

1. On Monday, 38 people went to a scary movie. 56 people went to a funny movie. How many people went to the movies on Monday?

2. On Tuesday, 23 people went to a dinosaur movie. 49 people went to a shark movie. How many people went to the movies on Tuesday?

Ongoing Review

3. Which combination does **not** make 100?

(A) 90 + 9   (B) 80 + 20   (C) 70 + 30   (D) 60 + 40

Session 4.2   Unit 8   49

▲ **Student Activity Book, p. 49**

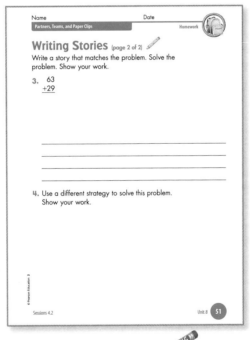

Name _____ Date _____
Partners, Teams, and Paper Clips   Homework

Writing Stories (page 2 of 2)

Write a story that matches the problem. Solve the problem. Show your work.

3. 63
   +29

_____
_____
_____

4. Use a different strategy to solve this problem. Show your work.

Sessions 4.2   Unit 8   51

▲ **Student Activity Book, p. 51**

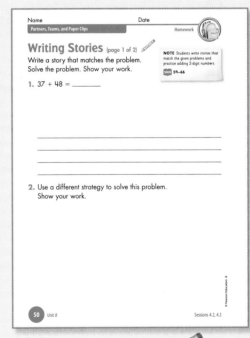

Name _____ Date _____
Partners, Teams, and Paper Clips   Homework

Writing Stories (page 1 of 2)

Write a story that matches the problem. Solve the problem. Show your work.

NOTE Students write stories that match the given problems and practice adding 2-digit numbers.
SMH 59–66

1. 37 + 48 = _____

_____
_____
_____

2. Use a different strategy to solve this problem. Show your work.

50 Unit 8   Sessions 4.2, 4.3

▲ **Student Activity Book, p. 50**

Adding Tens and Ones

Math Focus Points

◆ Adding 2-digit numbers by adding tens and ones

◆ Developing efficient methods for adding and notating strategies

Today's Plan		Materials
DISCUSSION ❶ **Adding Tens and Ones**	15 MIN · CLASS	• *Student Activity Book,* p. 50 • Chart: "Adding Tens and Ones"; connecting cubes; paper stickers
ACTIVITY ❷ **Practicing Adding Tens and Ones**	30 MIN · INDIVIDUALS	• *Student Activity Book,* pp. 52–53 • M32–M35* (as needed)
DISCUSSION ❸ **Adding Tens and Ones**	15 MIN · CLASS	• *Student Activity Book,* p. 52 • Connecting cubes; paper stickers; chart paper (optional)
SESSION FOLLOW-UP ❹ **Daily Practice and Homework**		• *Student Activity Book,* pp. 54–56 • *Student Math Handbook,* pp. 63–64, 65–66

*See *Materials to Prepare,* p. 111.

Classroom Routines

How Many Pockets? Comparing Data Ahead of time, collect pocket data from another class, recording the number of pockets beside each child's name on chart paper. During your Pocket Day, collect your class data on a similar list on chart paper. Then, ask students whether they think [fifth graders] wear more, fewer, or about the same number of pockets as second graders and why. Display the other class chart and focus the discussion on a comparison of the two sets of data.

DISCUSSION

1 Adding Tens and Ones

Math Focus Points for Discussion

◆ Adding 2-digit numbers by adding tens and ones

For homework last night, one of the problems you solved was 37 plus 48.

Remind students that a problem written vertically means the same thing as a problem written horizontally.

$$37 \\ +48$$ $$\qquad 37 + 48 =$$

Ask several students to share the stories they wrote to match this problem.

When you solved this problem, you probably used a variety of strategies. Whatever you did last night, I want everyone to think right now about this question: How could you use the strategy of adding tens and ones to solve this problem? ❶

Remind students that they can see examples of this strategy on your "Adding Tens and Ones" chart. Cubes in towers of 10 and paper stickers are particularly useful for modeling this strategy. Ask students to help you represent the problem by using one tool or the other.

Point out that the first step is to take the numbers being added and break them into tens and ones.

How many strips of 10 would you need to show the 37? How many singles? How many strips of 10 would you need for the 48? How many singles?

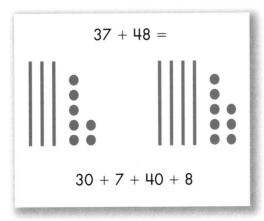

37 + 48 =

30 + 7 + 40 + 8

Algebra Note

❶ **Properties of Addition** The strategy of adding tens and ones (or adding by place) is an application of the commutative and associative properties of addition.

$37 + 48 = (30 + 7) + (40 + 8) =$
$30 + (7 + 40) + 8 =$
$30 + (40 + 7) + 8 =$
$(30 + 40) + (7 + 8)$

Second graders are not expected to know and use such terminology, but they can recognize that when they break up the 37 and 48, they have a new problem with four addends that can be combined in any order.

Math Note

❷ **Different Second Steps** After adding 30 + 40 or 40 + 30, some students add 7 to 70 and then 8 to 77. Others add 8 to 70 and then 7 to 78.

After breaking the numbers into tens and ones, you need to put all the tens together, put all the ones together, and then combine those totals. Think for a minute about how you would add tens and ones to solve this problem.

Give students a few minutes to think about and solve the problem. Encourage students who find this question difficult to work with the cubes or paper stickers.

Ask a student to share how he or she added by place to solve this problem.

$$30 + 40 = 70$$
$$7 + 8 = 15$$
$$70 + 15 = 85$$

Ask two other students to model the strategy with sticker notation and cubes in towers of 10.❷

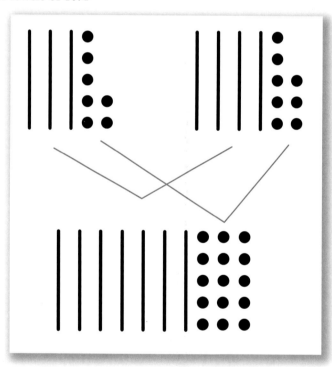

The problem was 37 plus 48. If you add the tens, you get 3 tens plus 4 tens or 30 plus 40. That's 7 tens or 70. Why wasn't our answer in the 70s?

Modeling the problem with paper stickers and/or sticker notation can help students see that there is another group of 10 in the 15 ones, which can be represented as another strip of 10. That makes 8 tens, which puts the answer in the 80s.

ACTIVITY

30 MIN INDIVIDUALS

② Practicing Adding Tens and Ones

Students use the strategy of adding tens and ones to solve Addition Problems, Set 4 on *Student Activity Book* pages 52–53.

✔ ONGOING ASSESSMENT: Observing Students at Work

Students practice using the strategy of adding tens and ones to solve addition problems.

- **Can students write an equation or a story problem that represents the problem?**

- **Are students able to add by place?** Do they accurately combine tens with tens and ones with ones? How do they keep track? What tools, models, or representations do they use? Do they get the right answer?

- **How do students record their work?** Are they using standard notation correctly?

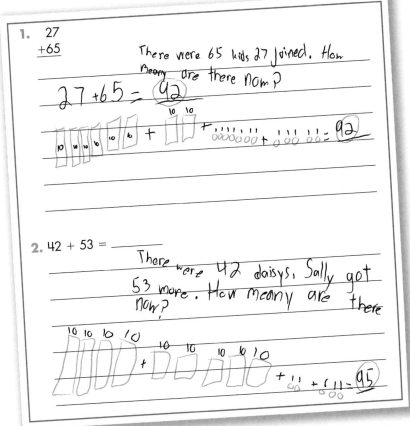

Sample Student Work

Name _____ Date _____

Partners, Teams, and Paper Clips

Addition Problems, Set 4 (page 1 of 2) ✏

Write a story that matches the problem. Try to solve the problem by adding tens and ones. Show your work.

1. 27
   +65

_____
_____
_____

2. 42 + 53 = _____

_____
_____
_____

52 Unit 8   Session 4.3

▲ **Student Activity Book, p. 52**

Name _____ Date _____

Partners, Teams, and Paper Clips

Addition Problems, Set 4 (page 2 of 2)

Write an equation. Try to solve each problem by keeping one number whole. Show your work.

3. Jake had 88 paper clips. He found 16 more paper clips in the hall. How many paper clips does Jake have now?

4. Sally had 73 marbles. Franco gave her 25 marbles. How many marbles does Sally have now?

Session 4.3   Unit 8 53

▲ **Student Activity Book, p. 53**

▲ Resource Masters, M32

Name _____ Date _____
Partners, Teams, and Paper Clips

Addition Problems, Set 4:
Variations (page 1 of 2)

Write a story that matches each problem.
Solve the problems. Show your work.

1. 41
   +26

2. 37 + 12 = ____

M32 Unit 8   Session 4.3

Name _____ Date _____
Partners, Teams, and Paper Clips

Addition Problems, Set 4:
Variations (page 2 of 2)

Write an equation. Solve the problem.
Show your work.

3. Sally saw 13 chickens in the yard. She saw
   25 chickens in the barn. How many chickens
   did Sally see in all?

4. Ms. Vale has 21 students in her class.
   Mr. Jones has 17 students in his class.
   Both classes went to the playground.
   How many students were at the
   playground?

Session 4.3   Unit 8 M33

▲ Resource Masters, M33

DIFFERENTIATION: Supporting the Range of Learners

Intervention Identify students who may benefit from working with
you in a small group. Have them retell the problem and identify the
action. Suggest that they use cubes in towers of 10 or paper stickers to
model and solve the problem. Some may benefit from first working on
the easier problems on Addition Problems, Set 4: Variations (M32–M33).

Extension Students who need more challenge can work on
Addition Problems, Set 4: Challenges (M34–M35).

DISCUSSION

3 Adding Tens and Ones

15 MIN   CLASS

Math Focus Points for Discussion

◆ Adding 2-digit numbers by adding tens and ones

◆ Developing efficient methods for adding and notating strategies

Call students together for a discussion of their work on Problem 1 in
Addition Problems, Set 4. Record the problem on the board or on chart
paper and remind students that a problem written vertically means the
same thing as a problem written horizontally.

$$27 \qquad 27 + 65 =$$
$$+65$$

Ask a student or two to tell a story that matches this equation. Then
remind them of the task, which is using the strategy of adding tens
and ones.

When you add tens and ones, you start by breaking the numbers into
tens and ones. How would you do that for this problem?

Ask students to help you represent the problem with cubes and/or paper
stickers.

After you broke the numbers into tens and ones, what did you do next?

Talk through the strategy with students, having volunteers model each step with the cubes and/or paper stickers.

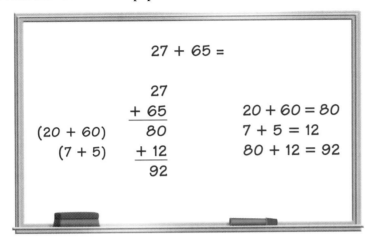

$$27 + 65 =$$

$$
\begin{array}{r}
27 \\
+\ 65 \\
\hline
80 \\
+\ 12 \\
\hline
92
\end{array}
$$

(20 + 60)
(7 + 5)

20 + 60 = 80
7 + 5 = 12
80 + 12 = 92

Finally, ask students to consider what is happening with the tens and ones in this problem.

The problem was 27 plus 65. If you add the tens, you get 20 plus 60. That's 80. Why wasn't our answer in the 80s?

Modeling the problem with paper stickers can help students see that there is another 10 in the 12 ones, which makes a total of 9 tens. Therefore, the answer is in the 90s.

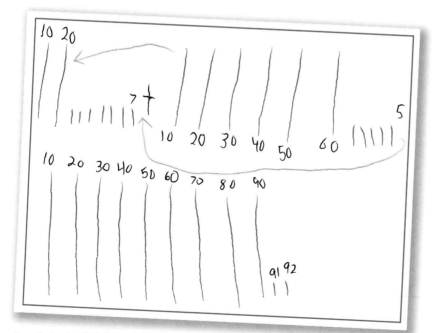

Sample Student Work

Addition Problems, Set 4: Challenges (page 1 of 2)

Write a story that matches each problem. Solve the problems. Show your work.

1. 39
   +67

   _____
   _____
   _____

2. 36 + 48 + 23 = _____

   _____
   _____
   _____

M34 Unit 8   Session 4.3

▲ **Resource Masters, M34**

Addition Problems, Set 4: Challenges (page 2 of 2)

Write an equation. Solve each problem. Show your work.

3. Jake had 74 pennies. He needed 48 more pennies to buy a baseball card. How many pennies did the baseball card cost?

4. Kira collected 49 shells. Franco collected 36 shells, and Jake collected 17 shells. How many shells did they collect in all?

Session 4.3   Unit 8 M35

▲ **Resource Masters, M35**

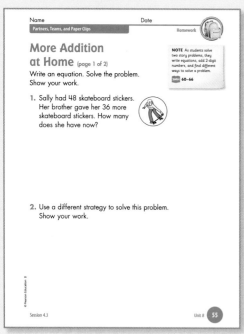

Name Date

Partners, Teams, and Paper Clips — Daily Practice

Today's Number: 12

Today's Number is 12.

NOTE Students write expressions that equal Today's Number by using only subtraction. There are many possible solutions.

SMH 55

42 – 30
50 – 20 – 10 – 8
12 – 0

1. Write at least five different ways to make Today's Number. Use only subtraction.

Ongoing Review

2. What time will it be in three hours?

(A) 3:45 (C) 6:45

(B) 5:45 (D) 12:45

54 Unit 8 Session 4.3 © Pearson Education 2

▲ Student Activity Book, p. 54

Name Date

Partners, Teams, and Paper Clips — Homework

More Addition at Home (page 1 of 2)

Write an equation. Solve the problem. Show your work.

NOTE As students solve two story problems, they write equations, add 2-digit numbers, and find different ways to solve a problem.

SMH 60–66

1. Sally had 48 skateboard stickers. Her brother gave her 36 more skateboard stickers. How many does she have now?

2. Use a different strategy to solve this problem. Show your work.

© Pearson Education 2 Session 4.3 Unit 8 55

▲ Student Activity Book, p. 55

SESSION FOLLOW-UP

4 Daily Practice and Homework

Daily Practice: For reinforcement of this unit's content, have students complete *Student Activity Book* page 54.

Homework: Students solve 2-digit addition problems and show their work on *Student Activity Book* pages 55–56.

Student Math Handbook: Students and families may use *Student Math Handbook* pages 63–64, 65–66 for reference and review. See pages 205–211 in the back of this unit.

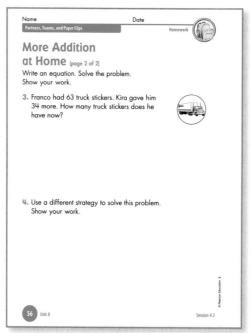

Name Date

Partners, Teams, and Paper Clips — Homework

More Addition at Home (page 2 of 2)

Write an equation. Solve the problem. Show your work.

3. Franco had 63 truck stickers. Kira gave him 34 more. How many truck stickers does he have now?

4. Use a different strategy to solve this problem. Show your work.

56 Unit 8 Session 4.3 © Pearson Education 2

▲ Student Activity Book, p. 56

Adding 2-Digit Numbers

Math Focus Points

◆ Developing efficient methods for adding and notating strategies

◆ Noticing what happens to place value when two 2-digit numbers with a sum over 100 are combined

Today's Plan		Materials
ACTIVITY ① **Practicing Addition** 40 MIN　INDIVIDUALS		• *Student Activity Book,* pp. 57–58 • M16*; M36–M39* (as needed); T81 • Connecting cubes; paper stickers
DISCUSSION ② **Strategies for Adding** 20 MIN　CLASS		• *Student Activity Book,* p. 57 • M16; T81 • Paper stickers; 100 charts
SESSION FOLLOW-UP ③ **Daily Practice and Homework**		• *Student Activity Book,* pp. 59–61 • *Student Math Handbook,* pp. 63–64, 65–66

*See *Materials to Prepare,* p. 111.

Classroom Routines

What Time Is It? What Time Will It Be?　Set the demonstration clock to 1:00. Ask students to set their clocks to the time it will be in 45 minutes and to record the time in digital format (1:45). Repeat, varying the starting and elapsed times and keeping both times on whole, half, or quarter hours. Depending on your students, choose times that will cross into another hour. For example:

• If it is now 3:45, what time will it be in 30 minutes?

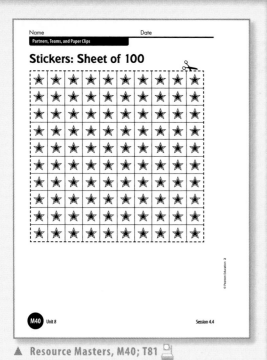

Stickers: Sheet of 100

M40 Unit 8   Session 4.4

▲ Resource Masters, M40; T81

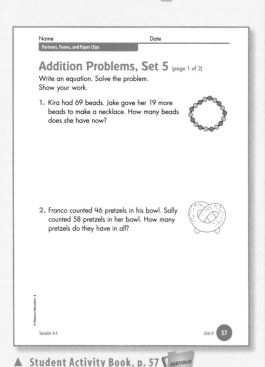

Name _____ Date _____
Partners, Teams, and Paper Clips

Addition Problems, Set 5 (page 1 of 2)

Write an equation. Solve the problem.
Show your work.

1. Kira had 69 beads. Jake gave her 19 more
beads to make a necklace. How many beads
does she have now?

2. Franco counted 46 pretzels in his bowl. Sally
counted 58 pretzels in her bowl. How many
pretzels do they have in all?

Session 4.4   Unit 8 57

▲ Student Activity Book, p. 57 PORTFOLIO

ACTIVITY

1 Practicing Addition

40 MIN INDIVIDUALS

Begin this activity by displaying Stickers: Sheet of 100 (T81) on the
overhead.

This year you have been working with stickers that come in strips of
10 and singles. Now that you are working with larger numbers, here's
another tool that will be useful to you: stickers that come in a sheet
of 100. How many strips of 10 equal one sheet of stickers? How many
singles equal one sheet?

Make available copies of Pages in a Sticker Book (M16) for students to
use while they work on Addition Problems, Set 5, on *Student Activity
Book* pages 57–58.

ONGOING ASSESSMENT: Observing Students at Work

Students practice adding 2-digit numbers.

- **Can students accurately write an equation or a story problem
  that represents the problem?**

- **What strategies do students use to solve the problem?** Adding
  tens and ones? Keeping one number whole? Another strategy?

- **What tools, models, or representations do students use to solve
  the problem?** Cubes? Stickers? 100 charts? Number lines?

- **How do students show their work?** Can you tell how they solved
  the problem? Are they using equations accurately?

1. Kira had 69 beads. Jake gave her 19 more beads to make a necklace. How many beads does she have now?

$$
\begin{array}{r} 69 \\ +19 \\ \hline 88 \end{array}
$$

$69 + 1 = 70$
$70 + 10 = 80$
$80 + 8 = 88$

2. Franco counted 46 pretzels in his bowl. Sally counted 58 pretzels in her bowl. How many pretzels do they have in all?

$$
\begin{array}{r} 46 \\ +58 \\ \hline 104 \end{array}
$$

$58 + 2 = 60$
$60 + 40 = 100$
$100 + 4 = 104$

Sample Student Work

1. Kira had 69 beads. Jake gave her 19 more beads to make a necklace. How many beads does she have now?

$69 + 19 = ?$

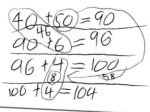

88 beads

2. Franco counted 46 pretzels in his bowl. Sally counted 58 pretzels in her bowl. How many pretzels do they have in all?

$40 + 50 = 90$
$90 + 6 = 96$
$96 + 4 = 100$
$100 + 4 = 104$

Sample Student Work

Name _____ Date _____

Partners, Teams, and Paper Clips

Addition Problems, Set 5 (page 2 of 2)

Write a story that matches each problem.
Solve the problems. Show your work.

3.
$$
\begin{array}{r} 41 \\ +74 \\ \hline \end{array}
$$

_____
_____
_____

4. 64 + 35 = _____

_____
_____
_____

58 Unit 8   Session 4.4

▲ **Student Activity Book, p. 58** PORTFOLIO WRITING

Name _____ Date _____

Partners, Teams, and Paper Clips

Addition Problems, Set 5: Variations (page 1 of 2)

Write a story that matches each problem.
Solve the problems. Show your work.

1.
$$
\begin{array}{r} 34 \\ +23 \\ \hline \end{array}
$$

_____
_____
_____

2. 27 + 16 = _____

_____
_____
_____
_____

M36 Unit 8   Session 4.4

▲ **Resource Masters, M36**

Algebra Note

❶ Multiple Addends Look for opportunities to point out that when students break one or both numbers into parts, they create a problem with multiple addends. Because of the discussions all year, students should be confident that they can combine those addends in any order and get the same answer.

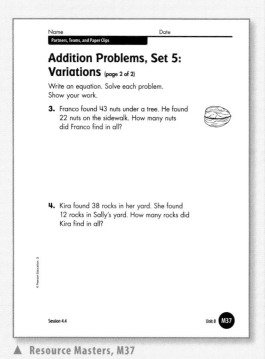

Name _____ Date _____

Partners, Teams, and Paper Clips

Addition Problems, Set 5: Variations (page 2 of 2)

Write an equation. Solve each problem. Show your work.

3. Franco found 43 nuts under a tree. He found 22 nuts on the sidewalk. How many nuts did Franco find in all?

4. Kira found 38 rocks in her yard. She found 12 rocks in Sally's yard. How many rocks did Kira find in all?

© Pearson Education 2

Session 4.4   Unit 8 **M37**

▲ Resource Masters, M37

DIFFERENTIATION: Supporting the Range of Learners

Intervention Identify students who may need help getting started and work with them in a small group. Have them retell the problem and identify the action. Encourage the use of cubes or paper stickers to model and solve the problem. Some may benefit from first working on the easier problems on Addition Problems, Set 5: Variations (M36–M37).

Extension Students who need more challenge can work on Addition Problems, Set 5: Challenges (M38–M39).

DISCUSSION

② Strategies for Adding

20 MIN   CLASS

Math Focus Points for Discussion

◆ Developing efficient methods for adding and notating strategies

◆ Noticing what happens to place value when two 2-digit numbers with a sum over 100 are combined

Call students together to discuss their strategies for Problem 2 of Addition Problems, Set 5.

Franco counted 46 pretzels in his bowl. Sally counted 58 pretzels in her bowl. How many pretzels do they have in all?

There are two equations that could represent this problem and two ways to write each equation. Record them on the board or on chart paper. ❶

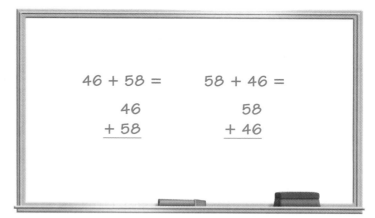

$$46 + 58 = \qquad 58 + 46 =$$

$$\begin{array}{r} 46 \\ + 58 \\ \hline \end{array} \qquad \begin{array}{r} 58 \\ + 46 \\ \hline \end{array}$$

Then ask students to share their strategies for solving the problem.

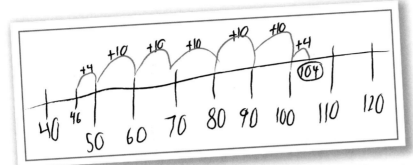

Sample Student Work

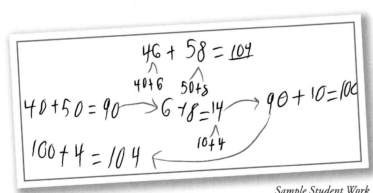

Sample Student Work

$46 + 58 = \underline{104}$

$40+6 \quad 50+8$

$40+50=90 \rightarrow 6+8=14 \rightarrow 90+10=100$

$100+4=104 \leftarrow \quad 10+4$

Sample Student Work

Name _____ Date _____

Partners, Teams, and Paper Clips

Addition Problems, Set 5:
Challenges (page 1 of 2)

Write a story that matches each problem. Solve the
problems. Show your work.

1. 56
    +86

_____
_____
_____

2. 58 + 45 + 17 = ____

_____
_____

M38 Unit 8   Session 4.4

▲ **Resource Masters, M38**

Name _____ Date _____

Partners, Teams, and Paper Clips

Addition Problems, Set 5:
Challenges (page 2 of 2)

Write an equation. Solve the problem.
Show your work.

3. Franco picked 34 flowers. Sally picked
49 flowers, and Jake picked 22 flowers.
How many flowers did they pick in all?

4. Jake counted 58 grapes on one vine and
62 grapes on another vine. How many
grapes did Jake count in all?

Session 4.4   Unit 8 M39

▲ **Resource Masters, M39**

As you have throughout this Investigation, focus on the strategies of keeping one number whole and adding tens and ones. Record students' strategies on the board or on chart paper and ask other students to model them with cubes, with paper stickers, on the 100 chart (or on Pages in a Sticker Book (M16)), and on the number line.

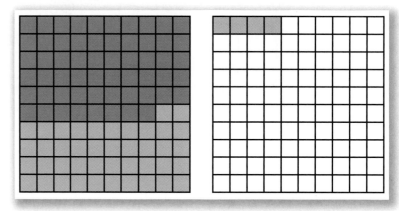

58 + 46 on Pages in a Sticker Book (M16)

This problem is challenging because the sum is over 100. Therefore, students who keep one number whole need to count past 100, and students who add by place need to deal with more than 10 ones and then with more than 10 tens. As you discuss both strategies, be sure to highlight the ways that students handled this.

The problem was 58 plus 46. If you add the tens, you get 50 plus 40. Why isn't our answer in the 90s? How could you combine two 2-digit numbers and get an answer that has three digits?

Modeling the problem with sticker notation or cubes in towers of 10 can help students see that when you "trade" ten of the 14 singles for a 10, you then have enough strips of 10 to "trade" for one "sheet" of 100. Demonstrate using a square to represent a sheet of 100 in sticker notation.

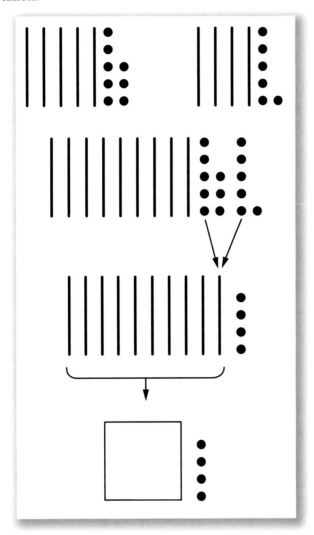

Use a set of transparent or paper stickers, including a sheet of 100 (T81), to display 104 (one sheet and four singles). Help students make the connection between the number of hundreds (sheets), tens (strips), and ones (singles) and the way we write the number one hundred four.

Teaching Note

❷ **Place Value: Hundreds, Tens, and Ones** This relationship is also illustrated in the *Student Math Handbook*.

How many sheets of 100 stickers are there in our final answer? *(one)* How many strips of 10? *(zero)* How many singles? *(four)* Then how do we write the number one hundred four?❷

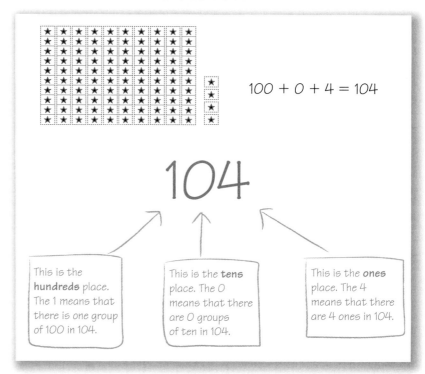

$$100 + 0 + 4 = 104$$

104

This is the **hundreds** place. The 1 means that there is one group of 100 in 104.

This is the **tens** place. The 0 means that there are 0 groups of ten in 104.

This is the **ones** place. The 4 means that there are 4 ones in 104.

Although the discussions in this investigation focus primarily on keeping one number whole and adding tens and ones, some students use other strategies, especially changing the numbers to make an equivalent problem that is easier to add.

Students might say:

"I took 2 from the 46 and gave it to the 58. Then I had 44 + 60. That's 104."

"I took 4 from the 58 and gave it to the 46. Then I had 50 + 54. That's 104."

"I know that 50 + 50 is 100. I still need to add 8 because it was 58, and I added 4 too many when I made 46 into 50. So, I have to do 100 + 8 − 4. That's 104."

As they move on into Grade 3, students will continue to refine and consolidate their strategies for keeping one number whole and adding the other on in parts and for adding tens and ones (which they will come to know as adding by place). They will also study strategies that rely on changing the problem to make numbers they find easy to work with, as in the examples above.

SESSION FOLLOW-UP

③ Daily Practice and Homework

 Daily Practice: For ongoing review, have students complete *Student Activity Book* page 59.

 Homework: On *Student Activity Book* pages 60–61, students review what they know about adding even and odd numbers and about addition combinations.

Student Math Handbook: Students and families may use *Student Math Handbook* pages 63–64, 65–66 for reference and review. See pages 205–211 in the back of this unit.

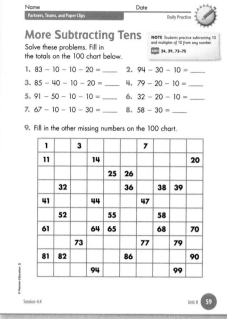

▲ Student Activity Book, p. 59

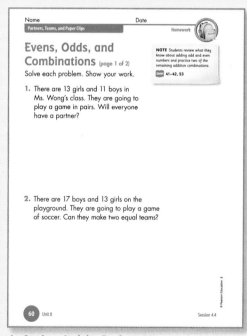

▲ Student Activity Book, p. 60

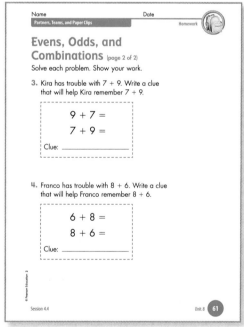

▲ Student Activity Book, p. 61

End-of-Unit Assessment

Math Focus Points

◆ Making and justifying generalizations about adding even and odd numbers

◆ Developing and achieving fluency with the Plus 9 and remaining combinations

◆ Adding 2-digit numbers accurately and efficiently

Today's Plan	Materials
ASSESSMENT ACTIVITY **① End-of-Unit Assessment** 60 MIN INDIVIDUALS CLASS	• M12, M13*; M41–M46* ☑ • Connecting cubes; paper stickers; 100 charts
SESSION FOLLOW-UP **② Daily Practice**	• *Student Activity Book,* p. 63–64 • *Student Math Handbook,* pp. 41–42, 52, 63–64, 65–66

*See *Materials to Prepare,* p. 111.

Classroom Routines

Quick Images: Cover Up with Tens and Ones Using the transparent stickers (T38–T39), display 62 with six strips and two singles. Follow the basic *Quick Images* activity. After students determine the total, cover 21 (two strips, one single) with a sheet of paper. Students use the number showing (41) to determine how many are covered. Discuss and model students' strategies. Then, keeping the total at 62, cover 31. Discuss strategies, including any that used the first problem to solve the new one. For example, "Last time there were 41 showing. This time there are 31. That's 10 fewer, so you must have hidden 10 more."

ASSESSMENT ACTIVITY

End-of-Unit Assessment

60 MIN INDIVIDUALS CLASS

This End-of-Unit Assessment addresses three benchmarks. ❶ ❷

Problems 1–3 assess Benchmark 2 and the student's ability to reason about partners, teams, and leftovers to make and justify generalizations about what happens when even and odd numbers are added. Problems 4–5 assess Benchmark 3 and the student's ability to add two 2-digit numbers accurately and efficiently. The final section assesses Benchmark 4 and the student's ability to demonstrate fluency with the Plus 9 and remaining combinations.

Provide students with copies of the End-of-Unit Assessment (M41–M45). With the class, go over all the pages in the End-of-Unit Assessment and review what students are to do on each. Explain that as students work on the first two sets of problems, you will also be meeting with individuals to review the addition combinations they have been learning.

▲ **Resource Masters, M42**

Professional Development

❶ **Assessment in This Unit,** pp. 14–15

❷ **Teacher Note:** End-of-Unit Assessment, p. 181

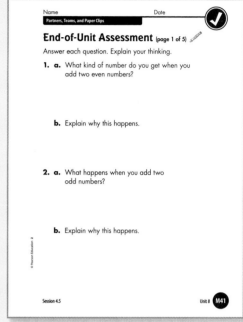

Name _____ **Date** _____

Partners, Teams, and Paper Clips

End-of-Unit Assessment (page 1 of 5)

Answer each question. Explain your thinking.

1. a. What kind of number do you get when you add two even numbers?

b. Explain why this happens.

2. a. What happens when you add two odd numbers?

b. Explain why this happens.

Session 4.5   Unit 8 **M41**

▲ **Resource Masters, M41**

Name _____ **Date** _____

Partners, Teams, and Paper Clips

End-of-Unit Assessment (page 3 of 5)

Write an equation. Solve the problem. Show your work.

4. Kira and Jake are on the same basketball team. During the game, Kira scored 48 points. Jake scored 34 points. How many points did they score?

Session 4.5   Unit 8 **M43**

▲ **Resource Masters, M43**

End-of-Unit Assessment (page 2 of 5)

3. a. What kind of number do you get when you add an odd number and an even number?

b. Explain why this happens.

M42 Unit 8   Session 4.5

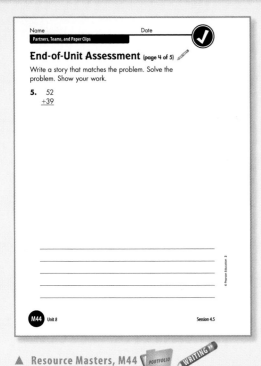

Name ___ Date ___

Partners, Teams, and Paper Clips

End-of-Unit Assessment (page 4 of 5)

Write a story that matches the problem. Solve the problem. Show your work.

5. 52
   +39

M44 Unit 8   Session 4.5

▲ **Resource Masters, M44** PORTFOLIO WRITING

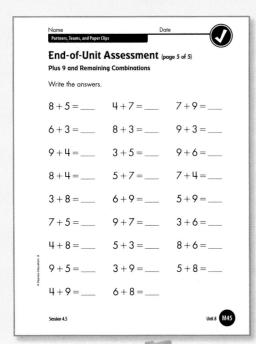

Name ___ Date ___

Partners, Teams, and Paper Clips

End-of-Unit Assessment (page 5 of 5)

Plus 9 and Remaining Combinations

Write the answers.

$8 + 5 =$ ___	$4 + 7 =$ ___	$7 + 9 =$ ___
$6 + 3 =$ ___	$8 + 3 =$ ___	$9 + 3 =$ ___
$9 + 4 =$ ___	$3 + 5 =$ ___	$9 + 6 =$ ___
$8 + 4 =$ ___	$5 + 7 =$ ___	$7 + 4 =$ ___
$3 + 8 =$ ___	$6 + 9 =$ ___	$5 + 9 =$ ___
$7 + 5 =$ ___	$9 + 7 =$ ___	$3 + 6 =$ ___
$4 + 8 =$ ___	$5 + 3 =$ ___	$8 + 6 =$ ___
$9 + 5 =$ ___	$3 + 9 =$ ___	$5 + 8 =$ ___
$4 + 9 =$ ___	$6 + 8 =$ ___	

Session 4.5   Unit 8 M45

▲ **Resource Masters, M45** PORTFOLIO

There are two alternatives for assessing the combinations. You may either observe individual students as they work on M45 or sit with them and go through a blank set of Addition Cards for the Plus 9 combinations (M12) and the remaining combinations (M13). If you use the cards, shuffle them and have a set with no clues written on the front. In either case, use the Assessment Checklist: Assessing the Plus 9 and Remaining Combinations (M46) to record your observations about each student.

Most students should be fluent with the plus 9 and remaining combinations by this point.

ONGOING ASSESSMENT: Observing Students at Work

Problems 1–3: Adding Even and Odd Numbers

● **Do students make accurate generalizations about what happens when you add different combinations of even and odd numbers?** What reasoning and evidence do they use? Are their explanations clear?

Problems 4–5: Adding 2-Digit Numbers

● **Can students accurately write an equation or tell a story that represents what the problem is asking?**

● **What strategies do students use to solve the problem?** Adding tens and ones? Keeping one number whole? Another strategy?

● **What tools, models, or representations do students use to solve the problem?** Cubes? Stickers? 100 charts? Number lines?

● **How do students show their work?** Can you tell how they solved the problem? Are they using equations accurately?

Plus 9 and Remaining Combinations

- **Are students fluent with the Plus 9 combinations?**

- **Are students fluent with the remaining combinations?**

DIFFERENTIATION: Supporting the Range of Learners

 English Language Learners may understand the tasks for assessment problems 1–3 but have difficulty writing their explanations in English. Ask these students to show you with cubes or counters what happens when they combine two even numbers, two odd numbers, or an odd and even number. Then ask questions about the specific representations they made. Restate their responses, and for those students who are ready, help them translate their oral responses into written form. Jot down the responses of students who are not yet able to do so themselves.

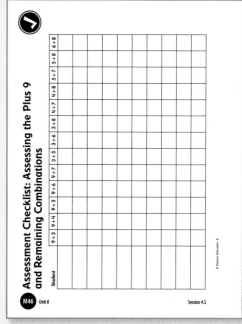

▲ Resource Masters, M46 ☑

SESSION FOLLOW-UP

2 Daily Practice

20 MIN   CLASS   PAIRS

 Daily Practice: For enrichment, have students complete *Student Activity Book* pages 63–64.

 Student Math Handbook: Students and families may use *Student Math Handbook* pages 41–42, 52, 53, 63–64, 65–66 for reference and review. See pages 205–211 in the back of this unit.

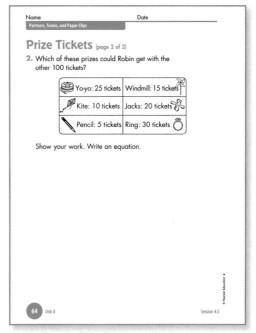

▲ Student Activity Book, p. 64

▲ Student Activity Book, p. 63

Partners, Teams, and Paper Clips

In Part 6 of *Implementing Investigations in Grade 2,* you will find a set of Teacher Notes that addresses topics and issues applicable to the curriculum as a whole rather than to specific curriculum units. They include the following:

Computational Fluency and Place Value

Computation Algorithms and Methods

Representations and Contexts for Mathematical Work

Foundations of Algebra in the Elementary Grades

Discussing Mathematical Ideas

Racial and Linguistic Diversity in the Classroom:
   Raising Questions About What Equity in the Math
   Classroom Means Today

Teacher Note

Defining Even and Odd

Many young students become intrigued by the patterns they notice with evens and odds as they work with whole numbers. An even number can be formally defined in several ways, including the following:

- A multiple of 2

- A number divisible by 2 (meaning a whole number that has no remainder when divided by 2)

- A number that results from multiplying any integer by 2

In Grade 2, students' work of defining even and odd is grounded in partners and teams, a context that is closer to students' experience. In this context, an even number is defined as follows:

- A number that makes two equal teams or groups, with none left over

- A number that can be made into partners or pairs, with none left over

Second graders need to develop mental images as they think about and make sense of any definition. Therefore, it is important to model the above ideas with students, using cubes and drawings.

A major idea for students to explore is that the two conditions that define even numbers are not independent but describe the same set; that is, if a number can be divided into pairs with none left over, can it also be divided into two equal teams with none left over, and vice versa? Students may answer this question by arranging the objects into an array.

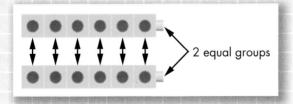

2 equal groups

If the objects can be made into two equal groups, they can be lined up in such a way that each object has a partner. Similarly, if the objects can be paired, they can be lined up in such a way that there are two equal groups.

An odd number is defined as follows:

- A number that has a remainder of 1 when divided into pairs or made into two equal groups

An effective representation of an odd number shows an "odd" member that either has no partner or makes the two teams unequal.

Second graders often make interesting observations about even and odd numbers.

- The [counting] numbers alternate: even, odd, even, odd, even, odd.

- When you double any number, the answer is even.

- Even numbers result from adding or counting by 2s, starting at 0.

- If the ones digit of a number is even, then the whole number is even (and if the ones digit is odd, the number is odd).

- Even numbers end in 2, 4, 6, 8, and 0. Odd numbers end in 1, 3, 5, 7, and 9.

Some students mistakenly associate even numbers with "friendly" numbers, thinking that if two and ten are even, then five must be as well. If students make this error, it is important to acknowledge that five is friendly, but bring them back to the idea of showing the number in partners of two or two equal teams. Because there is one left over, five must be odd.

Another common error is to associate even numbers with numbers that divide evenly (e.g., nine can be made into groups of three without a remainder, so nine is even). If students make this error, again acknowledge what is correct in the students' thinking—that three groups of three make nine—but emphasize that even numbers make groups of two or two equal groups.

Sometimes students will also say that any number is even because if there is one person left over after partnering up, that person joins a pair to become a partnership of three. Here, too, emphasize that although this is how such a situation can be handled in real life, even numbers mean that you have only groups of two.

One question that frequently arises is whether zero is odd or even. If students are interested, a discussion about zero can be very worthwhile. Some students may argue that it cannot be an even number because if you have zero objects, it cannot be made up of pairs. Other students may argue that zero is even because you can have two equal groups of zero. Still others may point out that the numbers alternate, and because one is odd and zero comes before it, zero must be even. All of these are valid points at the second-grade level.

From a mathematician's perspective, when the definitions of odd and even apply to all integers, zero is even. (Integers are the counting numbers [1, 2, 3, 4, . . .], their negative counterparts [−1, −2, −3, −4, . . .], and 0.) In later grades, students will learn that even numbers are defined as those that can be represented as $2n$, and odd numbers are those that can be represented as $2n + 1$, where n is an integer. By this definition, 0 is an even number because it can be represented as 2×0.

Note that the terms *even* and *odd* are defined only for integers and not for other numbers. For example, if the question arises whether the fraction $\frac{1}{2}$ is even or odd, the answer is neither because a fraction is not an integer.

Although students' earliest work with even and odd numbers typically stops with the observation that evens end in 0, 2, 4, 6, and 8 and odds end in 1, 3, 5, 7, and 9, students investigate in this unit why this is true.

Reasoning and Proof in Mathematics

As students engage in activities of the second-grade curriculum, they frequently find numerical relationships as they work. Part of your work is helping students notice those relationships, verbalize them, and consider such questions as, "Does this hold for *all* numbers? How can we know?" Finding ways to answer these questions will provide the basis for making sense of formal proof when it is introduced years from now. Consider the following vignette, in which second-grade students discuss their work with odd and even numbers.

Malcolm: If you add an odd and an odd, you'll always get an even.

Teacher: Always?

Malcolm: Yes!

Teacher: Do all of you agree with Malcolm? How do you know that will always happen?

Malcolm has made an assertion—mathematicians call such an assertion a conjecture—that the sum of two odd numbers is even. By asking, "How do you know that will always happen?" the teacher has challenged the class to find a way to show that this conjecture is true.

Tia: Every odd has a leftover, so you can just squish them together.

Teacher: What do you mean?

Tia: You can take the two leftovers and always squish them together.

The class has been working with the definition of even numbers as those numbers that can be arranged into pairs with nothing left over. Odd numbers, when arranged into pairs, have one left over. Tia now picks up two sets of cubes each arranged in pairs with one unpaired cube, showing two odd numbers. She then takes the two "leftovers" and brings them together.

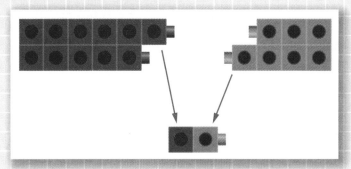

Tia: You squish the two leftovers together and now they all have partners.

Teacher: Is that true for all odds?

Tia: Yes, because all odds have a leftover.

Tia has presented a model of addition—joining two sets of cubes—and shows how she knows that the sum of two odd numbers will always be even. Because every odd number is made up of pairs and one leftover, you put the two leftovers together to make another pair. The total is made up of all pairs, so the total is an even number. This will work no matter which two odd numbers you pick; their total will *always* be even.

Students in Grades K–5 can work productively on developing justifications for mathematical ideas, as Tia does here. Before examining more closely what it looks like for second graders to prove an idea, consider what proof is in the field of mathematics.

What Is Proof in Mathematics?

Throughout life, when people make a claim or assertion, they are often required to justify the claim—to convince others that it is valid. A prosecutor who claims that a person is guilty of a crime must make an argument based on evidence to convince the jury of this claim. A scientist who asserts that the earth's atmosphere is becoming warmer must marshal evidence—usually in the form of data and accepted theories and model—to justify the claim. Every field, including the law, science, and mathematics, has its own accepted standards and rules for how a claim must be justified in order to persuade others.

When students in Grades K–5 are asked to give reasons why their mathematical claims are true, they often defend their claims as follows:

- "It worked for all the numbers we could think of."

- "I kept on trying and it kept on working."

- "We asked the sixth graders and they said it was true."

- "We asked our parents."

These are appeals to particular examples and to authority. In any field, there are appropriate times to turn to authority (a teacher or a book, for example) for help with new knowledge or with an idea that we do not yet have enough experience to think through for ourselves. Similarly, particular examples can be very helpful in understanding some phenomena. However, neither an authoritative statement nor a set of examples is sufficient to prove a mathematical assertion about an infinite class, such as all whole numbers.

In mathematics, a *theorem* must start with a mathematical assertion, which has explicit hypotheses (or "givens") and an explicit conclusion. The proof of the theorem must show how the conclusion follows logically from the hypotheses. A mathematical argument is based on logic and gives a sense of why a proposition is true. For instance, Malcolm asserted that if two numbers are odd, then their sum is an even number. In later years, Malcolm's theorem may be stated as follows: If two numbers, m and n, are both odd, then their sum, $m + n$, is an even number. The proof of this claim (see the right column) consists of a series of steps in which one begins with the hypotheses that m and n are odd numbers and forms a chain of logical deductions ending with the conclusion that $m + n$ is an even number. Each deduction must be justified by an accepted definition, fact, or principle, such as those used here—the definition of odd and even numbers and the laws of arithmetic.

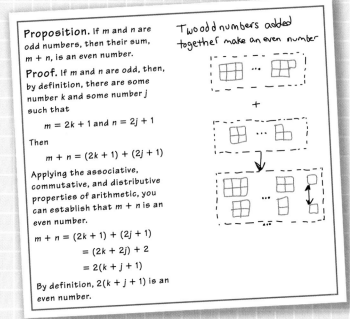

Mathematician's proof   *Tia's proof*

The model for such a notion of proof was first established by Euclid. In about 300 B.C., he codified what was known of ancient Greek geometry in his book, *Elements*. Euclid begins with the basic terms of geometry and, through hundreds of propositions and proofs, moves to beautiful and surprising theorems about geometric figures. What is remarkable is that, in each mathematical realm, you can get so far with such simple building blocks.

What Does Proof Look Like in Second Grade?

One does not expect the rigor or sophistication of a formal proof—or the use of algebraic symbolism—from young children. Even for a mathematician, precise validation is often developed *after* new mathematical ideas have been explored and are more solidly understood. When mathematical ideas are evolving and there is a need to communicate the sense of *why* a claim is true, then informal methods of proving are appropriate. Such methods can include the use of visual displays, concrete materials, or words. The test of the effectiveness of such a justification is this: Does it rely on logical thinking about the mathematical relationships, rather than on the fact that one or a few specific examples work?

Tia's argument, illustrated on the previous page, offers justification for the claim that "two odd numbers added together give an even number." The diagram shows two sets of cubes being combined. It indicates that each set has an odd number of cubes, showing pairs of cubes, with one cube left over in each set. When the two sets are combined, the two cubes that were not already paired join together to form a pair, showing that the total is an even number.

An important part of proving Malcolm's idea is Tia's claim that, at the start, her two sets of cubes represent any two odd numbers "because all odds have a leftover." Even though she has picked up particular numbers of cubes, they represent *any* two odd numbers, and the sum of the two sets *must* represent an even number. Tia's argument is not that $11 + 7 = 18$, so it works, but that *any* number with a leftover (i.e., an odd number) added to *any other* number with a leftover (i.e., another odd number) will result in a sum in which all cubes have a partner—an even number.

Proving by reasoning from representations of the operations, as these students do by joining two sets of cubes, is particularly appropriate in K–5 classrooms in which mathematical ideas are generally under construction and in which sense-making and diverse modes of reasoning are valued. Tia's argument offers justification for Malcolm's claim that if you add two odd numbers, the sum is even. It establishes the validity of the claim not only for particular numbers, but for any whole numbers, and it easily conveys *why* it is true.

To support this kind of reasoning, teachers should encourage students to use representations (cubes and number lines are good options) to explain their thinking. The use of representations offers a reference for the student who is explaining his or her reasoning, and it also allows more classmates to follow that reasoning. If it seems that students may be thinking only in terms of specific numbers, teachers may ask, "Will that work for other numbers? How do you know? Will the explanation be the same?"

Strategies for Learning the Addition Combinations

To develop efficient computation strategies, students need to become fluent with the addition combinations from $1 + 1$ to $10 + 10$. Fluency means that combinations are quickly accessible mentally, either because they are immediately known or because the calculation that is used is so effortless as to be essentially automatic (in the way that some adults quickly derive one combination from another—for example, thinking $8 + 9 = 8 + 10 - 1$). In *Investigations* students will be fluent with all of the addition combinations to $10 + 10$ by the end of Grade 2.

Why Do We Call Them Combinations?

The addition problems from $1 + 1$ through $10 + 10$ are traditionally referred to as "addition facts"—those combinations with which students are expected to be fluent. The *Investigations* curriculum follows the National Council of Teachers of Mathematics (NCTM) convention of calling these expressions *combinations* rather than *facts*. *Investigations* does this for two reasons. First, naming *only* particular addition and multiplication combinations as *facts* seems to give them elevated status and make them more important than other critical parts of mathematics.

Second, the word *fact* implies that something cannot be learned through reasoning. For example, it is a fact that the first president of the United States was George Washington, and it is a fact that Rosa Parks was born in Alabama in 1913. If these facts are important for us to know, we can remember them or use reference materials to look them up. However, the sum of the $7 + 8$ can be determined in many ways; it is logically connected to our system of numbers and operations. If we forget the sum but understand what addition is and know some related combinations, we can find the sum through reasoning. For example, if we know that $7 + 7 = 14$, we can add 1 more to get 15. If we know that $8 + 8 = 16$, we can take one away and get 15. If we know that $7 + 3 = 10$, we can then add the 5 that's left to get 15 ($7 + 8 = 7 + 3 + 5 = 15$).

The term *facts* conveys a meaning that is generally understood by some students and family members, so you might decide to use the term *facts* along with *combinations* in certain settings in order to make your meaning clear.

Learning the Addition Combinations Fluently

The *Investigations* curriculum, like NCTM, supports the importance of students' learning the basic combinations fluently through a focus on reasoning about number relationships: "Fluency with whole-number computation depends, in large part, on fluency with basic number combinations—the single-digit addition and multiplication pairs and their counterparts for subtraction and division. Fluency with basic number combinations develops from well-understood meanings for the four operations and from a focus on thinking strategies. . . ." [*Principles and Standards for School Mathematics,* pages 152–153].

In other words, students learn these combinations best by using strategies, not simply by rote memorization. Relying on memory alone is not sufficient, as many of us know from our own schooling. If you forget—as we all do at times—you are left with nothing. If, on the other hand, your learning is based on understanding of numbers and their relationships, you have a way to rethink and restructure your knowledge when you do not remember something.

Learning in Groups

Second graders will learn these combinations in groups (e.g., combinations that make 10; Plus 1, 2, or 10 combinations; doubles and near doubles) that help them learn effective strategies for finding solutions. Fluency develops through frequent and repeated use; therefore, as students work on a particular category of combinations, they play games and engage in activities that focus on those combinations. For example, in Unit 1, students reviewed the combinations that make 10 by playing *Make 10* and

Tens Go Fish, and by doing *Today's Number* for 10, or for other numbers, *using* combinations of 10.

Second graders will also be using Addition Cards to think about combinations they know and to practice those that they do not yet know. Over the course of the year, students get a set of Addition Cards for each category of combinations and sort them into two envelopes: Combinations I Know and Combinations I Am Still Working On. During Unit 1, students began to write clues that help them remember the combinations they find difficult.

Knowledge of the addition combinations should be judged by fluency in use, not necessarily by instantaneous recall. Through repeated use and familiarity, students will come to know most of the addition combinations quickly and a few others by using some quick and comfortable strategy that is based on reasoning about the numbers.

Categories of Addition Combinations

What follows is a list of the categories of combinations, sorted by the unit in which students are expected to achieve fluency with them. Note that some combinations fall into more than one category. For example, $1 + 9$ and $9 + 1$ is a Make 10 combination and a Plus 1 combination.

Counting, Coins, and Combinations

Plus 1 and Plus 2 Combinations Many children leave first grade fluent with the combinations that involve adding 1 or 2 to any single-digit number (e.g., $8 + 1$ and $7 + 2$). As your second graders come to understand that addition is commutative, they will become fluent with the reverse of those problems (e.g., $1 + 8$ and $2 + 7$).

Combinations that Make 10 These two-addend combinations of 10 were a benchmark at the end of Grade 1 and are reviewed in this unit.

Shapes, Blocks, and Symmetry

Doubles By the end of Grade 1, many children know their doubles combinations up to $5 + 5$. *Counting, Coins, and Combinations* introduces these combinations up to $10 + 10$.

Students practice and become fluent with these combinations in *Shapes, Blocks, and Symmetry*.

Stickers, Number Strings, and Story Problems

Near Doubles (Or, Doubles Plus or Minus 1) Students learn these combinations—those that are one more or one less than the doubles—by relating them to the doubles.

Pockets, Teeth, and Favorite Things

Plus 10 Combinations As students work on ideas in place value, they learn the Plus 10 combinations—all of the single-digit numbers (and 10) plus 10.

Partners, Teams, and Paper Clips

Plus 9 Combinations Students learn these combinations —all of the single-digit numbers (and 10), plus 9—by relating them to the Plus 10 combinations.

Remaining Combinations Eight combinations remain.

$3 + 5$ and $5 + 3$	$4 + 7$ and $7 + 4$
$3 + 6$ and $6 + 3$	$4 + 8$ and $8 + 4$
$3 + 8$ and $8 + 3$	$5 + 7$ and $7 + 5$
$5 + 8$ and $8 + 5$	$6 + 8$ and $8 + 6$

For students who are fluent with Doubles Plus or Minus 1, several are Doubles Plus or Minus 2. For students who are fluent with their Combinations that Make 10, and with breaking apart numbers, most problems can be solved quickly ($7 + 5 \rightarrow 7 + 3 + 2$). Similarly, students can use their knowledge of Combinations that Make 10 to solve Near 10 combinations ($6 + 3$, $7 + 4$, $8 + 3$).

Students should review the addition combinations that they have mastered throughout the year to maintain fluency.

Students' Subtraction Strategies

As students work on the activities in Investigation 3, you will see a wide range of understanding of the operation of subtraction. By the end of Grade 2, all students should have at least one strategy for accurately solving subtraction problems involving 2-digit numbers and notating their work. Students will vary in terms of efficiency and flexibility. Some work quite efficiently, completing a problem in just a few steps, and others make many small jumps. (At this point, students should no longer be counting by ones.) Some are quite flexible, choosing a strategy that fits the numbers in the problem, and others use one strategy exclusively.

Consider this problem:

> *Kira and Sally were playing* Cover Up *with 52 counters. Kira hid some of the counters, and then 29 were showing. How many counters did Kira hide?*

Students' strategies for subtracting to solve this problem fall into three basic categories.

Subtracting in Parts

At the end of Grade 2, many students see this problem as removing 29 from 52. There are several ways that they subtract the 29.

Some students, like Juan, use stickers or cubes to show 52, cross out or separate a group of 29, and then count how many are left. These students should be encouraged to use sticker notation to record their work and to add numbers and then use equations to explain what they did with the stickers or cubes.

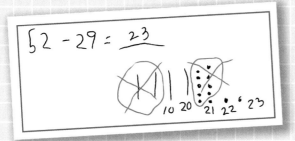

Juan's Work

Others break the 29 into parts and use equations and/or tools, such as the number line or 100 chart, to subtract it. Many break the 29 apart by place. Henry subtracts 20 and then 9. Amaya subtracts 10, then 10, and then 9.

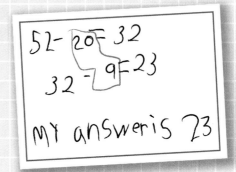

Henry's Work

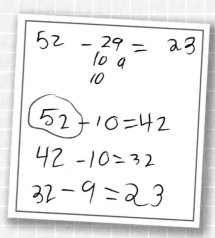

Amaya's Work

Others, like Gregory, subtract 2 to get to 50 (a multiple of 10). Then they subtract 10s (or a multiple of 10, such as 20) and any remaining 1s (in this case, 7).

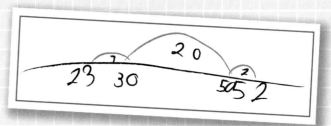

Gregory's Work

These students should be working to subtract the largest parts possible while still making sense of the problem and the numbers. For example, Amaya should be working toward subtracting multiples of 10 (e.g., 20) in one step.

Adding Up or Subtracting Back to Find the Difference

At the end of second grade, many students add up to find the difference between the two numbers in a subtraction problem. They see the problem as 29 + _____ = 52 and solve it by figuring out how much they need to add to 29 to get to 52.

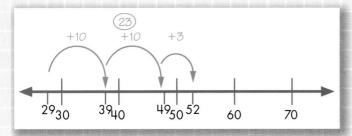

A few students see the problem similarly but use subtraction to find the difference between 52 and 29. They think 52 − _____ = 29, and solve it by figuring out how much they need to subtract from 52 to get to 29.

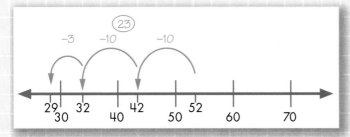

Some students may not necessarily think about adding up or subtracting back. Instead, like Melissa, they locate the numbers on the number line, label the space between them in useful parts, and combine those amounts to find the difference between them.

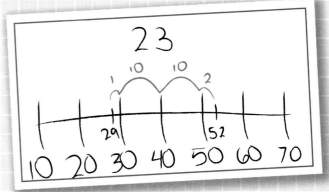

Melissa's Work

Keep in mind that students may use stickers, the number line, 100 chart, equations, or some combination of models as they work with this strategy, and that the amounts they add or subtract will differ. What all of the strategies in this category have in common is that they are finding the difference between 29 and 52.

I used the 100 chart

$29 + 1 = 30$

$30 + 20 = 50$

$50 + 2 = 52$

$2 + 1 + 20 = 23$

Carolina's Work

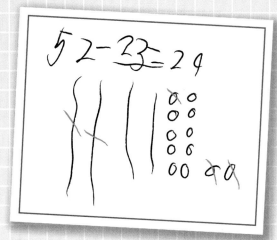

Chen's Work

$$52 - 10 = 42$$
$$42 - 10 = 32$$
$$32 - 2 = 30$$
$$30 - 1 = 29$$

$$10 + 10 + 2 + 1 = 23$$

Paige's Work

$$52 - \_ = 29$$

$$52 - 2 = 50$$
$$50 - 20 = 30$$
$$30 - 1 \quad 29$$

$$2 + 20 + 1 = 23$$

Travis's Work

As when they are subtracting in parts, students who are adding up or subtracting back should be using groups rather than counting by ones and should be moving toward a more efficient strategy. For example, those who are counting up or back by tens should be working to add or subtract multiples of 10, in this case, 20.

A note about adding up (or subtracting back) vs. subtracting in parts Modeling these strategies on the number line can highlight how they are different. When students subtract in parts, they start at 52, subtract 29, and land on their answer, 23.

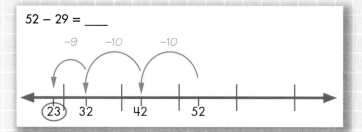

Subtracting in parts

When students add up or subtract back, their answer is the difference between the two numbers.

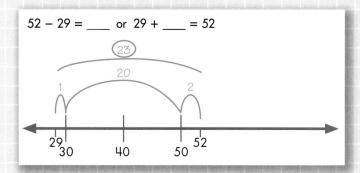

Adding up or subtracting back

It is important to help students see where the answer lies in these different strategies and why.

Other Strategies

At the end of Grade 2, a few students may use strategies that do not fall into either of the above categories.

Some students use strategies that rely on something they already know. For example, they add 1 to each number, maintaining the difference between them, to create an easier, equivalent problem (53 − 30). Others add or subtract 30 and then figure out how to compensate.

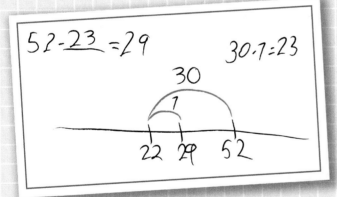

Alberto's Work

Yama's Work

Because many students use the strategy of adding by place successfully and efficiently, some assume that this strategy will work as efficiently with subtraction. Subtracting by place is fairly straightforward when there are more ones in the total amount than in the number to be subtracted; for example, 45 − 23. Students may think, "40 − 20 = 20, 5 − 3 = 2, and 20 + 2 = 22." However, when there are

more ones in the number to be subtracted, as in 45 − 27, students must think carefully about the amounts they are working with to subtract by place. If students are able to apply some of the work they have been doing in *Today's Number,* they may think, "45 is the same as 30 + 15, so 30 − 20 = 10 and 15 − 7 = 8." If they have some understanding of negative numbers or think of 5 − 7 as "owing 2," they can then proceed with 40 − 20 = 20, 5 − 7 = −2, and 20 + −2 = 18.

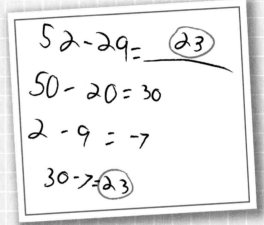

Monisha's Work

It is likely that some second graders will experiment with the U.S. standard algorithm for subtraction. Unlike the U.S. standard algorithm for addition, which is closely related to adding tens and ones, the subtraction algorithm does not closely resemble the typical second-grade strategies discussed in this Teacher Note.

Although a few students may be able to use this strategy with understanding, many see and use it as a series of steps they have memorized rather than relying on what they know about the numbers in the problem and the operation of subtraction. Students who misapply standard algorithms should focus on more accessible strategies for solving subtraction problems and notating their work. Students will have an opportunity to study the U.S. standard algorithm for subtraction in Grade 5.

Flexibility

At the end of Grade 2, some students have only one subtraction strategy that they use with understanding and are still working to use it efficiently. Others are comfortable enough with several strategies to choose a method based on the structure of the problem or the numbers in it. For example, you may see students who do the following:

- Count up if the numbers are close, but count back if they are far apart

- Almost always add up, unless the problem involves numbers close to landmark numbers such as 25 or 50

- Subtract in parts for a removal or "take away" problem, but add up for a problem about a missing part

A few students may be able to use several or all of the above strategies with understanding. They are developing fluency with the operation of subtraction—they have strategies that are accurate and efficient and they are flexible in their use.

However, the goal for the end of Grade 2 is that students have an understanding of the operation of subtraction, an ability to visualize a variety of situations that involve finding the difference between two quantities, and at least one accurate strategy for solving such problems. This foundation is built on in Grade 3 as students work to develop and refine subtraction strategies that are accurate and efficient.

Notation

All students should be able to write an equation that represents what a problem is asking, but second graders often use a variety of notational systems to solve problems and record their work, such as numbers, equations, the number line, and stickers as a model for representing the place value of our base-ten number system. See **Teacher Note:** Notating Subtraction Strategies, page 163.

Notating Subtraction Strategies

A challenge that students face as they develop and refine their strategies for subtraction in Grade 2 and beyond is finding clear and efficient ways to communicate their mathematical thinking on paper. Second graders have several models and representations available to them as they record their work, including drawings, the 100 chart, the number line, sticker notation, numbers, and equations.

Drawing All and Removing Some

A few students may draw all in a way that does not make efficient use of groups, cross out the amount subtracted, and then count those that remain. This is a time-consuming strategy for solving 2-digit subtraction problems and recording work. For example, Anita solves 48 – 24 by drawing 48 circles, crossing out 24, and counting those that remain. This strategy entails a great deal of counting and recounting.

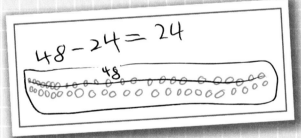

Anita's Work

Malcolm used a more efficient strategy to solve the problem. He used cubes in towers of 10, but when faced with the task of recording his work, he drew individual cubes—a challenging and time-consuming drawing task.

Malcolm's Work

Help students like Anita see how they can use cubes in towers of 10 or sets of paper stickers to represent the 48 and remove the 24 more efficiently. Encourage all students in this category to consider using sticker notation to record their work.

Sticker Notation

Many second graders use stickers or cubes in towers of 10 to solve subtraction problems. Using sticker notation to record what they did can be challenging, particularly when the number to be subtracted has more ones than the number they are subtracting from. Ending up with 10 too many, as Katrina and Esteban did, is a common error.

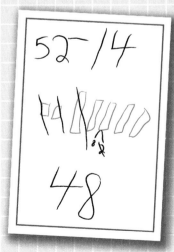

Katrina's Work

Esteban's Work

These students forget to cross out the strip of 10 when they break it into parts or trade it in for 10 singles. For example, Esteban draws 45 stickers and crosses out two strips and five singles. Because he still needs to subtract 2, he breaks one of the remaining strips into 2 and 8 and crosses out the 2. When he counts the stickers that remain, he counts that strip as both a 10 *and* an 8 because he did not cross it out when he broke it up. Therefore, he ends up with an answer of 28 (10 + 10 + 8) instead of 18. Ask these students to explain the steps they took to solve the problem so that you can discuss what happens with them at this point in the problem.

Also be on the lookout for students who painstakingly show every step and/or every amount in the form of stickers. For example, Juan adds up to solve 60 − 28. He shows that 28 + 2 = 30 and 30 + 30 = 60. Therefore, 28 + 32 = 60.

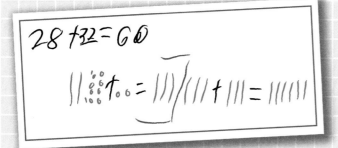

Juan's Work

As Juan becomes more fluent with this strategy and sees it modeled by his teacher and other students, he will develop more efficient ways of using stickers and then equations to represent his work.

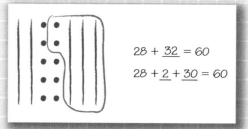

$$28 + \underline{32} = 60$$
$$28 + \underline{2} + \underline{30} = 60$$

Although not expected of students, be sure that when you use stickers to model strategies for the class, you do so step by step. For example, Jeffrey works through four steps as he uses stickers to represent his strategy for subtracting 14 from 42.

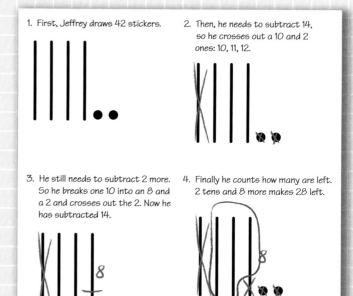

1. First, Jeffrey draws 42 stickers.

2. Then, he needs to subtract 14, so he crosses out a 10 and 2 ones: 10, 11, 12.

3. He still needs to subtract 2 more. So he breaks one 10 into an 8 and a 2 and crosses out the 2. Now he has subtracted 14.

4. Finally he counts how many are left. 2 tens and 8 more makes 28 left.

The image shown in Step 4 alone should be considered a complete piece of student work; it contains all the steps Jeffrey went through.

The 100 Chart

Many students who use the 100 chart (or a sheet of 100 stickers) to solve subtraction problems have difficulty recording what they did on paper. Some say, "I used a 100 chart" or "I counted on the 100 chart." Others try to draw the chart in whole or part. Encourage these students to describe the math of their strategy in writing; for example, "You said you counted on the 100 chart. *How* did you count? Did you count by ones? By tens?"

When students can do that, focus on helping them write equations and on connecting those equations to the jumps they are making on the 100 chart. For example, when the teacher visited Melissa, she was using a page in a sticker book to solve 38 + _____ = 65. After helping Melissa see that she did not need to fill in every number and working through the problem with her, the teacher helped her use equations to record her work by asking questions such as, "So you added up to find the difference between 38 and 65. You said you started at 38 and jumped 10. Where did you land? What did you do next?"

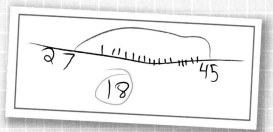

Melissa's Work

The Number Line

Many second graders use the number line to solve subtraction problems and to show how they solved them. For some students, drawing and labeling a number line and then showing a solution on it can be a challenging fine-motor task. For that reason, some teachers provide small prepared number lines for students to use to record their work.

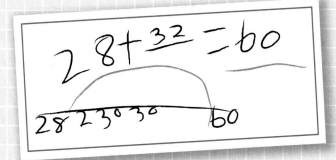

Nate's Work

For other students, the challenge is showing how they subtracted or added up, how they know they subtracted or added all that they needed to, and how to make their answer clear—all in such a way that someone else can read and understand their strategy. For example, to solve 60 – 28, Darren added up to find the difference. He thought, "28 + 2 = 30 and then 30 + 30 = 60. So, I had to add 32 to 28 to get 60."

Darren's Work

Darren is still learning the conventions of recording a strategy on the number line. Seeing his strategy modeled by his teacher and by classmates who use the number line will help him develop clearer methods for recording his work.

Numbers, Equations, and Vertical Notation

At this point in the year, many students use numbers and equations to show their strategies. There are some typical issues to look for as students use numbers and equations to record their work.

The run-on sentence Because students have been thinking about the meaning of the equal sign all year long, particularly during the course of *Today's Number,* you should not see many who record in this way.

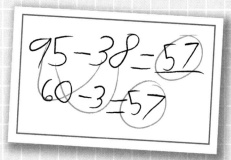

Tia's Work

It is clear that Tia is saying she subtracted 10 from 62 and then 7 from 52, but 62 – 10 does *not* equal 52 – 7. Question students who record in such a way, focusing on equality and what the equal sign means. For example, "I see here that you have an equation that says 62 – 10 = 52 – 7. Does 62 – 10 *equal* 52 – 7?"

Lines, carets, and arrows Some students who use lines, carets, or arrows to show their strategy for adding 2-digit numbers try to transfer that strategy to subtracting 2-digit numbers. As with addition, clarity and efficiency can be a problem with these recording methods. Subtraction, however, presents an additional difficulty.

Travis's Work

Although Travis's work looks neat, gives a pretty clear sense of his strategy, and gives the right answer, consider the explanation he gave his teacher (90 – 30 = 60, 8 – 5 = 3, and 60 – 3 = 57). For this reason, encourage these students to use horizontal equations, and do not use lines, carets, and arrows to model strategies for the class.

Vertical notation It is important that students be comfortable solving subtraction problems presented either horizontally or vertically by the end of Grade 2. Vertical notation does not suggest a particular strategy. Students should not see the way a problem is presented as a directive to carry out a particular strategy. Be on the lookout for students who believe that when they see a problem written vertically, they must carry out a particular algorithm rather than consider what they know about the numbers in the problem.

Most students record their strategies by using one of the above methods and/or horizontal equations. If you have students who are experimenting with ways to use vertical notation to record their strategies, there are some common issues to watch for. For example, Yama subtracts 10 from 50 and gets 40. She writes 4 in the tens place and then considers the ones. Because she cannot subtract 4 from 2, she subtracts 2, writes 0 in the ones place, and reminds herself that she still needs to subtract 2 more by writing another 2 to the right of the original problem. Then she subtracts that 2 from the 40 and gets her answer of 38.

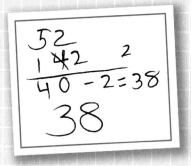

Yama's Work

Students like Yama compute accurately and use a strategy that is mathematically sound and makes sense to them. However, they need support finding a way to record their work clearly and efficiently.

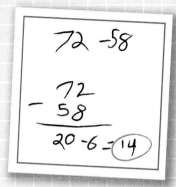

Simon's Work

Simon uses vertical notation to record a strategy much like Travis's.

$$72 - 58 =$$

$$70 - 50 = 20$$

$$2 - 8 = -6$$

$$20 + -6 = 14$$

Ask students who use this notation to explain how they solved the problem. Many students give problematic explanations like Travis's. Others may say, "70 − 50 = 20. You can't take 8 from 5, so that's 0. So my answer is 20." These strategies highlight the issues that come up when subtracting by place and the difficulty second graders have making sense of it.

Other students who use vertical notation are attempting to use the U.S. standard algorithm for subtraction.

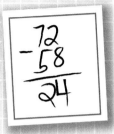

Alberto's Work

When you find students who are misapplying this strategy or using it without meaning, help them make sense of and practice a strategy that relies on what they know about the operation of subtraction and the quantities in the problem and offers a clear and efficient way to notate their work, such as subtracting in parts or adding up.

Assessment: Paper Clips and Cherries

Benchmark addressed:

Benchmark 1: Subtract 2-digit numbers.

In order to meet the benchmark, students' work should show that they can:

• Write an addition or subtraction equation that shows what a problem is asking;

• Compute accurately; subtract or add up in parts;

• Record their work.

Some students subtract in parts, some add up or subtract back to find the difference, and others use a fact they know to make the problem easier. They also use a variety of methods—equations, stickers, and the number line—to show their work.

Meeting the Benchmark

Subtracting in parts Some students subtract 36 from 100 or 14 from 52 in parts. Some use stickers or other representations of groups of ten to show the original amount; they cross out the amount subtracted and then figure out how many are left.

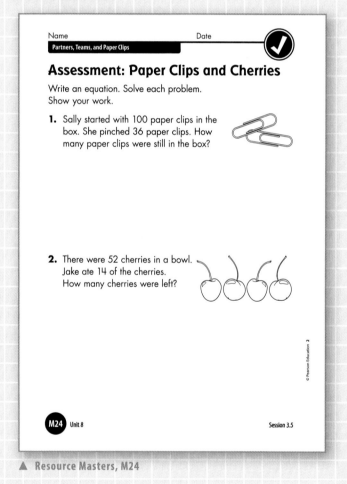

▲ Resource Masters, M24

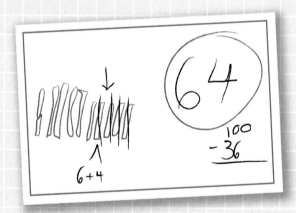

Juanita's Work

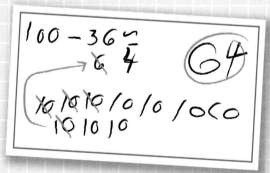

Esteban's Work

Others use the 100 chart or equations and/or the number line.

$$100 - 36 = 64$$
$$100 - 10 = 90$$
$$90 - 10 = 80$$
$$80 - 10 = 70$$
$$70 - 6 = 64$$

Paige's Work

$$100 - 36 = \underline{64}$$

$$100 - 30 = 70$$
$$70 - 6 = 64$$

Jacy's Work

$$52 - 14 = 38$$
$$10 \,\widehat{\,}\, 4$$

$$52 - 10 = 42$$
$$42 - 4 = 38$$

Darren's Work

Adding up or subtracting back to find the difference

Some students find the difference between 36 and 100 or 14 and 52 either by counting up or subtracting back. Again, they use a variety of tools and recording methods.

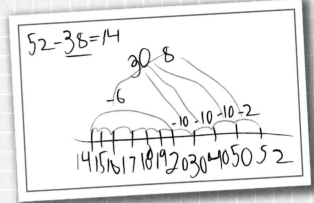

$$52 - 38 = 14$$

Luis's Work

$$36 + \!\!\text{\large\textcircled{64}}\!\! = 100$$

$$36 + \text{(bars)}\,\text{oooo} = 100$$

Anita's Work

$$100 - 36 = 64$$

$$36 \quad 40 \quad\quad\quad 100$$

Roshaun's Work

$$36 + \underline{64} = 100$$

$$36 + 4 = 40$$
$$40 + 60 = 100$$

Jeffrey's Work

Using something you know A few students may use an addition or subtraction problem they know to solve the problem.

Carla thought of the problem as 36 + _____ = 100. She knew that 30 + 70 = 100. If you take 6 from the 70 and give it to the 30, you have 36 + <u>64</u> = 100.

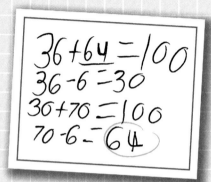

Carla's Work

Instead of subtracting 14 from 52, Simon subtracted 14 from 50 and then added the 2 back in because it was not part of the group that was being subtracted. (Imagine that you have a $50 bill and two $1 bills and that you use the $50 to pay for a $14 item.) Be sure to ask students who use this strategy how they knew to add the 2. Many second graders have trouble figuring out whether to add or subtract the 2 in this situation.

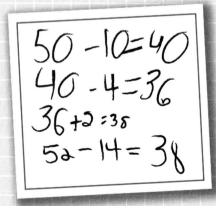

Simon's Work

Partially Meeting the Benchmark

Some students understand the structure of the problems but make errors as they count and keep track of the quantities.

Juan accurately shows 52 and crosses out 14, but he does not give one number to each remaining dot and ends up with an answer that is one off.

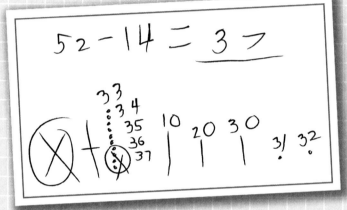

Juan's Work

Leigh accurately represents 52, but she forgets to cross out the ten that she trades in. So she ends up with an answer that is 10 too many.

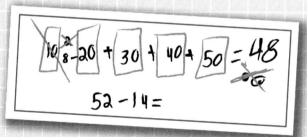

Leigh's Work

Note whether these kinds of errors are consistent across problems or more of a one-time occurrence. After reviewing their work, talk with these students to see whether they can find and correct such errors on their own and to decide whether such errors are a mark of quick and careless work or a mathematical misunderstanding.

Not Meeting the Benchmark

Some students understand the structure of the problem but use strategies that are inefficient and error-prone, such as counting back by ones or using ones to directly model the problem.

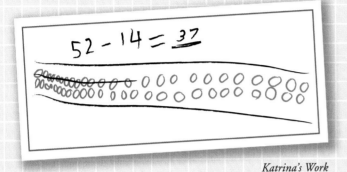

Katrina's Work

Nate's Work

Students who use these strategies do not meet the benchmark for this unit even if they get the right answer. However, it is important to consider each student's growth. Successfully solving this problem may represent a high level of work for a particular student. Support these students in

learning to work more efficiently. Encourage students who use or draw ones to use cubes in towers of 10 or stickers to model the problem and sticker notation to record their work. Help students who are counting back by ones see what happens when you subtract 10 from any number. For example, ask, "You said that you would start on 100 on the 100 chart and then count back 36. What if you started on 100 and subtracted 10? Where would you land?" The Daily Practice activities on *Student Activity Book* pages 19 and 59 provide further work with this idea.

Other students may be able to write an equation that represents the problem but do not have accurate strategies for computing. Their work does not give evidence of how they are thinking about the problem.

Leo's Work

Leo sets out the problem accurately but attempts to subtract by place. He is stumped by a problem that asks him to subtract 4 from 2. He arrives at the answer of 40 because he thinks, "Two minus 4 is 0 because you can't take 4 from 2."

It is important to talk with students like Leo to get a sense of what they do and do not understand about this problem. Can they retell the problem and visualize the action? Can they model it with stickers or cubes? If so, help them notate their steps, using horizontal equations. If you have students who cannot make sense of the action of the problem, spend time working on modeling and solving subtraction problems with smaller numbers.

Students' Addition Strategies

As students work on the activities in Investigation 4, you will see a wide range of understanding of the operation of addition. By the end of Grade 2, all students should be fluent with at least one strategy for solving 2-digit addition problems and notating their work. In Grade 2, fluency means that they have a strategy that they understand, that is efficient and accurate, and that works to solve addition problems with totals to just over 100. At this point, efficiency means that students are not counting on by ones. Students will vary in terms of flexibility; some are quite flexible, choosing a strategy based on the numbers in the problem, and others use one strategy exclusively.

Students' strategies for addition fall into three basic categories. Note that at this point in the year, it is assumed that students understand that addition is commutative and, therefore, that they can solve the following problem as 66 + 52 or 52 + 66:

> Franco had 66 car stickers. Jake gave him 52 car stickers. How many car stickers does Franco have now?

Keeping One Number Whole

At the end of Grade 2, many students keep one number whole and add the other one *in parts*. Fluency with this strategy means that students add on the other number in parts; that is, they do not count on by ones. Some students add on by place, adding the tens first and then the ones. They may add each ten in the number, as Chen and Carla did, or all of the tens at once, as Darren did. Others are more comfortable adding on to a number that is a multiple of 10, as Simon did. They add on enough to the other number to get to a multiple of 10 and then proceed.

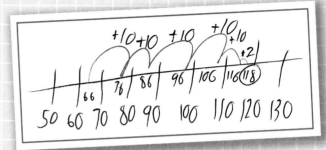

Chen's Work

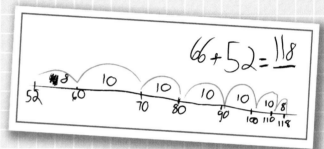

Carla's Work

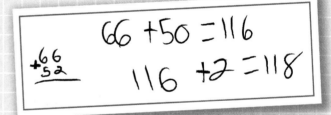

Darren's Work

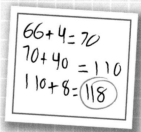

Simon's Work

Students should be working to add the largest parts possible while still making sense of the problem and the numbers. For example, students who are adding each individual group of 10 should be working to add multiples of 10, such as 50 or 60.

Adding Tens and Ones

At the end of Grade 2, many students add by place to combine 2-digit numbers. Whether they use a place-value model (e.g., the sticker notation used by Holly) or equations, these students break both numbers into tens and ones. Most combine the tens first, a strategy that provides useful information about the approximate size of the total. Their second step varies. Some, like Esteban, combine the ones (6 + 2) and then the subtotals (110 + 8), and others, like Henry, add each group of ones, one by one, onto the total (110 + 2 = 112, 112 + 6 = 118).

Holly's Work

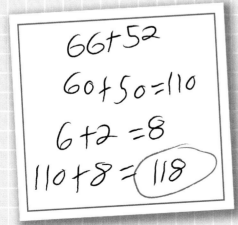

Esteban's Work

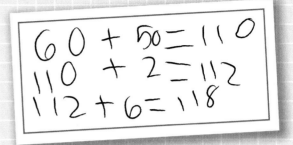

Henry's Work

Some students may use a place-value strategy but add the ones first and then the tens. There are several ways that students notate this strategy, including the U.S. standard algorithm for addition.

$$6 + 2 = 8$$
$$60 + 50 = 110$$
$$110 + 8 = 118$$

$$\begin{array}{r} 66 \\ + 52 \\ \hline 8 \\ + 110 \\ \hline 118 \end{array}$$

$$\begin{array}{r} 66 \\ + 52 \\ \hline 118 \end{array}$$

Use vertical notation to model adding tens and ones, but we do suggest that, for demonstration purposes, teachers record what was added (e.g., 60 + 50 =) to help students make sense of both the strategy and the notation.

$$\begin{array}{r} 66 \\ + 52 \\ \hline 110 \quad (60 + 50) \\ + 8 \quad (6 + 2) \\ \hline 118 \end{array}$$

Some students use vertical notation to record. As you model their strategies, emphasize that you are doing this for demonstration purposes. Students who use vertical notation do not need to write this extra information when they record.

The U.S. "carrying" algorithm, which some second grade students may be familiar with, is also an example of adding by place. Rather than beginning with the largest place, as students often do naturally, this algorithm begins with the smallest place. It includes a shorthand way of notating the value of numbers as the digits in each place are added. For many second graders, the compressed notation of this algorithm can obscure both the place value of the numbers and the meaning of each step of the procedure. This can lead to a more rote approach to solving addition problems, while students are still solidifying their understanding of the base-ten number system and the operation of adding in Grade 2—steps in students' development of computational fluency that take time and practice.

After students have developed good, efficient algorithms that they understand and can carry out easily, such as adding by place, some may also become fluent in the traditional or standard algorithm. Others will continue to use adding by place or adding on in parts fluently, which will also serve them well for their computation needs now and as adults. The U.S. "carrying" algorithm is not addressed directly in Grade 2, although some students may be able to use it with understanding. Note that the vertical notation of adding by place value shown on the previous page, in which the ones are added first, is closely related to the steps in the standard algorithm but makes these steps more transparent. When students use the standard algorithm, demonstrate this form of notation and help students compare the two. Students who use the standard algorithm should also learn other strategies that demonstrate their flexibility with and understanding of addition. The U.S. algorithm is included in a study of strategies for addition in Grade 4.

Changing the Numbers to Make an Equivalent Problem

At the end of Grade 2, a few students may "take" an amount from one of the addends and "give" it to the other addend, creating an equivalent problem that is easier to solve. For example, Jacy takes six from the 66 and gives it to the 52.

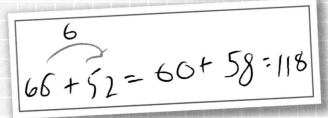

Jacy's Work

Similarly, Nadia takes 2 from the 52 and gives it to the 66, and Lonzell takes 4 from the 52 to turn 66 into 70.

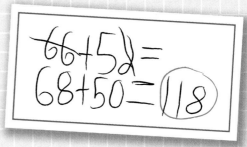

Nadia's Work

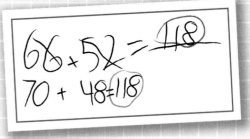

Lonzell's Work

Depending on how this strategy is conceptualized and carried out, it can also be seen as a variation of keeping one number whole and adding the other on in parts.

$$66 + 52$$
$$66 + 4 = 70$$
$$70 + 48 = 118$$

In Grades 3 and 4, students will study this strategy and others in more depth.

Other Strategies

There are a few other strategies to watch for. For example, depending on the numbers in a particular problem, some students change one or both of the numbers, or work with nearby friendly or landmark numbers, and then compensate for the changes. For example, consider these students' work with $66 + 52$.

66 + 52
70 + 52 = 122
I added 4 too many, so
subtract 4
122 - 4 = 118

Juanita's Work

66 + 52 = 118

If it was 50+50 that would = 100 but there
was an extra 10 from the 66 and that would
ouyel 110 and 6 +2 ayels 8 and
8+10 = 18 so add a hundred and you get 118.

Nate's Work

To some, Juanita's strategy seems similar to changing the numbers to create an equivalent problem, and Nate's looks like a variation of adding by place. It is not important that everyone agree on categorizing student strategies; rather it is important that the strategy be accurate, efficient, and understandable to the student.

Flexibility

At the end of Grade 2, some students can use only one of the above strategies fluently. Others are comfortable enough with several strategies to choose a method based on the structure of the problem or the numbers in it. For example, you may see a student who adds on one number in parts when combining a large number and a small number but who otherwise adds by place, or you may see a student who always adds by place unless the problem involves numbers close to landmark numbers, such as 25 or 50. Developing fluency with all these strategies is a focus of the Grade 3 work on addition.

Notation

All students should be able to write an equation (horizontally or vertically) that represents a given problem situation and interpret and solve a problem presented in either horizontal or vertical form. However, second graders often use a variety of notational systems—including numbers, equations, the number line, and stickers as a model for representing the place value of our base-ten number system—to solve problems and record their work. See **Teacher Note:** Notating Addition Strategies, page 176 for more information.

Notating Addition Strategies

One challenge students face as they refine and consolidate their strategies for addition in Grade 2 and beyond is finding ways to communicate their mathematical thinking on paper that are clear and efficient. Second graders have several models and representations available to them as they record their work, including the 100 chart, number line, sticker notation, numbers, and equations—written both horizontally and vertically.

The 100 Chart

At this point in the year, students should be moving away from using the 100 chart to solve problems. For example, most students should "just know" that $48 + 10 = 58$ without finding 48 on the 100 chart and moving down one row. However, some students may need this tool to orient and organize themselves and their thinking, and a few may still need this support to solve problems. Many of these students have difficulty recording what they did on paper. Some say, "I used the 100 chart" or "I counted on the 100 chart." Others try to draw the 100 chart—in whole or in part. Still others include a description of their strategy, "I started at 48 and added on 33."

Encourage students to describe the math of their strategy in writing; for example, "You said you counted on the 100 chart. *How* did you count? Did you count by ones? By tens?" The real focus, however, should be on helping students write equations and helping them connect those equations to the jumps they are making on the 100 chart; for example, "You said that you started at 48 and then jumped 10. Where did you land? What did you do next?"

$$48 + 33 = 81$$
$$48 + 10 + 10 + 10 + 3 = 81$$

I used the 100 chart.
I first was on 48 + 10 + 10 + 10 + 3
that's how I got to 81.

Luis's Work

$$48 + 33 = ?$$
$$48 + 2 \, ⓪ \, 31 = 81$$

I went to 48 on the 100's bord. Then I took away 2 from 33 to make 50 with 48. That left me with 31. Then I added on 30 to 50 that brout me to 80. Then I just added on 1 and my answer is 81.

Carolina's Work

The Number Line

Many second graders use the number line to solve addition problems and to show how they solved them. The number line is a particularly useful tool for using and representing the strategy of keeping one number whole. For some students, drawing and labeling a number line and then showing a solution on it can be a challenging fine-motor task. For others, the challenge lies in showing how they added on the other number, showing how they know that they added on all of it, and making their answer clear—all in such a way that someone else can read and understand their strategy. For example, to solve 48 + 33, Gregory kept the 48 whole and added on the 33 in chunks of 2, 10, 10, 10, and 1 (48 + 2 + 10 + 10 + 10 + 1). He shows that the 3 tens make 30, 2 and 1 makes 3, 30 and 3 makes 33, and his answer is 81.

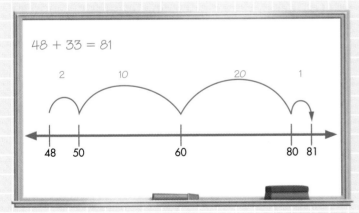

Gregory's Work

Although perhaps difficult to interpret at first glance, this sample is quite complete. As Gregory becomes more fluent with this strategy, and as he sees it modeled by his teacher and other students, he will trust that the amount added on can be seen in his jumps and that his answer is the amount recorded in his equation.

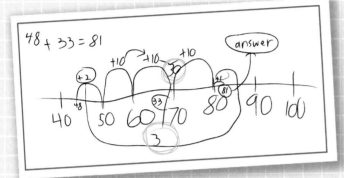

Sticker Notation

Many second graders use sticker strips and singles (or cubes in towers of 10) to solve addition problems efficiently and accurately. These tools are particularly effective for adding by place. But using sticker notation to record what they did can be challenging and cumbersome. Some students painstakingly show *every* step and draw out every amount in the form of stickers.

For example, Amaya shows 49 and 14 and then combines the tens (10 + 40 = 50). Then she takes a 1 from the 4 (4 − 1 = 3) and gives it to the 9 to make another 10 (9 + 1 = 10). She adds that 10 to the others (50 + 10 = 60) and then adds the 3 ones that are still left (60 + 3 = 63).

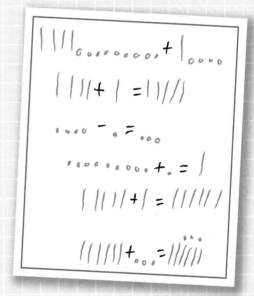

Amaya's Work

Again, this is a very complete description. As Amaya becomes more fluent with this strategy and sees it modeled by her teacher and other students, she will develop more efficient ways of using stickers and then equations to represent her work.

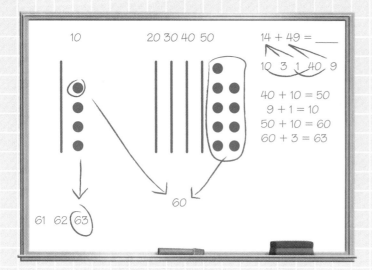

Numbers, Equations, and Vertical Notation

At this point in the year, most students use numbers and equations, in both horizontal and vertical form, to show their strategies. There are some typical issues to look for as students use numbers and equations to record their work.

The run-on sentence Because students have been thinking about the meaning of the equal sign all year long, particularly during their work on *Today's Number,* you should not see many who record in this way.

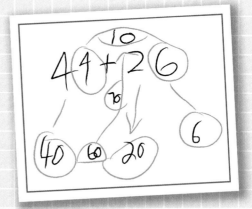

Alberto's Work

It is clear that Alberto is saying that he added (49 + 1) + 10, but 49 + 1 does *not* equal 50 + 10. Question students who record in such a way. Focus on equality and what the equal sign means. For example, "I see here that you have an equation that says 49 + 1 = 50 + 10. Does 49 + 1 *equal* 50 + 10?"

Lines, carets, and arrows Some students use lines, carets, or arrows to clearly and efficiently show their strategy for adding 2-digit numbers. Like Travis, they keep track of the place value of the numbers, and both their steps and answer are clear.

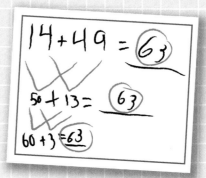

Travis's Work

Note that although carets can be a clear and efficient method for recording addition strategies, using carets becomes far more complicated and problematic when subtracting. For this reason—and because the field of mathematics agrees on certain notational conventions—all students should move toward using horizontal equations or vertical notation, with meaning, as they are ready.

Some students "try on" these methods of recording and use them accurately, but it is harder for others to clearly see and make sense of their strategies.

Anita's Work

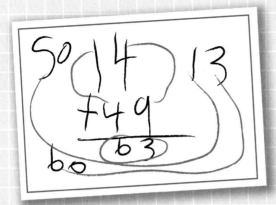

Lonzell's Work

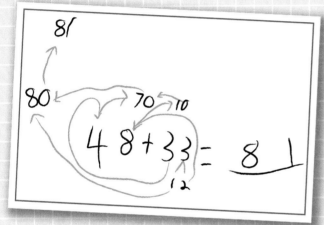

Malcolm's Work

Vertical notation It is important that students be comfortable with both vertical and horizontal notation by the end of Grade 2. Students should see both kinds of notation as efficient ways to record a problem and its solution, not as a directive to carry out a particular strategy. Some students believe that when they see a problem written in the vertical form, they must carry out a particular algorithm rather than consider what they know about the numbers in the problem. *Investigations* students are often more familiar with horizontal equations. Therefore, as they begin to see and use vertical notation, there are some common problems to watch for.

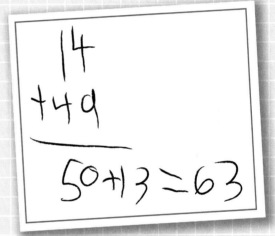

Katrina's Work

These students need support in developing clearer ways to record their strategies. Anita and Malcolm should be encouraged to use equations to show their steps, and Lonzell may benefit from a modified version of the standard algorithm's vertical notation.

$$\begin{array}{r} 14 \\ + \ 49 \\ \hline 50 \\ + \ 13 \\ \hline 63 \end{array}$$

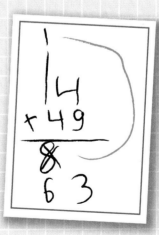

Leo's Work

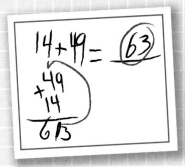

Paige's Work

These students compute accurately, but they need help finding ways to notate what happens to the extra group of ten. Consider modeling the slightly expanded form of the conventional notation to ensure that students understand the steps they are taking before teaching them the standard algorithm's notation.

$$
\begin{array}{r}
14 \\
+\ 49 \\
\hline
13 \\
+\ 50 \\
\hline
63
\end{array}
\qquad
\begin{array}{r}
1 \\
14 \\
+\ 49 \\
\hline
63
\end{array}
$$

Some second-grade students can use the U.S. standard algorithm and its notation with understanding. This is fine, although they are also expected to understand and be able to use other strategies and notations. Others misapply it and end with answers that do not make sense. These students may treat each number individually $(1 + 4 + 4 + 9)$ or not know what to do when the ones add to more than 10.

$$
\begin{array}{r}
14 \\
+\ 49 \\
\hline
513
\end{array}
\qquad
\begin{array}{r}
10 \\
14 \\
+\ 49 \\
\hline
153
\end{array}
$$

Bring these students back to the context and the action of the problem. Encourage them to model the problem and to make sense of and practice a strategy—such as adding by place or adding on one number in parts—that relies on what they know about the operation of addition and the quantities in the problem and offers a clear and efficient way to notate their work.

Teacher Note

End-of-Unit Assessment

Problems 1–3

Benchmark addressed:

Benchmark 2: Reason about partners, teams, and leftovers to make and justify generalizations about what happens when even and odd numbers are added.

In order to meet the benchmark, students' work should show that they can:

- Determine whether adding different combinations of even and odd numbers results in an even or odd sum;

- Provide evidence—based on partners, teams, and leftovers—that explains or shows *why* adding different combinations of even and odd numbers results in an even or odd sum.

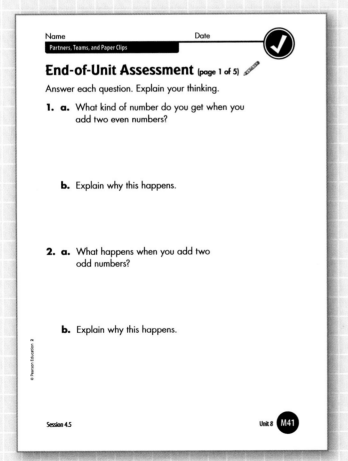

Name _____ Date _____

Partners, Teams, and Paper Clips

End-of-Unit Assessment (page 1 of 5)

Answer each question. Explain your thinking.

1. a. What kind of number do you get when you add two even numbers?

b. Explain why this happens.

2. a. What happens when you add two odd numbers?

b. Explain why this happens.

Session 4.5   Unit 8 M41

© Pearson Education 2

▲ **Resource Masters, M41**

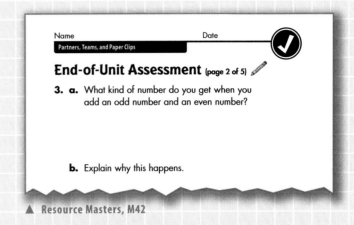

Name _____ Date _____

Partners, Teams, and Paper Clips

End-of-Unit Assessment (page 2 of 5)

3. a. What kind of number do you get when you add an odd number and an even number?

b. Explain why this happens.

▲ **Resource Masters, M42**

Meeting the Benchmark

The following examples of student work provide a range of typical responses. All of these students met the benchmark—they were able to accurately determine whether adding different combinations of even and odd numbers results in an even or odd sum and reason about partners, teams, and leftovers to explain why. (Note that the questions these students answered were worded slightly differently from those on M41–M42.)

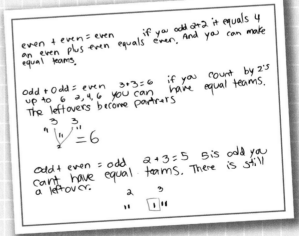

even + even = even if you add 2+2 it equals 4 an even plus even equals even. And you can make equal teams.

odd + Odd = even 3+3=6 if you count by 2's up to 6 2,4,6 you can have equal teams. The leftovers become partners

   3   3
" \|/ " = 6
      2

odd + even = odd 2+3=5 5 is odd you can't have equal teams. There is still a leftover.
      2   3
    " | 1 | "

Rochelle's Work

an even number has no left over so
if you add two even it will
be the same -even.

If you add two odds it will
be a even because the two
left over join and be a even

It will be a odd because
if you add an even to a
odd the left over will still
be there.

Jeffrey's Work

Some students accurately determine whether adding different combinations of even and odd numbers results in an even or odd sum but are unsure whether these generalizations are true for *all* numbers. These students convey their awareness that it is insufficient to test specific cases because other numbers—numbers with which they are less familiar—may behave differently. For example, even though Gregory can show—by reasoning about partners—why two odds make an even, he realizes that there are numbers he does not know.

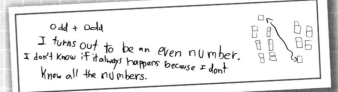

odd + odd
I turns out to be an even number.
I don't know if it always happens because I dont
know all the numbers.

Gregory's Work

Similarly, Jacy can show—by reasoning about teams—why two odds make an even, but she points out that there are numbers she did not test.

These types of arguments are powerful ones for young students who are just coming to realize that numbers are infinite and that there are numbers that they do not know about yet (e.g., very large numbers, negative numbers, and so on) to consider.

2. a. What happens when you add two odd numbers?

When you add two odd number
even because the 1s who don't have a parter they go together.

13

5

Lonzell's Work

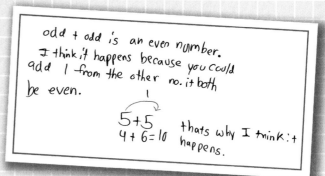

odd + odd is an even number.
I think it happens because you could add 1 from the other no. it both be even.

5+5
4+ 6= 10   thats why I think it happens.

Jacy's Work

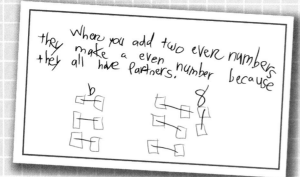

When you add two even numbers they make a even number because they all have partners.

6

8

Tia's Work

Although Gregory and Jacy have yet to learn that it is possible to prove claims for all even and odd numbers by reasoning from the definitions, their understanding of why the claim is true for familiar numbers indicates that they meet the benchmark.

Partially Meeting the Benchmark

Some students accurately determine whether adding different combinations of even and odd numbers results in an even or odd sum, but offer inadequate proof. For example, students may list many examples, as Malcolm does; only one example, as Anita does; or examples that include *only* one type of example, such as doubles, as Henry and perhaps Anita do. Some students, Anita for example, offer reasoning based on partners and teams, but for only one of the three questions.

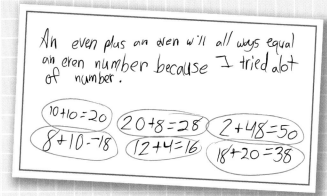

Malcolm's Work

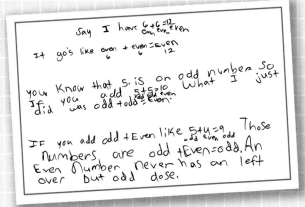

Anita's Work

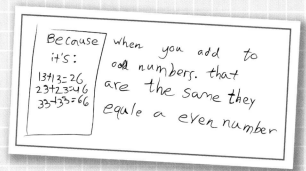

Henry's Work

Ask questions to encourage these students to expand on what they have written.

- "You listed many examples. Could you draw a picture or use cubes to show me *why* that happens for all of your examples? Does that show *why* an odd plus an odd is *always* an even?"

- "I noticed that all of your equations for Problem 1 and Problem 2 have the same two addends. Do you think that an odd plus an odd equals an even *only* if it's a doubles fact?"

Use students' responses to such questions to determine whether their work meets the benchmark or only partially meets the benchmark. Keep in mind that, particularly for this assessment, the most important thing is students' understanding of the ideas. If students can answer your questions well but do not communicate that understanding in writing, their work should be considered to meet the benchmark. It is also important to consider that doing more than giving examples and reasoning from those examples may be developmentally beyond some second graders.

Not Meeting the Benchmark

Some students cannot accurately determine whether adding different combinations of even and odd numbers results in an even or odd sum, or they provide no explanation or one that uses faulty reasoning.

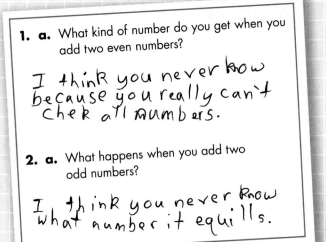

1. a. What kind of number do you get when you add two even numbers?

I think you never know because you really can't chek all numbers.

2. a. What happens when you add two odd numbers?

I think you never know what number it equills.

Yama's Work

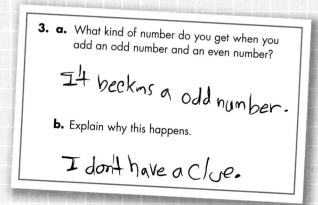

3. a. What kind of number do you get when you add an odd number and an even number?

It beckms a odd number.

b. Explain why this happens.

I don't have a clue.

Leigh's Work

Find out whether these students can determine whether a given number is even or odd and whether they can use partners or teams and leftovers to explain why. If students can do this, then they can work on story problems about adding two groups, such as those on *Student Activity Book* pages 1–3 and Problems About Two Small Groups (M2), and they can test examples that are given and that they make up on *Student Activity Book* pages 9–11. Encourage students to work carefully, to model problems in terms of partners and/or teams, to determine whether each addend and the resulting sum is even or odd, and to look for patterns and describe what they see.

Problems 4–5

Benchmark addressed:

Benchmark 3: Add two 2-digit numbers accurately and efficiently.

In order to meet the benchmark, students' work should show that they can:

- Write an equation that shows what the problem is asking (Problem 4);

- Write a story that matches a given equation (Problem 5);

- Add two 2-digit numbers accurately and efficiently (Problems 4 and 5);

- Record their work (Problems 4 and 5).

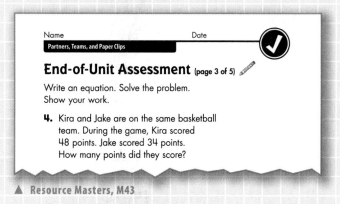

▲ **Resource Masters, M43**

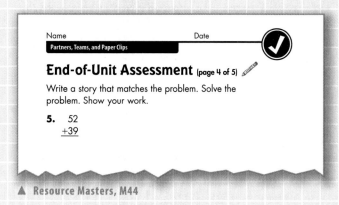

▲ **Resource Masters, M44**

Some students add by place, others keep one number whole, and still others change the numbers to make the problem easier. They use a variety of methods—equations, stickers, and the number line—to show their work.

As you look at students' work for these problems, be sure to note whether students can write an equation for Problem 4 and a story for Problem 5.

Meeting the Benchmark

The following examples of student work provide a range of typical responses. All of these students meet the benchmark—they were able to interpret the problem and solve it accurately and efficiently.

Adding tens and ones Many students add by place to solve these problems. They break both numbers into tens and ones, combine the tens, and then add on the ones in a variety of ways.

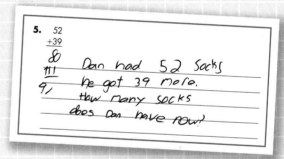

Dan has 52 dog stickers and 39 car stickers. How many stickers do's Dan have in all

$52 + 39 = 91$

$50 + 2 \qquad 30 + 9$

$1 + 1$

$50 + 30 = 80$
$9 + 1 = 10$
$80 + 10 = 90$
$90 + 1 = 91$

Darren's Work

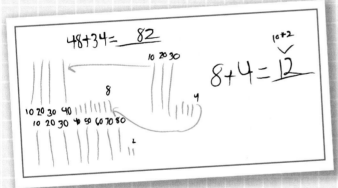

$48 + 34 = \underline{82}$

$10 \ 20 \ 30$

$10+2$

$8 + 4 = 12$

8

$10 \ 20 \ 30 \ 40$
$10 \ 20 \ 30 \ 40 \ 50 \ 60 \ 70 \ 80$

Jacy's Work

5. 52
   +39
   8
   11
   91

Dan had 52 sacks he got 39 more. How many socks does Dan have now?

Alberto's Work

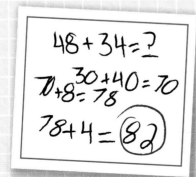

$48 + 34 = ?$

$30 + 40 = 70$
$70 + 8 = 78$

$78 + 4 = \boxed{82}$

Carla's Work

Keeping one number whole Some students keep one of the numbers whole and add the other on in parts. Many, like Leigh and Jeffrey, break the number they are adding on into tens and ones (52 + 30 + 9). Others, like Chen, add on enough to get to a multiple of 10 (48 + 2 = 50), then add on tens (50 + 10 + 10 + 10 = 80) or a multiple of 10 (50 + 30 = 80), and then add on the remaining amount (80 + 2 = 82).

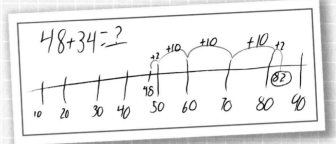

Chen's Work

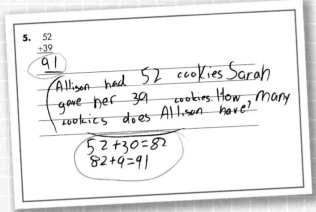

Leigh's Work

Making an equivalent problem A few students change the numbers to a multiple of 10, which is easier to work with, thus making the problem easier to solve. Students may say the following:

- Take 2 from the 34 and give it to the 48. 50 + 32 = 82.

- Take 6 from the 48 and give it to the 34. That's 40 + 42, and that's 82.

Partially Meeting the Benchmark

Some students understand the structure of the problem—that it is about combining to find the total—but make errors as they add and keep track of the quantities in the problem. For example, Monisha adds 38 + 4 and gets 41, Amaya gets 12 when she combines 2 and 9, and Gregory forgets the 2 ones from the 52 when he finds the total number of stickers.

Jeffrey's Work

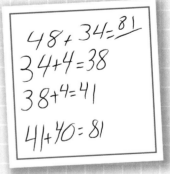

Monisha's Work

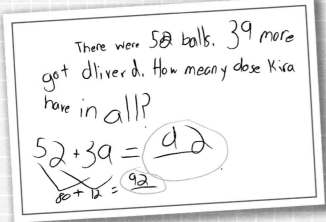

Amaya's Work

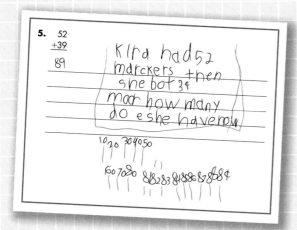

Gregory's Work

After you have reviewed their work, ask these students to see whether they can find and correct such errors on their own. Encourage them to take their time and work carefully to avoid such errors in the future. In addition, note whether these kinds of errors are consistent across problems or more of a one-time occurrence.

Not Meeting the Benchmark

Some students understand the structure of the problem but do not have efficient strategies for solving it.

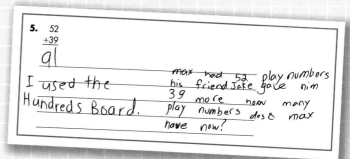

Yama's Work

When the teacher questioned Yama about *how* she "used the 100 chart" to solve 52 + 39, Yama demonstrated counting on from 52 by ones.

Students who count on by ones at the end of Grade 2 no longer meet the benchmark. However, it is important to consider each student's growth. Successfully solving this problem may represent a high level of work for a particular student. It is important to support these students in learning to count on in more efficient ways. Ask questions such as these:

- "You said that you would start on 52 on the 100 chart and then count on 39. What if you started on 52 and you added 10? Where would you land?"

- "If you start on 52, how many would you have to add to get to 60?"

You can also model such problems with cubes in towers of 10 or with a set of paper stickers. For example, "If we start with 52 stickers, how many would we have if we add another strip of 10?"

Other students understand the structure of the problem but do not have accurate strategies for solving it.

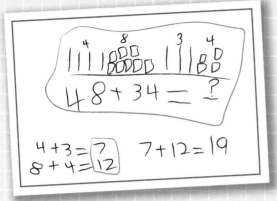

Henry's Work

Henry can write an equation to represent the first problem and can represent that problem in stickers. He also seems to have ideas about adding by place. However, he does not see the 4 in the tens place as 40 and the 3 in the tens place as 30. Instead of adding $(40 + 30) + (8 + 4)$, he adds $(4 + 3) + (8 + 4)$.

Other students who struggle with the place value of 2-digit numbers and/or with the vertical notation commonly associated with the U.S. standard algorithm for addition may end up with answers that are similarly unreasonable.

$$\begin{array}{r} 52 \\ + 39 \\ \hline 811 \end{array} \qquad \begin{array}{r} \overset{10}{52} \\ + 39 \\ \hline 181 \end{array}$$

These students are following a series of steps that are disconnected from the quantities in the problem and the properties of the operation of addition. Ask them to use a different strategy to solve the problem. If they cannot do this on their own, ask them to use cubes (in towers of 10) or stickers to represent the problem. Then ask these students to use the adding by place strategy to solve the problem. Help them use numbers and equations to record, as needed. Students who struggle with this need more practice adding smaller 2-digit numbers. Spend time working with them on smaller problems that do not require

regrouping and then move on to problems that do. Increase the size of the numbers as they become able to combine smaller 2-digit numbers.

Plus 9 and Remaining Combinations

Benchmark addressed:

Benchmark 4: Demonstrate fluency with addition combinations: plus 9 and remaining combinations.

In order to meet the benchmark, students' work should show that they can:

- Give the answers to these problems relatively quickly, without counting on their fingers or otherwise stopping to figure them out.

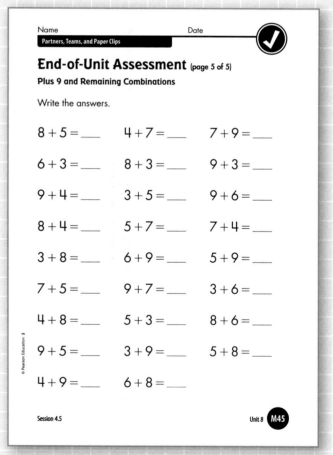

▲ **Resource Masters, M45**

Meeting the Benchmark

Students who are fluent with all or almost all of these combinations can hear or read a problem, think for a moment, and then say the answer. Most second graders should be in this category at this point in the year. Assessment Checklist: Assessing the Plus 9 and Remaining Combinations (M46) can be used to record student responses to Problem 6.

Partially Meeting the Benchmark

Students in this category are fluent with many of these combinations but pause to figure out the answer to some (e.g., 8 + 3 is 8, 9, 10, 11). Note which combinations still cause trouble and check that these match the cards in students' envelopes of "Combinations I'm Still Working On." Also point them out to students: "You've come a long way with these combinations, but a few of them still seem to give you some trouble. How could we make it easier for you to remember that 8 + 3 and 3 + 8 equal 11?" You may assign students two particular combinations per week to work on until they know them all.

Not Meeting the Benchmark

These students need to figure out many of these problems by using their fingers to count up or by using cubes to model the problem. There should be very few students in this category.

Students who partially meet or do not meet the benchmark need more practice with these combinations. To help students with the plus 9 combinations, assign *Plus 9 or 10 BINGO* (M10) during Math Workshop, during free time, and for homework. Also, work with these students to help them see the connection between plus 9 and 10 combinations, modeling the relationship with cubes and on the number line. Help students write clues and encourage them to use their Addition Cards to practice these combinations during Math Workshop, during free time, and for homework.

To assist students with the remaining combinations, help them write clues for the problems they find difficult. Model the relationships that these clues depend on with cubes or on the number line. For example, for 8 + 3, think "8 + 2 + 1." Also assign practice with their Addition Cards.

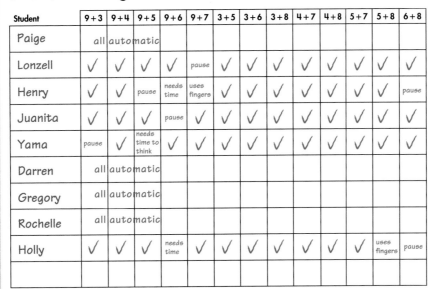

Assessment Checklist: Assessing the Plus 9 and Remaining Combinations

Student	9+3	9+4	9+5	9+6	9+7	3+5	3+6	3+8	4+7	4+8	5+7	5+8	6+8
Paige	all	automatic											
Lonzell	✓	✓	✓	✓	pause	✓	✓	✓	✓	✓	✓	✓	✓
Henry	✓	✓	pause	needs time	uses fingers	✓	✓	✓	✓	✓	✓	✓	pause
Juanita	✓	✓	✓	pause	✓	✓	✓	✓	✓	✓	✓	✓	✓
Yama	pause	✓	needs time to think	✓	✓	✓	✓	✓	✓	✓	✓	✓	✓
Darren	all	automatic											
Gregory	all	automatic											
Rochelle	all	automatic											
Holly	✓	✓	✓	needs time	✓	✓	✓	✓	✓	✓	✓	uses fingers	pause

▲ Resource Masters, M46

Two Leftovers Will Always Equal Another Pair

During Session 1.3, students work on two sets of *Student Activity Book* pages: Can You Make . . . ? and What Happens When . . . ? As this teacher observes pairs of students at work, she sees that they are at many different levels in terms of what it takes for them to accept the truth of a generalization. Some students state a generalization and then find examples, whereas others reason about an infinite class of numbers.

Holly and Melissa

Holly has written $22 + 2 = 24$ as proof that when you add two even numbers, you get an even number.

Teacher: Can you show me more about how you know that two even numbers will always equal an even number?

Holly turns back to her work and writes $24 + 2 = 26$.

Like many second graders, Holly believes that it is sufficient to test specific examples to prove a general claim. If they work, then the claim is true. What Holly does not appreciate yet is that in picking examples to test, she simply may not have come upon the ones that contradict the claim. Holly confronts this as she works on the first Can You Make . . . ? problem.

Holly finds two more combinations of even numbers that equal 24 fairly easily. She records $20 + 4 = 24$ and $10 + 14 = 24$. She quickly decides that it is impossible to make 24 with two odd numbers or with an even and an odd. In other words, having found two examples in which two even numbers make 24, she assumes that any other combination is impossible.

Melissa: You can too make 24 with two odds.

Holly reconsiders. She turns $10 + 14$ into $9 + 15 = 24$ and records it as an example of two odd numbers equaling an even.

In this case, Holly's partner challenges her to reconsider. However, the dilemma of what is known on the basis of particular examples is still at issue. What if Melissa had not challenged Holly? What if the class comes up with a conjecture and nobody finds the counterexample that proves that it is false? After all, because numbers go on infinitely, it is impossible to test all numbers.

Some students recognize the danger of making a claim on the basis of examples. They may voice such an argument: "Maybe somewhere out there, there are two numbers that . . ." These students are expressing an important idea.

It is also important to remember that it is possible to prove a general claim even when it is impossible to test all numbers, as long as one's argument relies on mathematical reasoning.

Simon and Juan

Simon and Juan are working on the first What Happens When . . . ? problem: What happens when you add two odd numbers together?

Simon: Here's 7 [holds up a tower of seven yellow cubes] and here's 5 [holds up a tower of five blue cubes]: 7 and 5 are odd numbers.

He breaks the tower of 7 into 3 pairs with 1 leftover and the tower of 5 into 2 pairs with 1 leftover.

Simon: Each one has 1 leftover. When you put all the cubes together, the 2 odd leftovers make another pair.

Teacher: We can see that this works when you add 7 and 5. How do you know that it will work with any two odd numbers?

Simon: With two odds there will always be 2 leftovers, and they make another pair.

Simon's argument, which relies on the definition of odd and even numbers and what it means to add, makes the case for any two odd numbers. Juan presents another argument.

Juan: All you have to do is take 1 cube off and put it on the other one.

Juan reassembles the tower of 7 and the tower of 5. Then he shows how, if you take 1 cube from the tower of 5 and give it to the tower of 7, you have towers of 4 and 8.

Teacher: How does that show us that the sum of two odd numbers is an even number?

Juan: Because both of those numbers [points to the 4 and the 8] can be made into pairs.

Not all 7- and 8-year-olds understand the difference between supporting a general claim with specific instances, as Holly does, and following a line of reasoning about an infinite class of numbers, as Simon does. The challenge is to encourage the kind of argument Simon makes without leaving behind students like Holly, who state a generalization and then find evidence that supports it.

Adding Two Evens or Two Odds

During Session 1.3, students have been thinking about what happens when you add different combinations of even and odd numbers. In this discussion at the end of the session, students use their definitions of odd and even as they justify what happens when *two odd* or *two even* numbers are combined. Notice that the teacher encourages students to explain their thinking by asking "Why?" and "Is that always true?"

Teacher: What did you find out about adding two even numbers?

Katrina: You can't make an odd by adding two evens.

Holly: You only get evens when you add an even plus an even.

Jeffrey: Yes; when we added two evens, we got an even.

Carla: It has to be even.

Teacher: Why do you say it has to be even, Carla?

Carla: Because an odd number has to have an extra number, and there isn't an extra number so it has to be even.

Darren: That's what we got, too. If the two numbers are even, it's always even.

Teacher: But does anyone have an idea why?

Katrina: Because it can't be odd. There's no way.

Jeffrey: If it's even, you can break it into 2s [takes cube towers of 6 and 4 and breaks them into pairs], 2, and 2, and 2, and 2, and 2. If you put them together or take them apart, it's still all 2s.

Teacher: What did you find out about adding two odds?

Gregory: If you plus an odd and an odd, you'll always get an even.

Anita: That's right. When we added 3 and 9, we got 12. That's even.

Darren: It's always even, no matter what you do. Everything we got was even.

Teacher: So Gregory, Anita, and Darren are saying that if you add two odds, you get an even. Is that always true? Can anyone explain why that might be true?

Jacy: With two odds—we did 7 and 5. It's really just like 6 and 6. If you take 1 off the 7 and put it on the 5 [demonstrates with cubes], it's all even again.

Teacher: So that's two odds making an even. Everyone build 7 and 5 with your cubes. Can anyone else add to what Jacy said?

Luis: It's like what Jeffrey said about 2s.

Tia: Even though an odd has a leftover, you can just squish them together.

Teacher: What do you mean by "squish them together"?

Tia demonstrates with cubes how you can break 7 into 3 groups of 2 with 1 leftover, and 5 into 2 groups of 2 with 1 leftover.

Tia: You can take the 2 leftovers and squish them together.

Teacher: Do you think that's true for all odds?

Tia: Yes!

Teacher: Why?

Tia: All odds have a leftover.

Simon: If you take two odd numbers, there are always 2 leftovers that can be partners.

Malcolm: I agree. It's like two evens. If you just had 6 and 4, it would be even, but there's 1 extra on each and that makes another 2, so it's still even altogether.

Notice that both parts of this conversation move from specific examples to general arguments aimed at explaining why the given generalization is true. The discussion about adding two evens moves from the unsuccessful search for two evens that add to an odd to arguments, such as Carla's and Jeffrey's, about why it is impossible for the sum of two even numbers to be odd. These arguments depend on the agreed-on definitions of even and odd numbers.

Similarly, the discussion about the sum of two odds moves from talk about specific instances to general arguments based on the one leftover from each odd number joining together to make another pair. Testing specific instances, as Anita did, is an important starting point. Such a test gives students a chance to state a generalization and offer evidence. The teacher's role is to encourage students to explain why it must always work that way.

Adding Nine

To introduce the plus 9 combinations at the beginning of Session 2.1, this teacher presents a pair of related problems that encourages students to use the relationship between adding 10 and adding 9. She writes $4 + 10 =$ _____ on chart paper.

Teacher: What do we know about adding 10 to another number?

Leigh: It becomes like 14; a 10 and a number.

Amaya: You replace the 0 with the 4 that's in the ones place. Because 0 plus 4 is 4.

Teacher: And when you put the 10 back in, what is the total?

Amaya: 14.

Teacher: How can you think about this using strips of 10 and singles?

Darren: If you add 10 you add 1 strip. So 4 plus 10 is 1 strip and 4 singles.

Teacher: I'm going to put up another problem. Remember that we've been talking about how things are related and about using what we know to solve a problem.

The teacher writes $4 + 9 =$ _____ on chart paper. Several students call out 13.

Teacher: Travis, you gave me an answer. Did you use anything you know to get the answer?

Travis: I know that $4 + 10$ equals 14. And I took the 1 away to get 13.

Teacher: Why did you have to take away the 1?

Travis: Because it isn't 10, it's 9, and 10 minus 1 is 9.

Anita: Yes, 10 and 4 is 14. Nine and 4 is 1 less, so it's 13.

The teacher records $4 + 10 = 14$ and $14 - 1 = 13$ and then directs students' attention to the number line.

Teacher: Travis and Anita said that $4 + 10$ is 14 [draws an arc from 4 to 14 and labels it +10] and $14 - 1$ is 13 [draws an arc from 14 to 13 and labels it –1]. But the problem was $4 + 9$. I see plus 10 [points to the +10 arc] and minus 1 [points to the –1 arc], but where's the plus 9?

Simon: From 4 to 13.

After asking Simon to count from 4 to 13 on the number line, the teacher draws a dotted line arcing from 4 to 13 and labels it +9.

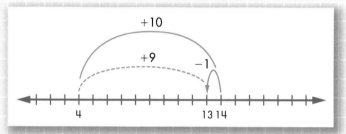

Teacher: Did anyone solve this a different way?

Jacy: You can flip the numbers for addition. So I thought 9 and 1 more makes 10, and then there's only 3 left to add.

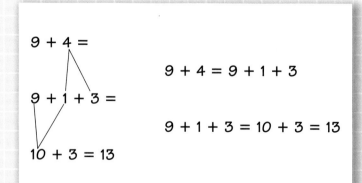

Teacher: Did anyone else change the order and think about it as 9 + 4 instead of 4 + 9?

Monisha: I started with 9 and then I went 10, 11, 12, 13.

Teacher: There's a tried and true strategy. You can start with the bigger number and count up.

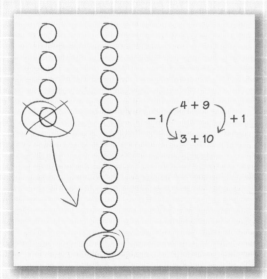

9   10   11   12   ⑬

Teacher: Any other strategies for solving 4 + 9?

Simon: You could give one number from the 4 to the 9 and then you have 3 and 10 and that equals 13.

Teacher: What Simon is saying is that I can take 1 from the 4 and give it to the group of 9, and then I have 10 and 3, and that's 13.

The teacher draws the following on the chart paper as she speaks:

Teacher: Why do you think Simon wanted to make this group have 10?

Melissa: Because 10 is easy to work with. If you know your plus 10s, then it's easy because you can take 1 from the 4 and add it to the 9, and then you have 3 + 10.

Chen: You just take 1 from the other number and add it to the 9 for 10, and then those numbers are easy to add.

Teacher: Let's look at that with cubes. Here's 4 + 9. Can someone show us what happens with the cubes in Simon's strategy?

Notice the way students use what they know to solve 4 + 9. Some reason that if 4 + 10 = 14, then 4 + 9 must equal 1 less. Others create an easier, equivalent problem (4 + 9 = 10 + 3) by taking 1 from the 4 and giving it to the 9. Still others know that you can add numbers in any order and count on from 9 or add on the 4 in useful groups (9 + 1 + 3). Note that these strategies rely on the following generalizations that students have been discussing over the course of the year:

- If you subtract 1 from one addend, the sum decreases by 1.

- If you take 1 from one addend and add it to the other addend, the sum remains the same.

- Order does not matter in addition.

- You can break numbers into parts to add them.

Modeling Students' Strategies for Pinching Paper Clips

After students have worked on the Pinching Paper Clips activity in Session 3.1, the teacher calls them together to discuss strategies. She poses a sample problem about 17 paper clips and asks students to think about how many are left in the box. Juanita announces that there are 87. The teacher asks how she figured that out.

Juanita: Because first you have the 10, so I went to this row [goes to the 100 chart and traces 91–100]. Then I still had 7 from the 17 and so I knew it was 87.

Teacher: So were you thinking about subtracting 17 from 100?

Juanita: Yes.

Teacher: And this . . . [traces 91–100]?

Juanita: That's the 10 and this [traces 81–87] is the 7.

Carla: No, you take away backward so it's 10 and then it's 7 more, so it's [goes to 90 on the 100 chart and counts back 7, ending at 84]. The answer's 83.

Juanita: Oh, so Carla and I are confused about which way to go—do we go this way [from 81 to 87] or that way [from 90 to 84]?

Teacher: What if we counted back by ones to solve 100 − 17? Let's look at it on the number line.

The teacher moves to the class number line and, with the class, first counts back 17 from 100 by ones, making 17 little jumps, then shows the same move in two jumps—one jump of 10 to 90, and another jump of 7 to 83.

Juanita: Carla's right.

Yama: Except if you think about it this way, it doesn't matter. You have to take away 17 paper clips and see how many are left. If you cross out this 10 [draws a line through 91–100], and then cross out these 7 [draws a line through 81–87], you still get 83 because there's 3 right here [traces 88–90], and then 80 more [gestures over 1–80].

1	2	3	4	5	6	7	8	9	10
11	12	13	14	15	16	17	18	19	20
21	22	23	24	25	26	27	28	29	30
31	32	33	34	35	36	37	38	39	40
41	42	43	44	45	46	47	48	49	50
51	52	53	54	55	56	57	58	59	60
61	62	63	64	65	66	67	68	69	70
71	72	73	74	75	76	77	78	79	80
81	82	83	84	85	86	87	88	89	90
91	92	93	94	95	96	97	98	99	100

80

3

Teacher: What Yama is saying is that there are two groups of paper clips—the ones that I took out of the box and the ones that are still in the box. She crossed out the 17 squares for the paper clips that I pinched—here are 10 and 7 more—and then she counted all the remaining squares that were left and got 83. Let's look at this on a sheet of 100 stickers.

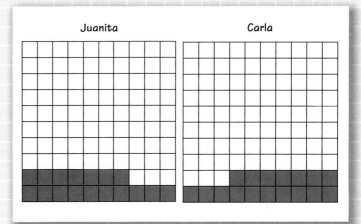

Juanita   Carla

The teacher spends some time talking through where in each representation you can see the 17 paper clips that were removed and the 83 that remain.

Teacher: Did anyone have a different way to think about how many are still in the box?

Alberto: You can start from 17 on the number line, then just keep plussing tens on, and then figure out the singles. [The teacher models the jumps of 10 on the class number line as Alberto counts by tens to 97 and then by ones to 100.] 83.

Nate: Carla went backward and Alberto started with 17, but they both had 83 left.

Teacher: Let's try another one. Chen said that he pinched 45 [circles 45 on the 100 chart]. What is an equation to show that?

Rochelle: 100 − 45 equals blank.

Chen: Or what plus 45 is 100?

Darren: Or 45 plus what? And you could also do 100 take away blank equals 45.

The teacher records and talks through the equations.

$$100 - 45 = \underline{\qquad} \qquad 100 - \underline{\qquad} = 45$$

$$\underline{\qquad} + 45 = 100 \qquad 45 + \underline{\qquad} = 100$$

She asks students what each number or blank represents in the problem. Then she asks for strategies. Because of the confusion about how to use the 100 chart to subtract, she asks Monisha to come to the class 100 chart and share how she has been using it to solve Pinching Paper Clips problems.

Monisha: I put a finger on 45. Then I start at 100 and count back to my finger: 10 [with her other hand she traces the 91–100 row], 20 [traces 81–90], 30 [traces 71–80], 40 [traces 61–70], 50 [traces 51–60]. Then 51 [touches 50], 52 [touches 49], 53 [touches 48], 54 [touches 49], 55 [touches 50]. I get 55.

Teacher: Would we get 55 if we thought about it the way Yama did? How many did Chen pinch?

Class: 45.

Teacher: These are the ones that Chen pinched [draws a line with her finger, separating the 100 chart into two parts], and these are the ones that are still in the box. Are there 55?

100 Chart

1	2	3	4	5	6	7	8	9	10
11	12	13	14	15	16	17	18	19	20
21	22	23	24	25	26	27	28	29	30
31	32	33	34	35	36	37	38	39	40
41	42	43	44	45	46	47	48	49	50
51	52	53	54	55	56	57	58	59	60
61	62	63	64	65	66	67	68	69	70
71	72	73	74	75	76	77	78	79	80
81	82	83	84	85	86	87	88	89	90
91	92	93	94	95	96	97	98	99	100

Teacher: What about Alberto's counting up method? Will we get 55?

Many students: Yes.

Teacher: Does anyone have another strategy?

Juan: I know that 40 + 60 is 100, but it's 45, so minus 5 from 60 and that's your answer.

Teacher: Juan used something he knew. Let's look at that with cubes.

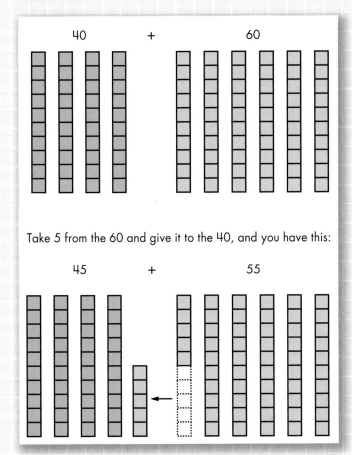

40   +   60

Take 5 from the 60 and give it to the 40, and you have this:

45   +   55

Leo: I have another way to do it. If you did 45 + 60, that would equal 105, so you would have to minus 5 to make it 100, and we know it's 45 paper clips, so you have to take it out of the 60 and that would be 55.

$$45 + \underline{60} = 105$$
$$45 + \underline{55} = 100$$

Leo's Work

The teacher takes the cubes she assembled to discuss Juan's strategy and uses them to model Leo's.

The students in this class visualize and solve Pinching Paper Clips problems in a variety of ways. Some subtract the amount pinched from 100, and others add up from the number pinched to 100. Some students use the 100 chart to subtract or add up, and others see it as a way to model the problem, with each square representing one paper clip. A few students reason numerically from facts they know to solve the problem.

Notice that the teacher decides to spend time with the 100 chart, given students' confusions about how to use it to subtract, and that she not only asks students to explain and model their thinking but also chooses particular tools to model particular strategies.

Dialogue Box

Subtraction Strategies

At the end of Session 3.4, these students have gathered for a class discussion of their strategies for solving Problem 1 on *Student Activity Book* page 35.

Jake had 72 pennies. He spent 58 on a new pencil. How many pennies does he have left?

Teacher: What do we know about this problem?

Amaya: Jake started off with 72 pennies.

Teacher: And then what happened?

Amaya: He spent 58 on a new pencil.

Teacher: Is he going to have more or fewer than 72?

Class: Fewer.

Teacher: How do you know?

Esteban: Because he spent some.

Teacher: What is an equation that would go with this story problem?

Amaya: 72 minus 58 equals blank.

The teacher records $72 - 58 = $ ____ on chart paper.

Teacher: Did anyone think about it differently?

Nadia: 58 plus blank equals 72.

The teacher adds that to the chart paper.

Teacher: Let's talk about how you solved it. Did anyone use the strategy we talked about the other day? Do you remember when I kept the bigger number together and broke the smaller number into pieces?

Gregory: But there aren't enough singles. You can't take 8 out of just those 2.

Teacher: That's an interesting point. Gregory is thinking about stickers. Where would I get the singles from?

Gregory: You have to break apart one of the strips.

Teacher: Let's use cubes to think about Gregory's idea. Here are 72 cubes [displays 7 towers of 10 and 1 tower of 2]. How could I take away 58?

Amaya: You can take away this 10, and this 10, and this 10, and this 10, and this 10 [removes 5 towers of 10 from the pile of cubes] and then break this [holds up a tower of 10] into 8 and 2 and take this 8 and then here's 58 [points to the towers of cubes she has removed from the original pile].

Teacher: And what do you have left?

Amaya: 14.

Teacher: Did anyone else subtract the 58 in parts?

Roshaun: I broke up the 58 into a 10, 10, 10, 10, 10, and 8. I took away 10 from the 72 and that's 62, and 62 take away 10 is 52, and 52 take away 10 is 42, and 42 take away 10 is 32, and 32 take away 10 is 22, and 22 take away 8 is 14.

Teacher: If you were going to do that on the 100 chart, what would it look like? How many tens did you take away?

Roshaun: Five.

Roshaun goes to the 100 chart, points to 72 and counts back by tens to 22. He then counts back by ones from 22 to 14, saying one number for each number he points to until he counts to 8 and lands on 14.

Paige: I did 72 minus 50 equals 22, and then I split the 8 into 6 and 2. Twenty-two minus 2 is 20 and 20 minus 6 equals 14.

The teacher uses equations to record Roshaun's and Paige's strategies.

Roshaun	Paige
72 − 10 = 62	72 − 50 = 22
62 − 10 = 52	22 − 2 = 20
52 − 10 = 42	20 − 6 = 14
42 − 10 = 32	
32 − 10 = 22	
22 − 8 = 14	

Teacher: How did Paige break up the 58 in order to subtract it?

Luis: 50, 2, and 6.

Teacher: What about Roshaun? How did he break apart the 58?

Luis: He broke the 50 into 5 tens. And then he did the 8 all at once.

Teacher: Gregory, Amaya, Roshaun, and Paige all took 58 away from 72. Did anyone use a different strategy?

Carla goes to the 100 Chart.

Carla: I started on 58 and to 68 is 10, and then I counted by ones to 72: 11, 12, 13, 14 [touches 69, 70, 71, and 72].

Teacher: Carla thought, "I have 58; how many to 72?" She counted up like this. [The teacher demonstrates on the class number line.]

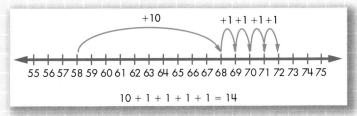

Because most of the class seems to be following these strategies, the teacher decides to extend the discussion and have a few other students share.

Teacher: You have many ways to solve this problem! Did anyone use another strategy?

Carolina: I did it a little different. I broke the 72 into 70 and 2 and the 58 into 50 and 8. Then I did 70 minus 50 is 20, and 20 minus 8 is 12. Then I had to add that 2 from 72 back in, so I did 12 plus 2 is 14.

The teacher talks through Carolina's strategy.

Teacher: Carolina, I'm curious about this last step, when you added the 2 back in. How did you know that you needed to add the 2?

Carolina: I already subtracted all of the 14. The 2 wasn't part of what I had to minus, so I had to add it.

These students have a variety of strategies for solving the problem, all of which are based on a sound understanding of the structure of the problem (i.e., it is about removing a part, 58, from a whole, 72) and of the operation of subtraction and on their flexibility with numbers and with breaking them into useful groups.

When Gregory says, "You can't take 8 out of just those 2," the teacher takes this opportunity to discuss an issue that commonly arises when working with subtraction. By modeling the problem with cubes, students are able to see the 72 as one whole group made up of tens and ones and also see the individual ones (cubes) that make up a tower of 10. The discussion focuses on first taking away 50 and then taking away 8 from the remaining 22 cubes.

Addition Strategies

To start Session 4.1, the students in this class solved the 2-digit addition problem on *Student Activity Book* page 40.

Kira had 48 balloons. Jake gave her 33 more balloons. How many balloons does Kira have now?

In this discussion, students share their strategies for solving $48 + 33$ and consider the efficiency of various strategies for solving and notating their work. The teacher focuses on two particular strategies: adding tens and ones, and keeping one number whole.

Teacher: What equations did you write?

Anita: 48 plus 33 equals blank.

Nadia: Or 33 plus 48 equals blank.

Chen: Or you can do it the stacking way, up and down.

The teacher records these suggestions on chart paper. Beneath them she writes "Adding Tens and Ones" and "Keeping One Number Whole."

$48 + 33 = \underline{\quad}$ $33 + 48 = \underline{\quad}$ $\begin{array}{r} 48 \\ + 33 \\ \hline \end{array}$

Adding Tens and Ones	Keeping One Number Whole

Teacher: Who used strips of 10 and singles to solve the problem?

Henry: I did 4 lines and then I put 3 more lines. And then I put 8 singles and then 3. I counted the strips first and I got 70. And then I did plus 8 equals 78. Then I knew that $78 + 3 = 81$.

Teacher: Where should I record Henry's strategy? Did he keep one number whole and add the other on in parts? Did he add tens and ones? Did he use another strategy?

Monisha: Tens and ones.

Teacher: How many people agree?

The rest of the class agrees. The teacher rephrases Henry's strategy as she records it beneath the heading "Adding Tens and Ones."

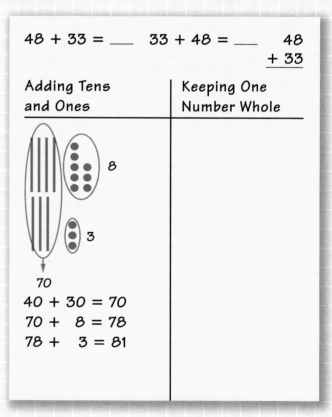

$48 + 33 = \underline{\quad}$ $33 + 48 = \underline{\quad}$ $\begin{array}{r} 48 \\ + 33 \\ \hline \end{array}$

Adding Tens and Ones	Keeping One Number Whole

70
$40 + 30 = 70$
$70 + 8 = 78$
$78 + 3 = 81$

Paige: I did it similar to Henry's. I did 40 + 30 = 70. 8 + 3 = 11. And you take the 10 and add it to the 70. That's 80. And then 80 plus 1 is 81.

Teacher: Which of our strategies would that go under?

Paige: The tens and ones.

The teacher records Paige's strategy under Henry's.

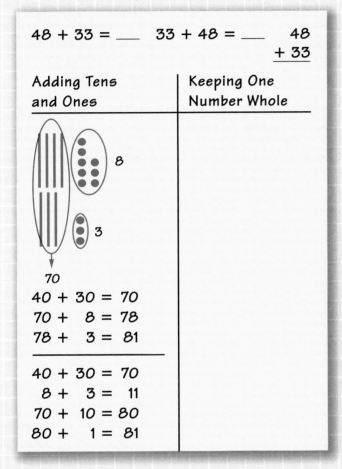

Teacher: Henry, do you agree that this is similar to yours? [Henry nods.] Henry used stickers in strips of ten and singles, and Paige used numbers and equations. Who else used adding tens and ones? [Eight students raise their hands.] Those of you who are using stickers, like Henry, can start to think about how to use numbers and equations to record when you add tens and ones. Did anyone try this other strategy of keeping one number whole?

Rochelle: I broke the 33. Then 48 and 10 is 58, and then 58 and 10 is 68, and 68 and 10 is 78. So it's 78 and then the 3 more is 79, 80, 81.

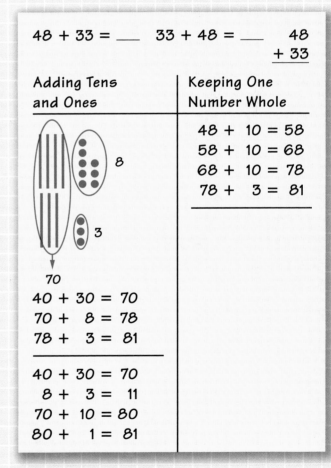

Teacher: Any other strategies?

Leo: I did 48 plus 30 is 78 and then 78 plus three is 81.

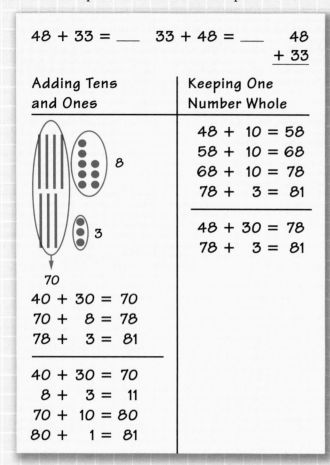

$48 + 33 = \underline{}$ $33 + 48 = \underline{}$ $\begin{aligned} 48 \\ + 33 \end{aligned}$

Adding Tens and Ones

70

$40 + 30 = 70$
$70 + 8 = 78$
$78 + 3 = 81$

$40 + 30 = 70$
$8 + 3 = 11$
$70 + 10 = 80$
$80 + 1 = 81$

Keeping One Number Whole

$48 + 10 = 58$
$58 + 10 = 68$
$68 + 10 = 78$
$78 + 3 = 81$

$48 + 30 = 78$
$78 + 3 = 81$

Teacher: Leo's strategy reminds me of another one on our chart.

Students: Rochelle's!

Teacher: How are they similar?

Lonzell: They both kept 48 whole and added on 33.

Teacher: How are they different?

Juanita: Leo did the 30 altogether. Rochelle did 10 plus 10 plus 10.

Teacher: Yes, Leo did it in two steps. People who are using this strategy can push themselves to add on the other number in fewer and fewer steps. I have one last question. The problem was 40 something plus 30 something. Why wasn't the answer in the 70s?

Luis: Because the somethings made more than 10. That put the number in the 80s.

Tia: It wasn't just 40 and 30. The 3 from the 33 and the 8 from the 48 made it go over into the 80s.

Teacher: Why did that happen?

Lonzell: Three and 8 is 11. And 70 plus 11 equals *eighty*-one.

Holly: The 10 from the 11 made it bump from 70 to 80. And then the 1 made it go to 81.

The *Student Math Handbook* pages related to this unit are pictured on the following pages. This book is designed to be used flexibly: as a resource for students doing classwork, as a book students can take home for reference while doing homework and playing math games with their families, and as a reference for families to better understand the work their children are doing in class.

When students take the *Student Math Handbook* home, they and their families can discuss these pages together to reinforce or enhance students' understanding of the mathematical concepts and games in this unit.

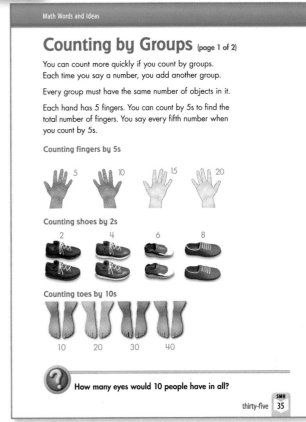

Math Words and Ideas

Counting by Groups (page 1 of 2)

You can count more quickly if you count by groups. Each time you say a number, you add another group.

Every group must have the same number of objects in it.

Each hand has 5 fingers. You can count by 5s to find the total number of fingers. You say every fifth number when you count by 5s.

Counting fingers by 5s

5   10   15   20

Counting shoes by 2s

2   4   6   8

Counting toes by 10s

10   20   30   40

? How many eyes would 10 people have in all?

thirty-five **35** SMH

◄ Math Words and Ideas, p. 35

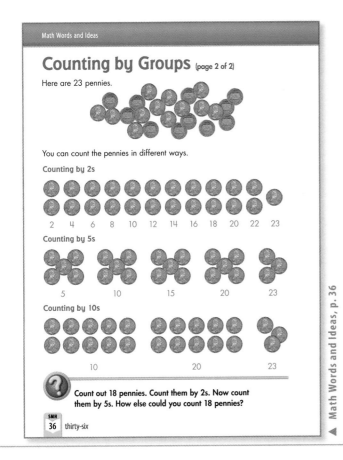

Math Words and Ideas

Counting by Groups (page 2 of 2)

Here are 23 pennies.

You can count the pennies in different ways.

Counting by 2s

2 4 6 8 10 12 14 16 18 20 22 23

Counting by 5s

5   10   15   20   23

Counting by 10s

10   20   23

? Count out 18 pennies. Count them by 2s. Now count them by 5s. How else could you count 18 pennies?

SMH **36** thirty-six

◄ Math Words and Ideas, p. 36

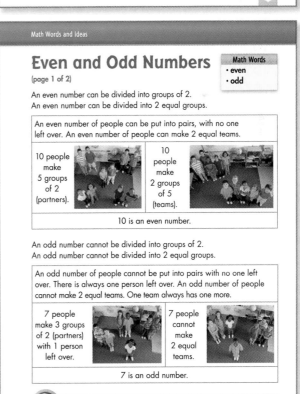

Math Words and Ideas

Even and Odd Numbers

(page 1 of 2)

Math Words
• even
• odd

An even number can be divided into groups of 2.
An even number can be divided into 2 equal groups.

An even number of people can be put into pairs, with no one left over. An even number of people can make 2 equal teams.

10 people make 5 groups of 2 (partners).

10 people make 2 groups of 5 (teams).

10 is an even number.

An odd number cannot be divided into groups of 2.
An odd number cannot be divided into 2 equal groups.

An odd number of people cannot be put into pairs with no one left over. There is always one person left over. An odd number of people cannot make 2 equal teams. One team always has one more.

7 people make 3 groups of 2 (partners) with 1 person left over.

7 people cannot make 2 equal teams.

7 is an odd number.

? Is 11 even or odd? How do you know? What about 16?

forty-one **41** SMH

◄ Math Words and Ideas, p. 41

Even and Odd Numbers

(page 2 of 2)

If you start at 0 and count by 2s, you say the even numbers.
If you start at 1 and count by 2s, you say the odd numbers.
On this 100 chart, the odd numbers are yellow.
The even numbers are green.

Odd and even numbers alternate in a pattern.

1	2	3	4	5	6	7	8	9	10
11	12	13	14	15	16	17	18	19	20
21	22	23	24	25	26	27	28	29	30
31	32	33	34	35	36	37	38	39	40
41	42	43	44	45	46	47	48	49	50
51	52	53	54	55	56	57	58	59	60
61	62	63	64	65	66	67	68	69	70
71	72	73	74	75	76	77	78	79	80
81	82	83	84	85	86	87	88	89	90
91	92	93	94	95	96	97	98	99	100

Is 35 even or odd? How do you know?
What about 60? 101?

SMH
42 forty-two

◀ Math Words and Ideas, p. 42

Plus 10 Combinations

Any single-digit number plus 10 is a Plus 10 combination.
So is 10 plus any single-digit number. Here are all of the
Plus 10 combinations you are working on.

Combination	
$10 + 0 = 10$ / $0 + 10 = 10$	
$10 + 1 = 11$ / $1 + 10 = 11$	
$10 + 2 = 12$ / $2 + 10 = 12$	
$10 + 3 = 13$ / $3 + 10 = 13$	
$10 + 4 = 14$ / $4 + 10 = 14$	
$10 + 5 = 15$ / $5 + 10 = 15$	
$10 + 6 = 16$ / $6 + 10 = 16$	
$10 + 7 = 17$ / $7 + 10 = 17$	
$10 + 8 = 18$ / $8 + 10 = 18$	
$10 + 9 = 19$ / $9 + 10 = 19$	

What patterns do you notice in the Plus 10 combinations?
Which ones do you know? Which are you still working on?

fifty-one 51
SMH

◀ Math Words and Ideas, p. 51

Plus 9 Combinations

Any number plus 9 is a Plus 9 combination. So is 9 plus
any number. Here are the Plus 9 combinations you are
working on.

$9 + 1 = 10$ $9 + 2 = 11$ $9 + 3 = 12$ $9 + 4 = 13$
$1 + 9 = 10$ $2 + 9 = 11$ $3 + 9 = 12$ $4 + 9 = 13$

$9 + 5 = 14$ $9 + 6 = 15$ $9 + 7 = 16$ $9 + 8 = 17$
$5 + 9 = 14$ $6 + 9 = 15$ $7 + 9 = 16$ $8 + 9 = 17$

$9 + 9 = 18$ $9 + 10 = 19$ $10 + 9 = 19$

Some children learn the Plus 9 combinations by relating
them to Plus 10 combinations they know.

$9 + 6 = 15$
$6 + 9 = 15$

Clue: $9 + 1 + 5 = 15$

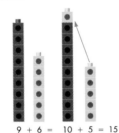

$9 + 6 = $ $10 + 5 = 15$

What helps you remember the Plus 9 combinations?
Which ones do you know? Which are you still working on?

SMH
52 fifty-two

◀ Math Words and Ideas, p. 52

The Remaining Addition Combinations

You have learned these addition combinations so far.

Plus 1   Doubles
Plus 2   Near Doubles
Combinations of 10   Plus 10
                                Plus 9

Now there are just a few addition combinations left.
Here they are.

$3 + 5$	$3 + 6$	$3 + 8$	$4 + 7$	$4 + 8$	$5 + 7$	$5 + 8$	$6 + 8$
$5 + 3$	$6 + 3$	$8 + 3$	$7 + 4$	$8 + 4$	$7 + 5$	$8 + 5$	$8 + 6$

Here are some clues to help remember $6 + 8$ and $8 + 6$.

Kira thinks about doubles.

"I know $6 + 6 = 12$.
8 is 2 more than 6, so
$6 + 8$ is 2 more than
$6 + 6$. So, $6 + 8$ is 14."

"$8 + 6$ is the same
as $8 + 2$, which is
10, plus 4 more.
The answer is 14."

Jake uses 10.

Which of these combinations are hard for you to remember?
Can you think of a clue to help you remember them?

fifty-three 53
SMH

◀ Math Words and Ideas, p. 53

An Addition Story Problem

Here is a story problem.

Sally has 10 crayons. Jake gave her 12 more crayons. How many crayons does Sally have now?

In this problem, two groups are being combined or joined. This equation shows what is happening in this problem.

$$10 + 12 = \underline{\ ?\ }$$

 Does Sally have more crayons at the beginning of the story or at the end?

fifty-nine **SMH 59**

◀ Math Words and Ideas, p. 59

Solving An Addition Story Problem

Here is the story.

Sally has 10 crayons. Jake gave her 12 more crayons. How many crayons does Sally have now?

There are many ways to solve this problem. Here is what some students did.

Jake counted on from 10.

$$10 + 12 = \underline{\ 22\ }$$

11 12 13 14 15 16

17 18 19 20 21 22

Sally used what she knew about addition combinations.

 I know
10 + 10 = 20,
so
10 + 12 = 22.

Leigh split 12 into 10 and 2. Then she used the number line to add.

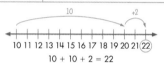

10 11 12 13 14 15 16 17 18 19 20 21 (22)

$$10 + 10 + 2 = 22$$

 How would you solve this problem?

SMH 60 sixty

◀ Math Words and Ideas, p. 60

Addition Notation

Sally has 10 crayons. Jake gave her 12 more crayons. Now Sally has 22 crayons.

Here are 2 equations for this problem.

Math Words
- equation
- equal to
- addend
- plus
- sum
- equal sign

$$10 + 12 = 22$$

10 plus 12 is equal to 22.

$$22 = 10 + 12$$

22 is equal to 10 plus 12.

10 and 12 are the addends. 22 is the total or sum.
The equal sign shows that 10 + 12 is the same amount as 22.

 What is the same and what is different about these two equations?

sixty-one **SMH 61**

◀ Math Words and Ideas, p. 61

Another Addition Story Problem

Here is another story problem.

Sally went to Sticker Station. She bought 42 moon stickers and 35 star stickers. How many stickers did Sally buy?

In this problem, groups are being combined or joined. This equation shows what is happening in this problem.

$$42 + 35 = \underline{\ \ \ }$$

 How many strips of 10 did Sally have? How many singles? How many stickers altogether?

SMH 62 sixty-two

◀ Math Words and Ideas, p. 62

Solving Another Addition Story Problem (page 1 of 2)

Here is the story.

Sally went to Sticker Station. She bought 42 moon stickers and 35 star stickers. How many stickers did Sally buy?

There are many ways to solve this problem.

Some children think about tens and ones.

Chen used strips and singles to show the stickers Sally bought.	Holly and Simon broke both numbers into tens and ones. They added the tens first, and then the ones.

$42 + 35 = $ ___

42   35

He put the tens together and the ones together.

7 strips of 10 is 70.   7 singles is 7.

Then he added. 70 + 7 = 77.
Sally bought 77 stickers.

Holly recorded like this:

$35 + 42 = $ ___
$30 + 40 = 70$
$5 + 2 = 7$
$70 + 7 = 77$

Simon recorded like this:

$$\begin{array}{r} 35 \\ + 42 \\ \hline 70 \\ + 7 \\ \hline 77 \end{array}$$

▲ Math Words and Ideas, p. 63

Solving Another Addition Story Problem (page 2 of 2)

Other children keep one number whole and add the other number on in parts.

Henry thought about stickers.	Carla used the 100 chart. She added 35 stickers onto the 42 Sally already had.

42 + ☐ 77
      ☐ 76
      ☐ 75
      ☐ 74
      ☐ 73

52 62 72

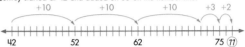

+ 8
+10
+10
+ 2 + 5

$$\begin{array}{r} 42 \\ + 35 \\ \hline 77 \end{array}$$

Jeffrey started at 42 and added on 35 on the number line.

+10   +10   +10   +3 +2

42   52   62   75 ⑦⑦

Simon broke 35 into 30 and 5 to add it onto 42.	Leo kept the 35 whole. He added the 42 by adding 40 and then 2 more.

$42 + 35 = $ ___
$42 + 30 = 72$
$72 + 5 = 77$
77 stickers

$35 + 42 = $ ___

$$\begin{array}{r} 35 \\ + 40 \\ \hline 75 \\ + 2 \\ \hline 77 \end{array}$$

❓ **Tia solved this problem by adding 40 + 37. What did she do? Why does that work?**

▲ Math Words and Ideas, p. 64

Solving an Addition Problem (page 1 of 2)

Here is another problem.

$38 + 23 = $ ___

$$\begin{array}{r} 38 \\ + 23 \end{array}$$

There are many ways to solve this problem.

These children broke both numbers into tens and ones. They added the tens together and the ones together, and then added those totals.

Juan used stickers.	Monisha's Solution

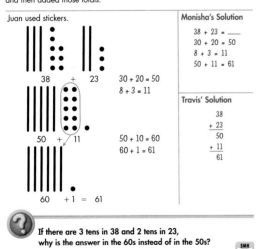

38   +   23

50   +   11

60   + 1 = 61

$30 + 20 = 50$
$8 + 3 = 11$

$50 + 10 = 60$
$60 + 1 = 61$

Monisha's Solution

$38 + 23 = $ ___
$30 + 20 = 50$
$8 + 3 = 11$
$50 + 11 = 61$

Travis' Solution

$$\begin{array}{r} 38 \\ + 23 \\ \hline 50 \\ + 11 \\ \hline 61 \end{array}$$

❓ **If there are 3 tens in 38 and 2 tens in 23, why is the answer in the 60s instead of in the 50s?**

▲ Math Words and Ideas, p. 65

Solving an Addition Problem (page 2 of 2)

These children keep one number whole and add the other number on in parts.

Amaya thought about stickers.	Luis used the 100 chart.

$38 + 23 = \underline{61}$

38 + ☐ 59
      ☐ 60
      ☐ 61

48 58

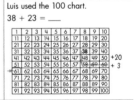

$38 + 23 = $ ___

+20
+ 3

Jacy started at 38 and added on 23 on the number line.

$38 + 23 = $ ___

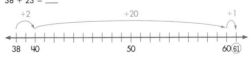

+2   +20   +1

38 40   50   60 ⑥⑥

Leo and Nate broke 23 into 20 and 3 and then added it onto 38.

Leo recorded like this:	Nate recorded like this:

$38 + 23 = \underline{61}$
$38 + 20 = 58$
$58 + 3 = 61$

$38 + 23 = $ ___

$$\begin{array}{r} 38 \\ + 20 \\ \hline 58 \\ + 3 \\ \hline 61 \end{array}$$

❓ **Esteban solved this problem by adding 40 + 21. What did he do? Why does that work?**

▲ Math Words and Ideas, p. 66

A Subtraction Story Problem

Here is a story problem.

Carla had 16 shells. She gave 7 of them to Juanita. How many shells did Carla have left?

In this problem, Carla starts with a group of shells and gives some away.

This equation shows what is happening in this problem.

$$16 - 7 = \underline{\quad}$$

 Does Carla have more shells at the beginning of the story or at the end?

sixty-seven **SMH 67**

◀ Math Words and Ideas, p. 67

Solving a Subtraction Story Problem

Here is the story.

Carla had 16 shells. She gave 7 of them to Juanita. How many shells did Carla have left?

There are many ways to solve this problem. Here is what some students did.

Yama broke apart 7 into 6 and 1 and then subtracted from 16.	Gregory used a number line and counted back 7. He got to 9.
$16 - 7 = \underline{\quad}$ $16 - 6 = 10$ $10 - 1 = 9$ So, $16 - 7 = 9$.	$16 - 7 = \underline{\quad}$ 9 10 11 12 13 14 15 16
Katrina drew 16 shells and crossed out 7. There were 9 left. $16 - 7 = \underline{\quad}$ 	Malcolm used an addition combination he knew. The problem is asking $7 + \underline{\quad} = 16$. I know $7 + \underline{10} = 17$, so $7 + \underline{9} = 16$. If $7 + 9 = 16$, then $16 - 7 = 9$.

 How would you solve this problem?

SMH 68 sixty-eight

◀ Math Words and Ideas, p. 68

Subtraction Notation

Math Words
• minus
• difference

Carla had 16 shells. She gave 7 of them to Juanita. Then Carla had 9 shells left.

Here are two equations for this problem.

$$16 - 7 = 9$$

16 minus 7 is equal to 9.

$$9 = 16 - 7$$

9 equals 16 minus 7.

The difference between 16 and 7 is 9.
The equal sign shows that $16 - 7$ is the same amount as 9.

 What is the same and what is different about these two equations?

sixty-nine **SMH 69**

◀ Math Words and Ideas, p. 69

Another Subtraction Story Problem

Travis had 48 circus stickers. He gave 22 to Nadia. How many circus stickers does Travis have left?

In this problem, Travis starts with 48 stickers. He gives 22 to Nadia.

This equation shows what is happening in this problem.

$$48 - 22 = \underline{\quad}$$

 Does Travis have more stickers at the beginning of the story or at the end?

SMH 70 seventy

◀ Math Words and Ideas, p. 70

Solving Another Subtraction Story Problem (page 1 of 2)

Here is the story.

Travis had 48 circus stickers. He gave 22 to Nadia. How many circus stickers does Travis have left?

There are many ways to solve this problem. Some children show 48 stickers. Then they remove or cross out 22 of them, and count how many are left.

Leigh drew 48 stickers, crossed out 22, and counted how many were left.	Gregory broke up the 48 so he could subtract 22.
48 − 22 = ___ 10 20 and 6 more is 26 She has 26 stickers left.	$48 = 20 + \cancel{20} + 6 + \cancel{2}$ 26 are left!

Other children subtract 22 from 48 in parts.

Jacy used a number line to subtract 22 from 48.	Malcolm broke 22 into 20 and 2. First he subtracted 20, then he subtracted 2.
  48 − 22 = 26	48 − 22 = ? 48 − 20 = 28 28 − 2 = 26

seventy-one **71**

◄ Math Words and Ideas, p. 71

Solving Another Subtraction Story Problem (page 2 of 2)

Other children think, "22 + ___ = 48." They think about how much they have to add to 22 to get to 48.

Roshaun used a number line.

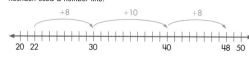

22 + 26 = 48

Travis used the 100 chart.	Paige used equations to record her thinking.

8
10
+ 8
26

100 chart showing 1–100 with 22, 30, 40, 48, 49 highlighted

22 + _26_ = 48

22 + _20_ = 42

42 + _6_ = 48

20 + 6 = 26

 How would you solve this problem?

72 seventy-two

◄ Math Words and Ideas, p. 72

Solving a Subtraction Problem
(page 1 of 3)

Here is another problem. 72 − 38 = ___

$$72 \atop -38$$

There are many ways to solve this problem.

Some children show 72 stickers. Then they remove or cross out 38 of them, and count how many are left.

Amaya drew 72 stickers.	Carla used the 100 chart.

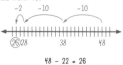

To cross out 38, she had to change one strip to singles.

100 chart showing 1–100
+ 2
+10
+10
+10
+ 2
34

She counted how many were left. "10, 20, 30, and 4 more is 34."

72 − 38 = 34

Henry thought:	Roshaun drew 72 stickers, crossed out 38, and counted how many were left.

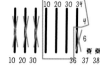 You can break 72 into 40 + 30 + 2. If you take the 38 away from the 40, there's 2 left. 2 + 30 + 2 = 34.

10 20 30 34 / 4 / 6 / 36 37 38 / 10 20 30

seventy-three **73**

◄ Math Words and Ideas, p. 73

Solving a Subtraction Problem
(page 2 of 3)

Other children subtract 38 from 72 in parts.

Tia used the 100 chart. She started at 72 and counted back 38. She subtracted 2 first, then 30, then 6 more. 34 were left.

72 − 38 = 34

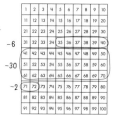
−6
−30
−2

Melissa used the same strategy as Tia, but she used the number line to subtract in parts. She subtracted 2 first, then 30, then 6 more.

72 − 38 = ___

72 − 2 = 70
70 − 30 = 40
40 − 6 = 34

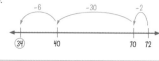
−6 −30 −2
34 40 70 72

Alberto broke 38 into 30 and 8. First he subtracted the 30. Then he subtracted the 8.

72 − 30 = 42
42 − 8 = 34
72 − 38 = _34_

74 seventy-four

◄ Math Words and Ideas, p. 74

Solving a Subtraction Problem

(page 3 of 3)

To solve 72 − 38, other children think, "38 + ___ = 72."
They think about how much they have to add to 38 to get
to 72.

Anita used the 100 chart
to add up.

10 + 10 + 10 + 4 = 34

1	2	3	4	5	6	7	8	9	10
11	12	13	14	15	16	17	18	19	20
21	22	23	24	25	26	27	28	29	30
31	32	33	34	35	36	37	38	39	40
41	42	43	44	45	46	47	48	49	50
51	52	53	54	55	56	57	58	59	60
61	62	63	64	65	66	67	68	69	70
71	72	73	74	75	76	77	78	79	80
81	82	83	84	85	86	87	88	89	90
91	92	93	94	95	96	97	98	99	100

Henry kept adding 10 until he got close to 72.

$$38 + 10 = 48$$
$$48 + 10 = 58$$
$$58 + 10 = 68$$
$$68 + 4 = 72$$

$$10 + 10 + 10 + 4 = 34$$

Lonzell used the number line to add up.

$$30 + 2 + 2 = 34$$

30

2   2

38   68 70 72

seventy-five **SMH 75**

◀ Math Words and Ideas, p. 75

Plus 9 or 10 BINGO

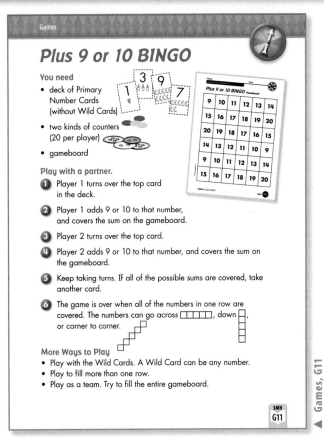

You need
- deck of Primary Number Cards (without Wild Cards)
- two kinds of counters (20 per player)
- gameboard

Play with a partner.

1. Player 1 turns over the top card in the deck.

2. Player 1 adds 9 or 10 to that number, and covers the sum on the gameboard.

3. Player 2 turns over the top card.

4. Player 2 adds 9 or 10 to that number, and covers the sum on the gameboard.

5. Keep taking turns. If all of the possible sums are covered, take another card.

6. The game is over when all of the numbers in one row are covered. The numbers can go across ⬚⬚⬚⬚⬚, down ⬚, or corner to corner. ⬚

More Ways to Play
- Play with the Wild Cards. A Wild Card can be any number.
- Play to fill more than one row.
- Play as a team. Try to fill the entire gameboard.

SMH G11

◀ Games, G11

Index

IN THIS UNIT